WILLIAMSBURG

DECORATING WITH STYLE

WILLIAMSBURG

DECORATING WITH STYLE

The Colonial Williamsburg Foundation

Produced by Tricia Foley

Photographs by Jeff McNamara

Text by Catherine Calvert

Design by Dina Dell'Arciprete-Houser

Clarkson Potter/Publishers

New York

Published by Clarkson N. Potter, Inc.,
201 East 50th Street, New York, New York 10022.
Member of the Crown Publishing Group.
Random House, Inc. New York, Toronto,
London, Sydney, Auckland
www.randomhouse.com

CLARKSON N. POTTER, POTTER, and colophon
are trademarks of Clarkson N. Potter, Inc.

Williamsburg and the Hallmark are trademarks of
The Colonial Williamsburg Foundation.

Printed in China

Library of Congress Cataloging-in-Publication Data
Williamsburg: Decorating with Style / by the
Colonial Williamsburg Foundation; text by
Catherine Calvert; produced by Tricia Foley;
photographs by Jeff McNamara—1st ed.
1. Decoration and ornament—Virginia—
Williamsburg—History—18th century. 2. Interior
decoration—Virginia—Williamsburg—History—
18th century. 3. Williamsburg (Va.)—Social life and
customs. I. Calvert, Catherine. II. Foley, Tricia.
III. Colonial Williamsburg Foundation.
NK1411.W54D43   1998
745'.09755'4252—dc21   97-42917
ISBN 0-609-60049-4

10 9 8 7 6 5 4 3 2 1
First Edition

ACKNOWLEDGMENTS

We are indebted to many creative and energetic people whose talents, knowledge, and vision joined to make this book possible. Its beauty lies not only with the intrinsic appeal of Williamsburg—it largely results from the way Colonial Williamsburg's charms inspired the creative team. Trish Foley and photographer Jeff McNamara worked magic together, capturing Williamsburg's timeless elegance. Writer Catherine Calvert caught the spirit of the place—past and present—in her vibrant text. Alexandra Randall's floral arrangements made every room they graced into a special occasion place.

Over several years, from initial discussions about a collaboration with Colonial Williamburg to the final text corrections, we have been pleased to work with all those at Clarkson Potter whose efforts helped to bring the book to publication: Chip Gibson, Lauren Shakely, Andrew Martin, Marysarah Quinn, Dina Dell'Arciprete-Houser, Mark McCauslin, Joan Denman, and Kathryn Crosby.

Many Colonial Williamsburg staff members contributed time and knowledge to this project. In particular, Liza Gusler, curator of museum education, contributed significantly to the creation of the text. Linda Baumgarten, curator of textiles and costumes, Janine Skerry, curator of ceramics and glass, Margaret Pritchard, curator of prints and maps, and Betty Leviner, curator of exhibition buildings, generously shared knowledge in their areas of expertise. In addition, Jan Gilliam, Tanya Wilson, Don Thomas, Judy Kristoffersen, Dennis Cotner, and Gloria McFadden helped the stylist and photographer with the intricate logistics of photography in historic buildings. Thanks to architectural research staff members Mark R. Wenger, Ed Chappell, and Willie Graham for reviewing the architectural text. They also, along with senior furniture conservator Carey Howlett, identified historic paint colors. From the landscape department Laura Viancour and Gordon Chappell helped with gardens, advising where to find the best photo opportunities of seasonal blooms. Thanks also to Larry Griffith for reviewing the garden photography.

While curators and researchers provided the essential base of knowledge, many other Colonial Williamsburg staff members played important roles in developing this book. Charles Driscoll, vice president, products and commercial properties, provided his invaluable eye for style and appearance with his critique of the book. Joe Rountree and Donna Sheppard gave insights gleaned from years of experience with Colonial Williamsburg publications.

Innumerable members of the products team helped make this book a reality. The product management staff—Gail Burger, Kris Fischer, Alice Watkinson, Sara Lewis, and Beth Emerson—provided the backbone of the project. We called on colleagues at our Historic Area stores, Craft Houses, Colonial Williamsburg Mail Order, Merchandise Management, and Distribution Center to help gather furnishings for contemporary scenes photographed in the Nelson-Galt House. Anne Oren did an outstanding job organizing products from our *Williamsburg* licensees for the project.

Two wonderful shops in nearby Yorktown, Virginia, came to our aide with great products and antiques. Ginny Lascara, Rob Hunter, and Michele Erickson at Period Design provided good ideas and beautiful objects; at Nancy Thomas, Sandy Mottner provided more beautiful accent pieces for photographs.

Colonial Williamsburg works with an excellent team of licensed manufacturers who produce products that carry the *Williamsburg* brand. Many of the home furnishings and accessory manufacturers were especially helpful in making their products available. We are especially indebted to Baker Furniture Company and F. Schumacher and Company, who led the charge.

CONTENTS

Even at nearly three centuries old, Williamsburg is a trendsetter. The twentieth-century restoration of Williamsburg to its eighteenth-century origins has influenced the look of American architecture and interior decoration and affected the tastes of generations. Millions of homeowners, inspired by a trip to Colonial Williamsburg, have embraced the timelessness of these designs, and as new discoveries change the look of Williamsburg itself, new generations embrace them in turn.

This book explores the power of the historic town's mystique to influence our taste and our notion of American decorating history, and in the process shares ideas for bringing the Williamsburg style into American homes. The symmetry of Georgian buildings, furnished sumptuously or sparsely with time-mellowed antiques; the elegant practicality of even the simplest accessories; the delight of formal topiary and crisp hedges evoke an emotional reaction. In the interiors of Williamsburg, Americans find themselves to be at home, in the deepest sense of the word.

The restoration of Williamsburg sparked the imagination of a generation. By the mid-1930s visitors to Colonial Williamsburg were clamoring to take home a bit of the splendors they saw. Indeed, many wanted to re-create whole Williamsburg houses, from cellar to chimney, from carpet to chandelier. To satisfy their desires, the *Williamsburg* Reproductions Program was created. Using the collection of antique furnishings as inspiration, Colonial Williamsburg partnered with manufacturers of impeccable caliber to supply eighteenth-century-style furnishings for twentieth-century living. *Williamsburg* reproductions have been a powerful and far-reaching extension of Colonial Williamsburg's educational mission—"that the future may learn from the past." These scrupulously accurate historical reproductions bring the past into today's homes.

Williamsburg's museum interiors continue to influence home decoration. In 1981, our curators installed accurate marbleized floorcloths and checked slipcovers in the Governor's Palace. Quickly this historical presentation moved beyond the province of house museums and into the realm of show houses, decorating magazines, and now, into smartly decorated homes, leading one design magazine to call the 1980s the "decade of the floorcloth." Why did these period design details translate so easily into today's lifestyles? Because they are classics, and classics by definition stand the test of time.

The furnishings, fabrics, chinaware, and silver the great men of Williamsburg sought to own two hundred years ago were novelties—the products of discoveries of new worlds and inventions of new manufacturers' methods, yet remarkably, this moment in design history has endured, as has America herself, as a synthesis of influences from many parts of the world.

We hope that you may be inspired not only by the grand historical origins of Williamsburg, but by the perennial freshness of its design traditions, to let our past become part of your future. In order to guide your eye through the authentic museum of Williamsburg homes, each chapter is divided into a tour of carefully selected rooms, followed by "Contemporary Interpretations" that demonstrate how eighteenth-century design elements, along with the fine reproductions of the *Williamsburg* program, can be used in the settings of today.

Robert Wilburn

President, The Colonial Williamsburg Foundation

March 1998

*These buildings here described are justly
reguted the best in all the English America.*
—HUGH JONES,
PRESENT STATE OF VIRGINIA, 1724

WILLIAMSBURG

came of age when all seemed possibility, when the future was glorious and there for the grasping. Williamsburg in full bloom was a town that held dear the talismans of the time—the eighteenth-century Virginian's belief in the might of the British crown, in the potential that lay before anyone with ambition, in the force of man on the landscape, in the suavities of civilization and the amusements and possessions that marked a cultured person. Here was the capital of the wealthiest colony, the center for scholarship and sociability, for politics and trade, where the hum of the streets was the very sound of a civilization shaping itself. For a century's span, Williamsburg's world was a rich one. ◆ Originally, of course, this was a crossroads in the wilderness, where a few planters drawn by offers of free land for settlers chopped their clearings and planted tobacco and corn. Virginia's origins lay at nearby Jamestown, settled in 1607, but always a precarious perch, with its swamps and diseases and frequent fires. In 1699 Governor Nicholson and the House of Burgesses decided the small village growing at what was known as Middle Plantation would serve as a better capital, though it was still a small settlement in the woods with some marks of progress—a church, some taverns, a few shops, and the newly established College of William and Mary. The location was deemed to be "healthy and agreeable" with a "serene and temperate Aire, dry and champaign Land and plentifully supplied with wholesome springs." ◆ And, with a vote, the legislature moved to the little town, and shaped its future. The pattern was set with a pen stroke—a plan for the town was sketched, most probably under the Governor's supervision, organized along a broad main street that passed straight for nearly a mile between the College building and the Capitol building that was begun in 1701. Provisions were made for a Market Square, for a grander church, for a residential quarter, and by 1716 the Royal Governor occupied his large house, dubbed the Palace by those still living in the typical Virginia dwelling of two or three rooms.

The Colonial Williamsburg we see now follows the pattern of what was created as the rich and the poor and the enslaved circled this center for commerce, political power, and social life. The colony was still primarily agrarian, towns were small, and farmers and planters, especially the wealthy on their thousands of country acres, were isolated. Williamsburg became the stage where power was bartered and friendships made, where fashions were imported and carried home in a cart, where elegant balls brought the glittering summit of society to caper by candlelight, and the craftsmen and -women set their shop windows to catch the town's attention.

Although some were born in the colony, most came from England: At society's pinnacle were the wealthy adventurers, planters, and investors, joined by a thriving middle class of small holders and merchants alive to the town's possibilities, and supported by indentured servants and others willing to bet their future on weeks in a boat bouncing on a broad sea, and years spent working to save a stake. And, of course, there were Native Americans who lived nearby, and, for instance, sold pottery to the new householders, and African slaves whose labor was everywhere.

England remained the focus, the "mother country," for many, a value that transcended later political agitations. England, after all, controlled the colony's trade and was determined to keep it, but, more subtly, England was the origin of intellectual concerns and the books and newspapers that discussed them, of laws and of manners, of fashions in dress and the rituals of life—tea and the cups to put it in, brocade and the pattern for a cloak, wallpaper in the newest tints—all delivered to the docks in the ships that sailed away with hogsheads of tobacco. But, English as the colonists considered themselves to be, something new was building here too, a way of life that matched the colony's own rhythms, where climate and distance and new influences made Williamsburg something other than just a displaced English village. By the time America broke with Britain, the colonists who chose to remain had come to think of themselves as altogether different, and made their lives accordingly.

The town that was created with a vote and a map lost its center in a show of hands as well, when the legislature decided in 1779 to move the capital to Richmond, leaving the graceful brick buildings empty, the streets quiet, the tavern keeper and silversmith, the cabinetmaker and carpenter with fewer customers. The nineteenth century saw a town where cows grazed on the College green that had been the site of a fine ornamental garden, and those townspeople with the wherewithal tacked a veranda trimmed in Carpenter Gothic onto the front of a Georgian house and sat in a rocker and watched the dust rise on Duke of Gloucester Street. Tourists came now and then to "walk where Washington walked" and visit a tearoom to be served by a colonist's great-granddaughter, perhaps, who might have stored her Bible and her silver spoons in the family mahogany chest of drawers and longed for something more up-to-date. Well into this century, Williamsburg slumbered, a town that remembered its glories while electric wires were strung along the streets and the eighteenth-century harmonies of proportion and planning were covered in the gas stations and plate glass the new generations required.

Yet the very slumbering was a great boon to historic preservation, as no factories replaced the colonial structures, no grand civic improvements swept away the great Palace or widened the Duke of Gloucester Street into a highway. Although Williamsburg was not completely a town that time forgot, it was enough of one that the aura of the eighteenth century clung to it until enough generations had passed to appreciate not only the old capital's contributions to history, but also its remarkable living "library" of design.

THE RESTORATION

But some were able to see beyond the twentieth-century layer. "Williamsburg . . . offered an opportunity to restore a complete area and free it entirely from alien or inharmonious surroundings as well as to preserve the beauty and charm of the old buildings and gardens of the city," wrote John D. Rockefeller Jr. And that is what he did, in a long process that was begun when he secretly wrote a check in 1926 for $8,000 to buy the Ludwell-Paradise House, convinced by the enthusiasm and scholarship of Dr. W. A. R. Goodwin, who had served as priest of Bruton Parish Church.

Goodwin was a rare example of a romantic with the push and pull of a born salesman. As a boy he'd dreamed over the book *Hidden Cities Restored;* as a man he was known for his persuasiveness, dynamism, and charisma. He had spent years on his own small preservation efforts in the town, before finding the man with the foresight—and the fortune—to see what lay buried here. For him, it was a crusade, a chance to reveal in the city "an outward and visible sign of spiritual truth and beauty, through which the lives of visitors to the place would be inspired and enriched."

Rockefeller was not immediately won over; secretaries shrugged off the importuning rector. But he did eventually pay the town an anonymous visit, viewing the Wythe House with Goodwin, then asking to wander alone through the quiet streets and woods. The town itself spoke to him evocatively, and most convincingly, and Rockefeller then began the relationship with the place and its inhabitants that continued throughout his

life. He underwrote the restoration of the town and received in turn what seemed more than ordinary satisfactions, especially after he bought Bassett Hall and spent several months of the year here. He and his wife, Abby Aldrich Rockefeller, were happy with the simplest of pleasures in the town, among them a nightly walk. "We look in the windows, and we look at the moon and the stars. You can't appreciate Williamsburg unless you walk through the town. Always you see something different: a fence or a chimney from some angle you never saw before. I feel I really belong in Williamsburg."

Millions of visitors since have shared this sentiment, as well as the many delights afforded by a walk down Williamsburg's streets. The peace and the beauty of this space, the simple geometry of the eighteenth-century town plan filled with the blooming gardens and houses on a human scale, exemplifies many visitors' sense of a comfortable urban plan. Some take home a

A marble mortar in the Pasteur & Galt Apothecary shows its years of use.

tricorn hat, most a roll or two of photographs, others an idea for the cut of a curtain, or a dream of a tall-post bed. For there is something about the scale and the execution of the restoration of the town, with attention paid to the tiniest detail, that has persuaded Americans that here was a way of life that has meaning for contemporary householders, too.

THE REVIVAL OF "COLONIAL STYLE"

Visitors are responding not only to the past of two hundred years ago, but also to the "colonial" influences that have long been part of the country's design choices. Each era has plucked from the past what suits its present. As soon as they had enough history to celebrate it, Americans made a point of the past, even as they worshiped the future. And enthusiasm for things "colonial" began as soon as the memories of the early days of settlement began to fade; by the 1860s "olde tyme kitchens" were a feature of charity fairs, where ladies in hoop skirts sat gingerly on hundred-year-old chairs and tried a bite of apple pie from an old recipe. Furnishings almost always included a spinning wheel, a musket over an open fireplace, candlesticks and pewter plates, and an attendant in a "mobcap." One New England writer said the idea was "to reproduce the manners, customs, dress, and if possible, the idiom of the time—in short, to illustrate the domestic life and habits of the people, to whose determined courage . . . we owe that government, so dear to every loyal heart." Many contemporary restoration programs share a similar aim. At home, however, the Victorians still saw much of eighteenth-century design as too plain, too old-fashioned, too out-of-date to tolerate on a daily basis, except as a curiosity from great-grandmother's day. Old photographs of the interiors of Williamsburg houses where descendants of original families lived show their attempts to soften and enhance eighteenth-century spaces by draping frilly lace curtains over a fine chair rail, covering a graceful Pembroke table until only the legs peeked out from beneath a fringed patterned tablecloth in the parlor.

But the Centennial of the Revolution in 1876, and the ensuing growth in national pride, prompted a new interest in interpreting design elements from the eighteenth century—the first "Colonial Revival," a mining of a rich dictionary of ornament for the new spaces, new possessions that would call to mind the era, if not replicate it faithfully. At the same time that Frank Lloyd Wright was sculpting his ground-hugging Prairie homes and the Beaux Arts architects were erecting French palaces in midwestern towns, Charles Follen McKim, William Rutherford Mead, and Stanford White devoted much of their architectural practice to designs that captured the doorway, the window, the shutter of earlier times. In 1876 the three young men had gone on a tour of New England towns, sketching and measuring surviving eighteenth-century buildings, excited by the riches that lay before them, however drowsy and derelict. The newly wealthy merchants about to build a house to crown their labors in Newport or on a New York estate were happy to choose one of their designs that implied family roots stretching back to the beginnings of the country, though a cornice shape might come from Connecticut, a window from Richmond.

And there was a growing demand at all levels for furnishings that called the time to mind, though, as Clarence Cook wrote in 1878 in *The House Beautiful,* it was the "spirit" of the past that needed reviving, not an exact replication of the antique; it was the "charm of bygone days" that was to be pursued. Still, he preached the joys of what had gone before, and the beauty of what remained, like the fine sideboard he found serving as a chicken coop for a farm family. Beyond mere beauty, antique objects had a symbolic value, something we

In the front hallway of the Christiana Campbell Tavern, a red cape hanging on a peg brings the past to life.

The Governor's butler kept not only the crystal and plate at the ready, but also his articles of grooming.

are as likely to respond to—the warmth of the hearth, for instance, where a family could gather was a romantic remnant of the past—and a cheering ritual for the present that we recognize as well.

By the 1920s, when Colonial Williamsburg's restoration was begun, more architects and their patrons were interested in authenticity, in exact replicas of houses that had stood two hundred years before, complete to the contents. Architectural historians and archaeologists were more and more involved in mapping out the regional and individual variations in the houses of colonial times. The great antiques collectors of the age, such as Henry du Pont at Winterthur and Henry Ford at Greenfield Village in Michigan, were able to buy not only exquisite examples of American antique furniture but whole houses, or just their prime portions—a stair hall, a paneled wall—in which to put them, and set the pace for scholarship and display.

On a domestic level, the affection for Colonial Revival, which dates officially from America's first centennial celebrations in 1876, has remained a constant throughout this century. An eagle might hang over the front door or a family room center around a broad fireplace; Chinese wallpapers might adorn the dining room or candlesticks dress the table. One of the most winning examples of the revival is in Williamsburg, at Bassett Hall, the eighteenth-century frame house on the fringe of the Historic Area that was the Rockefellers' favorite refuge. Abby Aldrich Rockefeller decorated the house with the fine folk art she collected, a good highboy and handsome china, and the cushioned sofas and up-to-date curtains that made for comfort— "authentic" Colonial Revival. Mrs. Rockefeller was one of the first to show how to mix early American with contemporary art.

THE INFLUENCE OF THE COLONIAL WILLIAMSBURG FOUNDATION ON DECORATION

Williamsburg spread the taste for the best of eighteenth-century design from the moment visitors opened the doors of the first few restored houses. Rockefeller always intended the town's primary purpose to be educational, a way to inculcate the values and lessons of early American history. But other lessons were learned as well, such as a new appreciation of the way of life many members of this small society enjoyed. Although these first visitors saw rooms very different from the ones we now explore, the same sigh often came—"I could live there."

And magazines like a 1937 *House and Garden,* for instance, made it possible. Devoting a whole issue to the town, it both chronicled the passionate interest the public had in its history, and the growing desire to own examples of its designs. The editors exhort the readers to the "absorbing and illuminating study" to be found here, the opportunity to examine, by actually standing in a room or studying the front door, to "ask ourselves exactly what it is about that room that we like. It may be the size, and the proportions; it may be a certain finely balanced arrangement of the windows and doors and wall areas; it may be the details, the color scheme, the decoration." Visitors today, at whatever level of consciousness, go through the same process.

Perry, Shaw, and Hepburn, the Boston architectural firm that supervised the restoration of Williamsburg, was asked by the magazine to produce plans for contemporary readers to build from, not exact copies of existing houses, but fine examples of houses that typify their own era—where there was always space for a maid's room, but rarely for a second family bathroom. The houses were built all over America: "Williamsburg Colonial" was a line looked for on a real estate advertisement, ensuring charm, boxwood hedges, and fireplaces in the living room and dining room.

House and Garden advocated filling the rooms inside with *Williamsburg* reproductions, exact copies of chairs and tables and glassware that were appropriate to Williamsburg. The reproductions program, just eight years old, had been a radical advance for the restoration, developed at the prompting of Rockefeller himself. In 1930 the Raleigh Tavern was to be reopened as an inn where the public might dine, and the furniture and fabrics planned as a mix of antique and reproductions. But for mealtimes, there was a need to order some modern china for the tables, to stand up to daily use. Rockefeller was discontented with this lapse in authenticity, and asked that England's Josiah Wedgwood & Sons, the company that had made much of the chinaware whose fragments were found in excavations on the tavern's site, produce more of the Queen's Ware the previous patrons had known. "The purpose of education might be furthered by the sale of this ware," Rockefeller suggested, and there lay the beginnings of the reproductions program. By 1937 it had grown enough to fill a first mail-order catalog, which allowed even more people to enjoy the reproductions of textiles and wallpapers, pewter, crystal, brass, carpets, and lighting.

Some reproductions were needed for proper interpretation of the historic houses. When, for instance, a bed was to be hung properly with the many yards of fabric required, reproductions true in design and coloring were developed to stand up to the rigors of display. But the enthusiasm of the public for well-made replicas, when antiques were expensive and, often, impractical, meant a growing market for products made to the exacting standards of *Williamsburg*. Soon, builders wanted paints and moldings; interior designers sought out fabrics; home decorators from the White House to the suburbs discovered that Colonial Williamsburg furniture would outlast a generation and survive changing styles with dignity.

Reproductions have always had appeal—even the Romans made copies of fine Greek statues—but

Williamsburg's program has always been uniquely vigorous in its scholarship and attentive to authenticity and quality, demanding much of its suppliers. Sometimes, as with Wedgwood, factories familiar to the colonists could be called upon; on other occasions, manufacturers willing to resurrect the colonists' handwork or other traditional techniques joined the roster of reproduction craftsmen. A manufacturer who earns a license from Colonial Williamsburg will work carefully with curators to determine possible candidates for reproduction, as well as to ensure the accuracy of the product. With the extensive collections on display in the restoration and in the DeWitt Wallace Gallery, and the Abby Aldrich Rockefeller Folk Art Center, inspiration for pieces grand and humble is easy to find.

And each generation, for the almost sixty years the reproductions have been available, has found its own way with these classics. The sideboard Grandmother loved in her formal dining room, where she set the table with care and linen table mats, serves just as happily at family meals in today's informal homes. A change of upholstery, and the scroll-armed love seat travels from room to room before settling at the foot of the bed. Mrs. Peyton Randolph, who loved her Chelsea tea set in 1775, might have been surprised to see its descendant carried into the kitchen for tea with a friend, but she would have recognized the pattern of the china, and the friendship.

"Designs based on antiques in the Colonial Williamsburg collections work in both traditional and contemporary settings," says Elizabeth Gusler, the curator of museum education who knows a great deal about the way eighteenth-century residents furnished their houses, and appreciates the ease with which reproductions inhabit our own time. "We repeat the same trends century to century. These reproductions are based on proportions and decorative elements that have stood the test of time. They have become classic, transcending a specific time or place."

THE WILLIAMSBURG WAY OF LIFE

Perhaps the aspect of eighteenth-century living that would most surprise us now was a room's flexibility. While we are used to a single-purpose area labeled for dining or for sleeping, both the terms and the uses for a room were much less rigid in colonial Williamsburg. The gradual desire for privacy, for distinguishing between a public and private side of a house, is part of the changing vision of a residence and its framing of a family's relationship with the world outside.

In the early days of settlement, it was a rare family who had more than a room or two to live in, and even then, with constant travelers' visits and servants busy about their work, these were spaces filled with people and activity until everyone fell asleep. This central room served many purposes and was furnished for practicality, oriented to the broad fireplace, where food was cooked and the fire warmed the room. Furniture was made to be adaptable—stools and chests were for sitting, a long board could be brought out to serve as a table at dinnertime, and a well-trimmed bed along one wall was—when curtains were drawn—the preserve of the master and mistress of the house. Even well into the eighteenth century, quite successful planters inhabited such one-up, one-down houses; prosperity was revealed in the fine woodwork or finishes within what seemed a simple building from without.

This main room devoted to dining and entertaining, in its more sophisticated incarnations, as well as the work of the household, was called a hall, a term that originated in grand medieval houses where master and mistress and all their household occupied one large room. The use of "hall" or "hall-parlour" lingered into the eighteenth century; for instance, Colonel Thomas Jones of Williamsburg settled his property on his wife in

1732, and detailed seven punch bowls "all of which are now in a room . . . called the Hall, and most of them are part of the usual furniture of the hall." Those punch bowls were probably handily placed for an evening's entertainment, held ready in a corner cupboard.

By the mid-eighteenth century an ambitious home builder, typically a plantation owner or wealthy town dweller, like George Wythe at colonial Williamsburg, would include a broad hallway or passage as the first element of the house encountered by a visitor. The long passageway in the middle of the house, with its doors open at either end, could allow a sweep of a breeze, and be a pleasant place to sit with a friend or two. Often with a magnificent stairway as its centerpiece, the passage was calculated to impress any visitor with the grandeur of the occupant, and the progression from outside to inside the family circle. A few very rich citizens built houses with magnificent stairways that led to entertaining spaces on the upper floor, as in the Governor's Palace. But everywhere the passage continued to be an assembly room for many occasions, not simply a space devoted to traffic. There are mentions of harpsichords being played there, of ladies receiving their guests while seated there: "We took our seats in a cool passage where the Company were sitting," Philip Fithian, a tutor to the Carter family, wrote of a visit to a neighbor. Clearly, Williamsburg's hot and humid summers encouraged use of the breeziest spot in the house.

In the seventeenth century a "hall" had been a multipurpose chamber, full of furniture, such as a dining table, chests, cupboards, and chairs, as detailed in one 1674 inventory. But by the middle of the next century, men and women with bigger houses that allowed a separation between social and family spaces, and more formal ideas of how to meet the world had begun to devote separate rooms to different activities. The lucky few enjoyed a dining room and a gathering place that became known as the parlor. Even as these rooms evolved as places where particular activities were carried on, families still treated their functions as flexible. In the Governor's Palace, for instance, the dining room contained several desks and worktables which remained even when the expansive dining table with its panoply of plate and white damask was carried into place by the servants.

The true luxury was space, accompanied by improvements in the physical makeup of the house that allowed rooms' uses to change. Windows were bigger, with more light to illuminate a far corner, and the smaller fireplaces with, sometimes, by the 1770s, a handsome iron coal grate, meant visitors and family could make use of the whole of a room in comfort. No longer did they need to draw quite so close to the fireside to stay warm, or stitch and read next to a small window in search of light. As colonial society matured and shed its wilderness roots, members wanted to draw a line between the private activities of the family, the domestic tasks it took to run the house, and the elegant occasions when guests came to call.

A contemporary room decorated completely in authentic colonial style would look spare, unsettled, to our eyes. We would recognize, however, the era's zest for acquiring the newest, the most fashionable, the ornamental as well as the merely useful. As the eighteenth century progressed, the enthusiasm for acquiring things beyond what was strictly necessary for daily living spread throughout society. This consumer revolution was driven by increasingly sophisticated manufacturing methods that allowed goods to be sold at more affordable prices, as well as a public that simply wanted more, its enthusiasms stoked by the newest imports —tea and Chinese porcelain, Indian fabrics, Virginia tobacco—that encouraged new social rituals, and the equipment to serve them.

Virginians were as anxious to follow fashion as their fellows in London; many had been educated in England and continued ties based on trade and family relationships that kept them up to date. Those with money to spend collected enormous stashes of silver and finely worked mahogany, bales of silks, and buckles for their shoes. William Nelson was obviously of two minds about the growing wealth of the colony when he wrote his agents in London in 1772: "I am much obliged to you for the elegant mahogany cistern as well as the convenience to preserve the gravy warm, but do you observe that these elegancies are so many incitements to luxury to which Virginians are but too prone." With a gleeful self-assurance, those with the disposable income for such luxury goods were likely to display them in a pointed manner; paint analysis reveals that the open-shelved cupboards, called a "bowfat" or "buffet" in eastern Virginia, were sometimes painted a particularly eye-catching orange, for instance, to ensure the attention of the visitor and to set off the fashionable "Queen's China."

Williamsburg had many stores and importers offering lavish lists of things to be bought, which brought visitors and townspeople alike to browse through the newest goods from the latest shipment from London. Traces of surprisingly high-flown tastes have been found in archaeological digs in Williamsburg, implying that those just ascending the social scale would often splurge on a fine piece of creamware or a set of silver spoons. The very wealthy planters would instruct their agents in London to search for whatever was in the newest taste, though often adding the caution that what was chosen be "plain but neat." In fact, furniture made in this period in Virginia is remarkable for its restrained styling in contrast to Northern examples, as Virginians found true elegance in understatement.

Today, we love the neoclassical elements that were all the rage in Chippendale's workshop, we savor color and texture, just as our ancestors did, we appreciate the arts of the dining table, even if candlelight is now our choice rather than our only option. And much of the material culture of the eighteenth century makes sense to us, feels right, because in the harmony of its proportions it still suits our ideas of how a chair, a table, a chest of drawers should be formed. Thomas Chippendale, in his *Gentleman and Cabinet-Maker's Director,* the design book we know was in Williamsburg cabinetmaker Edmund Dickinson's workshop, cites both the laws of perspective and the ancient orders of architecture as the proper fitting for furniture. He speaks of designs as being "intelligible," a good word for the almost indefinable way we still respond to these designs that were worked out with mathematical precision as certain as the sun's setting, as well as the individual grace that a love of beauty yields.

The ongoing work of historians and archaeologists has revealed more to us about the way of life that was lived here, and the story told in the houses and on the streets of Williamsburg has subtly changed from the first days, when modern habits based on the hangovers from the Victorian love of ornament and "what looked nice" had more to do with how the draperies and furniture and plantings were first placed in the town. Insights have widened, and there is a new appreciation of vivid colors, for instance, or rooms that were much more sparely furnished than was first thought.

Williamsburg has never been a richer resource for those seeking design inspiration. The quality of scholarship at work behind the scenes means that what we see is as close as we can approach to the life that vanished two hundred years ago. The active reproduction program means we can command just the chair and table and candlestick that suit our own ideas of beauty at home. Inspiration lies all around us, in the pathways and the Palace, the gardens and the parlors, the bar rooms and the bedrooms of the restored colonial capital. "There are windows here . . . through which unparalleled vistas open," said Dr. Goodwin of the Williamsburg he hoped to restore. And those who love fine design will never stop walking the streets and pausing to peer into windows that open on another world. ◆

For six decades, the *Williamsburg* Reproduction Program has filled homes with beautiful furnishings such as this side table.

LIVING ROOMS *and* GATHERING PLACES I

No people can entertain their friends with
better cheer and welcome.
—HUGH JONES,
PRESENT STATE OF VIRGINIA, 1724

Few accounts of colonial Virginia omit accounts of merrymaking, of balls that went on for four days and nights, of parties when, as Philip Fithian observed, "the ladies were dressed gay and splendid & when dancing their skirts & Brocades rustled and trailed behind them," or musical evenings in Williamsburg when, as the irascible visitor Landon Carter complained to his diary, "I hear from every house a constant tuting." Such grand and formal occasions were not uncommon, especially during Publick Times when planters in from their acres and members of the House of Burgesses flooded the town for sessions at the capitol, and filled the taverns, two to a bed. Of course, on ordinary days there were more informal gatherings, perhaps a few women collecting to share some tea on the new china set fresh from London, or men who sat round the punch bowl replenished regularly with hot spiced wine and spent the evening puffing on long clay pipes full of the local leaf and talking politics.

OPPOSITE The imposing doors of the Supper Room at the Governor's Palace feature a chinoiserie door surround based on designs by eighteenth-century Chesapeake designer William Buckland, who was probably influenced by English furniture-maker Thomas Chippendale. The stove, with its (very modern for the time) neoclassical designs of urns and garlands, RIGHT, was ordered from London to warm the room during winter parties.

So this society that was so fond of its sociability embraced the parlor—a room whose very name recalls conversation—which became the chief public room of the house, where company was entertained and on display were the finest furniture, the most expensive wallpapers and paints and cabinetwork. The expensive bed that once was often centered in the main room was relegated to a separate chamber, but there were many other ways to acquaint the visitor with the taste and the deep pockets of the home owner. The Brush–Everard House's vivid verdigris paint in the parlor, for instance, is a powerful statement of fashion, fancy, and finances on the part of Thomas Everard, a wealthy leader of the community.

As was common throughout a house of this period, furniture was chosen for versatility as well as the taste of the moment. Especially in the parlor, the eighteenth-century approach to the room as a constantly changing background to the requirements of hospitality is clear. Within the frame of a fine finished room were chairs and tables that could be placed anywhere—next to the window on a sunny day, drawn near the fire on a winter's

Side chairs, **OPPOSITE,** could be moved to suit the activities of a room. Fine examples of Chippendale chairs usually came in sets of twelve; these were reproduced from a partial set of chairs that were in the Palace when Lord Dunmore, Virginia's last governor under the crown, was in residence. **ABOVE** Lord Botetourt had two such stoves in the Palace. **RIGHT** Four glass transfers from a set of designs depicting the seasons are in a bedchamber in a surround of fancy molding.

evening—and reconfigured for an intimate gathering or a grand entertainment. If an evening's activities were to flow from cards to some late refreshments, the furniture obliged: Chairs that by day served a tea table could be pulled to the card table, and the drop leaves on the table by the window could be raised and secured to hold the punch bowl and the plates. Moved into place by servants, each piece of furniture was returned to its proper position against the chair board on the wall, when a room was deemed to be "at rest." It was as if the room were a stage, a set readied for each performance of daily life.

We would find this a much more sparsely furnished room than we are used to in our own time, with no draperies at the windows, perhaps a Wilton carpet laid wall to wall or a small precious rug in the center of the room. Seating came in great abundance and variety, a forest of mahogany legs and arms of all shapes and sizes. There might be an "elbow chair" with short arms, a corner chair, also called a smoking chair, high-back, low-back, or cane chairs, Windsor chairs, or even, as a

RIGHT The Governor's visitors must have marveled at the dazzling Wilton carpet and bright blue wallpapers in an Adam-inspired neo-classical decorating scheme. The wallpaper edges, **BELOW**, were outlined with gadrooned papier-mâché borders molded from a fragment that Chippendale supplied to Harewood in England.

COLOR

Visitors to Williamsburg today, who often think of the typical Williamsburg interior as a harmonious blend of "Williamsburg blue" and pure white, are surprised when they enter the houses that reflect the newest research into colonial color schemes. From the first efforts at restoration, the houses here were carefully examined for clues to their original shapes and colorings; researchers painstakingly scraped back layers of paint. But increasingly sophisticated techniques have allowed a sharper view into the palette that pleased those who built these houses. Chemical analysis and historical research have revealed that, although the exterior of an eighteenth-century Williamsburg house may have been unpainted or covered in a wash of white, the rooms within were often vibrant with colors that can seem flamboyant to our eyes. • Certainly many houses were full of the ocher or dull brown paint, pale blue, and white that householders ordered as neat and practical—at one point the Randolph House was painted Spanish brown both inside and outside, surely a conservative choice. But such owners as Thomas Everard, intent on a dazzling new look when he renovated his house around 1770, chose a different color as the main motif for every room. He had the parlor painted in a verdigris glaze, a bright green that was obviously expensive and, when seen under the glitter of candlelight, must have come alive in an interplay of shadow and shimmer. And the dining room cupboard, once bright orange, received another greenish glaze coat, since Virginians were likely to draw attention to the place where their best was displayed with an emphatic tone in the paintwork—an inspiration to contemporary home owners.

LEFT *The wall behind this post-Revolutionary mantel is painted bright yellow, similar to a color found on an early wallpaper at the Brush-Everard House. A fashionable portrait in wax hangs against paneling in the Governor's Palace dining room,* **RIGHT,** *painted in pearl color, as noted in the Virginia House of Burgesses orders for painting the room. This color is available from Martin Senour as Palace Diningroom Pearl Blue.*

The view through the ground floor of Christiana Campbell's Tavern, LEFT, *reveals a succession of color in pleasing combination, a decorating scheme that works with very little other decoration. In the red dining room of the King's Arms Tavern,* RIGHT, *a handsome pierced-back chair and raised panel door are the only other decoration.*

A silk robe and a Chippendale chair mark the room beyond, painted in Palace Chambers Yellow from Martin Senour as the Governor's dressing room, LEFT. *The walls of the Governor's library, in the foreground, are in Palace Study Blue.* RIGHT *Wetherburn's Tavern, with a lighter look than the King's Arms, is home to a splat-backed chair. The chair rail behind, painted in a rich brown, protects the lighter walls from scuff marks.*

This reconstructed workshop, **LEFT,** is painted with an iron oxide pigment often used on simple early Virginia buildings. **RIGHT** The white, brown, and ocher color scheme of the St. George Tucker House was ordered by Tucker himself in 1798, according to the contract with Jeremiah Satterwhite. Exteriors were generally painted either very dark hues or white.

LEFT The Brush-Everard House's vivid verdigris paint in the parlor is a powerful statement of fashion, fancy, and finances on the part of Thomas Everard, a wealthy leader of the community. **RIGHT** Recent microscopic analysis has revealed a pretty sky blue used on the Nelson-Galt House woodwork in the third quarter of the eighteenth century.

The color scheme of the front public room of the Raleigh Tavern features Raleigh Tavern Green on the woodwork. Thin fluted pilasters frame the spaces on either side of the fireplace in the large front room.

collection is a handsome desk and bookcase made by local cabinetmaker Anthony Hay, of walnut with cubbyholes, a drop front, and a closed cupboard above. Simply styled, it was owned by Dr. John Minson Galt, and shows even the solid middle class of the town could aspire to a handsome piece probably meant for the parlor.

Colonists could, increasingly, depend on local tradespeople for some of their furniture, though most still saw England as the main supplier, or, more rarely, bought

Williamsburg cabinetmaker advertised in a *Virginia Gazette* of 1766, a "mathematical gouty chair." Rush-bottomed or brocade-seated, with "Russian-leather" or "Turkey-work," and often ordered in sets to match, these were chairs that could be placed in the hall or around a table. The most precious, with fine upholstered seats, were likely to be protected with less-expensive materials, like the loose checked slipcovers we see in the Palace.

And there were tables to suit many purposes, too, a round tea table, its tilt-top an aid to stowing it against the wall, or a card table with a folding top and a green baize surface. There might be a musical instrument, such as the "very neat hand organ in a mahogany case with gilt front" advertised in the *Gazette* in 1752, or a secretary that could store a few precious books; in the Colonial Williamsburg

OPPOSITE Set up to display their spare elegance, pierced splat chairs fill an office in the Governor's Palace. **ABOVE LEFT** Chairs in the parlor of the Peyton Randolph House await duty. **ABOVE** Nearby, a tray of glasses and a few open bottles stand ready to make guests feel at home. Beneath the table is a "spirit case."

The dining room of the Peyton Randolph House was a large multipurpose room that could be arranged to suit the activity of the hour—from dining to dancing to musical diversion. As an important public room it displayed the family's wealth and refined tastes. The view through the ground floor, OPPOSITE, recalls the enfilade arrangement of rooms in grand English country houses.

STAIRCASES

In the beginning, there were ladders to lofts, but as the century progressed, any house grand enough to claim a proper second floor was designed around a handsome stair hall, for progressing properly upstairs could be an important social ceremony. The careful carpentry details that mark an important room in the house are found here, too, in the decoration that marks the moldings and the choice of woods that made the balustrade and turned posts. A grand open staircase wasn't practical—heat escaped, and broad stairs required more space. Clearly, there were other important elements at work than practicality. The first object to confront a visitor entering a passageway was this staircase, an important element in the hall's design. A handsome stairway signaled that important rooms lay upstairs and, in a time when a party might drift all over the house, led the way to more imposing spaces, as at the Governor's Palace, where ascending the stairs was part of a grand party's panoply, and the Governor undoubtedly made the most of a formal descent. Even Peyton Randolph's staircase, with its floods of light from the curved window at the top and a multiplicity of beautifully turned banisters, announced from the hallway that this was a household of some ceremony. There might be dark and narrow stairs at the rear of a house where servants could scuttle up and down, but in the main stair hall a household's formality was revealed.

LEFT *The stair hall of Bassett Hall, built in the third quarter of the eighteenth century and restored after a fire in 1932, is a fine example of how a staircase can add drama to the visitor's first view of a grand house. The railing curves upward at the turning, emphasizing the line of the staircase. The detail,* RIGHT, *shows the delicate S-curve in the spandrel over the wainscoting that protects the wall side of the staircase.*

One of the first things Peyton Randolph planned as he renovated his father's house in the mid-eighteenth century was a grand staircase to the upper story. The open string stair with its square newel and turned baluster, LEFT, marches toward the large north-facing window. The scrolling that incorporates acanthus leaves and little flowers decorates a staircase at the Brush-Everard House, RIGHT, and dates to about 1740.

George Washington may well have mounted Christiana Campbell's tavern staircase, LEFT, with its broad short sweep of steps and a turned newel. The back stairs at the Nelson-Galt House, RIGHT, dates to the early eighteenth-century. Baker's reproduction chairs, covered with Schumacher's Tavern Check, stand guard in the hallway.

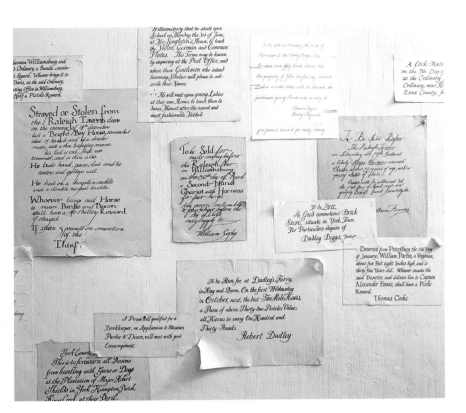

Taverns like the Raleigh, located on Duke of Gloucester Street, resembled home, with furnishings that were plainer versions of the chairs and tables in fine houses, **OPPOSITE**. The walls, painted in the color now available from Martin Senour as Raleigh Tavern Green, set off the mellow tones of the wood, **BELOW**. The wall in the passageway, **LEFT**, would have been plastered with notices—the bulletin board of its day.

furniture from ships that brought the products of other colonies to Virginia. An order to England would produce furniture in the latest style, but new ideas also came directly with cabinetmakers' apprentices when they arrived from London. An inventory of the effects of Williamsburg cabinetmaker Edmund Dickinson listed a copy of Chippendale's *Director*, the all-important pattern book for furniture—as its title page states, the "Most elegant and Useful designs of Household Furniture in the Most Fashionable Taste." Williamsburg cabinetmakers could command the patronage of some of the colony's most discerning individuals. Certainly men as sophisticated and well-off as Robert Carter of Nomini Hall ordered furniture, including an expensive desk and bookcase, from Williamsburg cabinetmakers, and a table in the Colonial Williamsburg collection attributed to Anthony Hay offers a fine example of fanciful and finely made fretwork that incorporates a small bird, perhaps the sign it was made for Colonel William Byrd. And in 1766 "B. Bucktrout, cabinet-maker from London" could advertise in the *Virginia Gazette* that he was doing "all kinds of cabinet-work in the newest fashions."

LIGHTING

Candles, for us the accompaniment to romance and special occasions, were a precious necessity for Williamsburg households. Oil lamps became a possibility late in the century, but only the wealthy could afford the costly whale oil that fueled them. Candles were also expensive in money or labor; made of wax or spermaceti, they were carefully hoarded: Governor Botetourt's inventory included a package of broken wax candles, among the "5 doz. long wax candles" and five dozen "middling wax tapers" and green wax tapers. Even the wealthy Carter family lit their dining room for a party with just seven candles—and that was considered a lavish display. Certainly grand houses like the Palace had rooms with multibranched hanging chandeliers, so a formal occasion was literally dazzling. But candlesticks, easily carried to a dark corner, were much more common. Such candlesticks' designs reflected fashion; for instance, London's taste for the baroque surfaced in a well-turned baluster shape worked in silver. A chamberstick might be made in flowered china or of glass. To increase the refraction of light, candlesticks often came with a backing of mirrored glass, a glass globe that protected a flame and increased its power, or dangling glass lusters that shimmered and cast rainbows around the room. • But these were pieces for the ballroom or parlor; daily needs or more workaday parts of the house were served with iron "hogscraper" sticks; a fragment of one was found in the Geddy shop site, with a brass reinforcing band, dating to 1750. Tin sconces on the wall or tin sticks also lit the more informal parts of the house, such as a passageway or the kitchen.

Whether a wealth of bayberry tapers hung by their uncut wicks in the butler's pantry of the Governor's Palace, LEFT, or a modern interpretation of candlelight in a delicate wall sconce, RIGHT, the lights of Williamsburg suggest intimacy and the pace of a gentler time. The glass shade in the entrance hall of Bassett Hall would have protected the candle flame from sudden breezes, the wall from soot, and the passerby from the danger of fire.

LEFT *A chandelier in the Governor's Palace was designed to light up a grand party with the least number of expensive candles; myriad pieces of crystal, called "glass lustres," refracted and magnified the light.* RIGHT *A night light, indoors, shows one more variation on the colonial lighting theme. Its spare lines make it look almost modern.*

Outdoors, then as today, lights meant safe passage on town streets. Though a lantern such as this, LEFT, *might seldom have been lit, it would have been invaluable when due occasion merited. Today, its design is an unobtrusive solution to illuminating the front door. A brass candlestick was the simplest means to illuminate the stairs up to bed,* RIGHT.

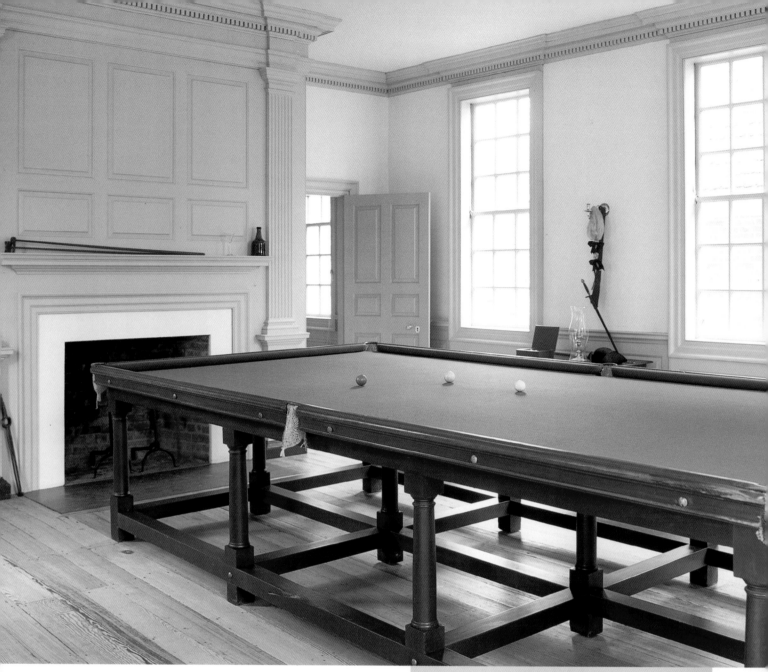

Besides handsome furniture, the features of the parlor were likely to include paintings, like the "neat landskip" George Washington ordered, or, more commonly, framed prints on the wall, bought at the printers and booksellers. Often, the subject matter was both decorative and informative. A collection of well-chosen prints could provide a suitable topic for conversation with visitors—Fithian writes of visiting a friend and having a pleasant time leafing through his folders of prints—and a way of indicating the educated and cultured interests of the owner. The excitement of the time's scientific inquiry and new explorations of the world could be brought home with an engraving of North American birds by Mark Catesby, or a folio of botanical illustrations, displaying flowers in fine detail. Those with a less serious turn of mind might put themselves down for a delivery

LEFT *A contemporary mantel is in the Craft House, where reproductions are shown in room settings. Even today, the fireplace is often the focus of a room, and the most honored place for a work of art is over the mantel.* RIGHT *A paneled wood surround ends a few feet above the hearth with space above for framed botanical prints.*

Some elaborate mantels, such as this one in the Peyton Randolph House, with a pattern of acanthus leaves in high relief, LEFT, *featured carving. Distinctive blue-and-white delft tiles with Dutch landscapes (here in a Palace bedroom),* RIGHT, *were an attractive way to line the fireplace, but would have been available only to the wealthiest citizens, who could afford to import them from Holland.*

CONTEMPORARY INTERPRETATIONS

EVEN BEYOND THE LIGHT, THE WARMTH, AND

the soft upholstery, much has changed in today's living rooms that would mystify our eighteenth-century ancestors. The number of the furnishings, the new uses to which old forms are put, and, above all, the placement of chairs and tables would have surprised them, though they would certainly share our pride in handsome possessions and the warmth of gathering friends and family around the hearth.

No colonist had the luxury of space to nominate one room as a "living room," decorate it, and ironically then do most of the "living" in the rest of the house, preserving the "best" for rare formal occasions. In the eighteenth century, all was there to be used, with the adaptability of the room's contents allowing gatherings both formal and family-oriented. If we do keep a formally decorated room just for visitors, we're honoring the Victorians, who loved their parlors and made them into rooms meant more for display, where proper behavior was expected and furniture was stiff, horsehair-covered, and intended to maintain decorum.

In our own time, as houses grow smaller and reflect more closely how we actually live, we are moving toward a more free and less defined use of space that echoes the colonial

Full of light and pattern, this living room brings together many colonial design influences, using the reproductions from the Williamsburg program. **OPPOSITE** A comfortable easy chair, candlelight, and wine in handblown flutes provide the perfect ingredients for a mellow evening. The tea table, **RIGHT** and **BOTTOM**, serves its original purpose in front of the fire and also acts as a coffee table for the sofa and chairs. The toile de Jouy on the chair, Pleasures of the Farm from Schumacher, plays against the simple stripes on the sofa, pillow, and walls.

Virginians' ideas of entertaining with ease in adaptable rooms. And we can learn much about decorating from following colonial models. Contemporary plans now often include a common room, a "great room" near the kitchen, perhaps, where the whole family can involve itself in lots of different activities—and visitors can be welcomed into the heart of the family.

Schumacher's Greenhow Stripe fabric completely changes the look of the caned sofa from Baker Furniture in this passageway transformed into a sunroom. With a tea table and plain white curtains reminiscent of "Virginia Cloth," the sunroom is a cheerful place to entertain.

The caned sofa, here with a single pillow instead of cushions, lends an appropriately tropical air to the Virginia setting. The tea table, from Tradition House, is based on an antique tray in the Williamsburg collection. The tray can be lifted off the base for ease of serving. Chippendale's designs inspired the shape of the stand.

Here the forms of furniture common to Colonial Williamsburg come into their own, made as they are for serving different uses and for ease in adaptability. Some pieces of furniture we would find useful just as they did—a gaming table will suit bridge and Monopoly players, too. But chairs and tables chosen for the many ways they work in a room multiply the pleasure. One of the early archaeological finds in Williamsburg was a castor, showing that a chair or table could be drawn easily into place. Think of a tall tea table that *Williamsburg* reproduces—lift it to rest before the fire and you have a perfect setting for an easy supper or a card game with a child. Return it to the side of the sofa where it will collect this week's magazines and the coffee cup in the morning. Put it under the window to display your favorite collection.

Upholstered pieces were much rarer, and much less cushioned, than those we know; for instance, *Williamsburg* reproductions of

With at emphasis on a more period look that allows the fine moldings to take center stage, **OPPOSITE**, this room takes advantage of the arresting tones of Galt Sky Blue paint; the roll of a wing chair's arm, the circle of a side table, the play of the light are all elements in the design. Magnolia leaves in a jug are a simple arrangement on a side table, **LEFT**. The telescope box, **BELOW**, reveals and eighteenth-century-style coverlet and blanket to cozy a winter evening.

THIS PAGE and OPPOSITE A change in furniture has recast the living room of the Nelson-Galt House seen on pages 52–53. Now a more informal Baker sofa in a cheerful furniture check anchors the place before the fire. With the bare swept floorboards and undraped windows, the richness of detail in the furniture—the fretwork on the parlor table, the warm wood tones—stands out. A tall cupboard, BELOW, which follows a design for a clothes press, serves as an "entertainment center." More storage comes from the telescope box on a low stand, holding trays of glasses, ABOVE, and beneath the sofa table, OPPOSITE, helping keep clutter hidden.

wing chairs can be ordered with the authentic small pad, or the downier cushions we're used to. There were few if any sofas in early Williamsburg. But choosing a small settee, perhaps a rolled-arm love seat size, for a living room rather than a full-size sofa will also open new possibilities. Try it next to a table for extra seating, or balancing two armed chairs, and most of us will choose to orient it toward a fireplace for the luxury of sitting comfortably and watching the flames. Just as the colonials lived with sets of matching chairs intended to be moved where need or impulse required, we can be less rigid in our thinking about that wooden armchair, which might move from the desk to the side of a sofa to the tea table. The lesson the era has to teach us is easily read in new ways to arrange a living room for comfort and use, rather than a strict formation to which we must accommodate ourselves.

Contemporary decorators have a wealth of fabric and color to choose from, beyond the dreams of kings of old. Our color schemes can be temporary, due to the ease of wallpaper and paint applications and access to ready lengths of material, and we can rely on four-color pictures in catalogs or swatches, rather than an agent far away for our choices. A living space can be cast as formal or informal by the choice of paint and fabric. While a colonial Virginian would select a fine fabric like brocade and use just a few measures at the window and almost always in a bedchamber, a few more on chair seats, to create a room where elegance was the prime value, we can tilt the formality of the space with our choice of fabric, echoing the elegance of their choice with our own damasks or fine-printed chintzes, or encourage relaxation with a furniture check used everywhere in the room, from simple curtains to its customary place as a slipcover.

The new paint schemes from Williamsburg are interesting as starting points for inspiration. In the last ten years, there has been an increasing interest in paint effects beyond slapping some buckets of off-white on the walls of our own homes; the familiarity with rag-rolling, stenciling, and sponge-painting may make the bright green glaze in the Brush-Everard parlor less of a shock. And the range of colors contains many mood makers: Texture as well as color are elements to work with in choosing a paint; for example, the rougher cast of a milk paint is appealing for a less important room. And the increasing discoveries of the importance of wallpaper are adding to the repertoire of Williamsburg; the definite statement that these boldly patterned papers makes is an important addition to the design scheme of a room. It's tempting to adopt the

eighteenth-century touch of a golden fillet or border around a room, outlining and defining the space.

As they did, we admire well-worked moldings, used as chair rails or lining the ceiling or fireplace, or we might choose to demarcate the space by using paneling that extends from floor to chair rail, with wallpaper or paint above. The Georgian emphasis on the architecture of the room, on enhancing the geometric play of the shape that contains our living, is something we can adopt and adapt to a modern room, where lack of ornament has been a twentieth-century enthusiasm. Fine moldings, chosen for the scale and formality of the room, are like a good bone structure on which to build the form of a living room. The rooms of even the most severely "off the rack" developer's design will seem less boxlike with the finishing touch of molding.

Beyond the structure of the room and the furniture and fabrics that fill it, there are the personal touches that we choose to make our house our own. Interesting or amusing prints like those made

The "great room" at the Craft House shows how Williamsburg designs work for today's lifestyles. The table is modeled on a New England table, with fine carving and cabriole legs even at the back, a feature that adds versatility. There are few sofas associated with Colonial Williamsburg; this one, upholstered in Randolph Stripe Schumacher fabric, is based on an English original with graceful rococo curves in the arm, **BELOW LEFT,** and leg, **OPPOSITE.** The chest, **ABOVE,** is modeled on an original that Mr. and Mrs. John D. Rockefeller Jr. purchased for Bassett Hall, their Williamsburg home. The leather chest, **RIGHT,** is worked with nails in a tulip design.

from Mark Catesby's early bird studies are beautiful in their own right, as well as being insights into the interests of the age. We might adopt the use of handsome mirrors as a focal point in a room; the sense of space and light their reflections add are as welcome now as they were two hundred years ago.

We are more collection-minded than the average early Williamsburg resident, though the rising middle class was increasingly able to collect. If the truly wealthy, like the Governor or George Washington, could afford "ornamental china" like porcelain figures made at London's Chelsea manufactory, the middle class enjoyed pottery variations made in Staffordshire. If a family collected candlesticks in various materials it was because each and every one was put to use, then stored during the daytime. For us, such useful and handsome relics of the time

The black-and-white painted floorcloth was a popular fixture in well-traveled spaces like the passageway; now we enjoy its strong background to the damask-covered sofa, **LEFT**. Like the floorcloths, which imitated more costly stone tile floors, Schumacher's Pillar and Arch wallpaper, **ABOVE**, adds the feeling of grand architecture in two dimensions. The girandole sconce provides an enticing light reflected in the mirror and the gold leaf. A capacious and cozy wing chair, **OPPOSITE**, would have been found only in a bedroom—such upholstered pieces were rare—and often hid a chamber pot, as did the original of this New England easy chair. The chinoiserie fabric reflects the eighteenth-century passion for all things Oriental.

are wonderful to gather and mass on a mantelpiece ready to be used on a late-winter afternoon, a point of interest every day. We do carry on their impulse to display what we love in the living room, where we can enjoy it daily, and share our pride and enthusiasms—the delft dishes, the botanical prints, the tea chest of fine mahogany—with friends.

the BEDCHAMBER 2

> *"[We] live in this House with great Neatness, &*
> *convenience; each one has a Bed to Himself . . ."*
> —PHILIP VICKERS FITHIAN, 1774

Then, as now, the most intimate space in a household was that where the master and mistress slept, in the major bedchamber, surrounded by some of their finest possessions. In the simplest houses, with only one or two rooms, or in a rough inn, everyone slept together by necessity, as Colonel William Byrd, the wealthy diarist whose wide-ranging life brought him to the Palace as well as humbler houses, writes, "pigging lovingly together." But the first step toward gentility and a more refined way of life came when the heads of the household withdrew at bedtime to their own chamber—or, in the grandest households, the lady to her own, the gentleman to his—and shut the door. In this most private of spaces, women performed their toilette, or invited their closest friends to draw a chair to the tea table for a gossip, or reached in the darkness of the night to rock the cradle of their newest child, or a gentleman tilted his shaving mirror to catch the light by the window or drowsed by the fire in a capacious wing chair.

OPPOSITE The inventory of Lord Botetourt listed chintz bed curtains and green window curtains in the Governor's Palace; curators chose Jones toile, a copy of an original fabric that, dating to 1760, is the earliest dated English copperplate printed fabric. The rather startling purple-and-green combination is based on a fashionable installation recorded by Thomas Chippendale, and reflects the vivid colors discovered to be typical of the period. RIGHT It was not unusual to share tea with a friend in the bedchamber.

With just a few pieces of furniture in an exquisitely paneled room, the might and richness of the occupant is revealed. In this Palace bedchamber, a tall clothes press provides storage for folded clothing and other possessions. The bed curtains were drawn at night, securing privacy and conserving warmth. Feet were protected from the bare floorboards by a bed round, a U-shaped woven carpet.

tains to match; six mahogany chairs, with gothic arch backs and seats of yellow silk and worsted damask, an elbow chair, a fine neat mahogany serpentine dressing table, with a mirror and brass trimmings, a pair of fine carved and gilt scones." The handsome room that resulted would surely have had much in common with a wealthy man's chamber in Williamsburg, where Washington spent so much of his time as a burgess.

A bedstead with its hangings—"bed furniture"—was the most valuable piece in a household, expensive in the quantities of cloth required to drape it in the current fashion, in the services of the upholsterer who came to make it up, and in the sheets and counterpanes that made it comfortable. They held pride of place in the house, and in a will: Williamsburg resident Orlando Jones left his best feather bed and furniture to his wife, his second best to his daughter, while George Washington's mother, Mary, inherited from her father "the feathers in the kitchen loft to be put in a bed for her."

Old inventories indicate that bedchambers typically had one or more bedsteads, with, perhaps, a cradle and a trundle bed made to fit under the high main bed. There was a chest of drawers or clothespress in which clothes could be folded—built-in closets were still rare—and, more unusually, a table, a looking glass, perhaps a chair or two. Wing chairs, called easy chairs, with their side pieces that protected a lounger from the drafts, and often a chamber pot concealed in the seat, were bedroom furniture, not parlor pieces. And here was the place to find a bit of carpeting, perhaps next to the bed, and curtains that could be drawn against the glare of day. An elaborate room could result, as witnessed by the order George Washington, still a bachelor, placed for his Mount Vernon bedroom in 1757: "a mahogany bedstead with carved and fluted pillars and yellow silk and worsted damask hangings; window cur-

The chairs, **ABOVE** and **RIGHT**, in the Wythe House are dressed in expensive textiles with simple tie closures. Such covers were both practical and fashionable, saving the more expensive fabrics underneath. The bed, **OPPOSITE**, in the Governor's Palace is hung in a crisp white cotton, in a style Hepplewhite called "loop and button," suggesting it be paired with a japanned cornice.

The Governor's Palace bedroom features a
dramatic white-draped bed. The curtains are
based on a Hepplewhite design, which would
originally have been made of white calico. Virginia
cloth was the patriotic choice of the time after
Peyton Randolph, who encouraged the independence of the colony, promoting this home-grown,
home-woven material as a solution to the burden
of duties on imported textiles. Even the royal governor valued the local cloth; the inventory listed a
white Virginia cloth counterpane for the bed. In
spite of the grandeur of the carved urns and
painted decorations, this is a cost-conscious presentation. Paint made humble woods appear to
be finer than they were, and the hangings are
simple, fastening up for the day with a button
and a loop of cotton tape.

FABRICS

Oznaburg and dowlas, pondicherry, huckabuck, sarcenets, and Persians—the materials offered for sale in eighteenth-century advertisements would mean little to us until we come to linen, worsted, chintz, and silk. Textiles for dress and for decorating were varied, expensive, and precious, made in India and exported to England, then to America, or manufactured in the mill towns of Britain, with taxes and duties at many points in the process. Even homemade materials were costly in the labor-intensive time and effort required to create a simple fabric in the process from sheep or cotton field to spinning wheel or loom. So fabrics chosen for decoration, whether wool worsted or cotton, linen or silk, were used carefully and in a limited way; bed hangings represented the major expanse—and expense. Fabrics were protected from everyday wear; even the richest family ordered "case covers," slipcovers in a less expensive fabric, such as a checked linen over a silk brocade. The Governor's Palace inventory listed crimson damask chairs with red check covers. • A red check or a stripe was suitable for a curtain on a tavern or a tradesman's bed, while the master and mistress hung their bed with a copperplate printed textile or silk. Indian chintzes were coveted for their pretty patterns and polished surface; a fine example was almost as expensive as the rare and costly silks. By midcentury, evolving technology permitted the mass production of printed textiles in India and England; copperplates engraved with designs inked in monochromes easily printed yards of material at a time, known as "copperplate calicoes." Their cheerful designs were drawn from nature, or even from the topics of the times—many post-Revolutionary-era prints feature George Washington.

Although the Georgian interior relied on harmony, proportion, and color for its initial effect, the delights of pattern were available—to those who could afford them—in lengths of fabric, wallpaper, and carpeting. The finest brocaded silks, LEFT, were too fine even for interiors, but would have brightened a room when made up into ladies' dresses. Fewer color variations were possible with indigo resist printing, as in the sample, RIGHT.

LEFT *Copperplate printing on fabric made possible a host of landscape and fanciful scenes, here inspired by the Orient, one of the eighteenth century's fascinations.* **RIGHT** *Athena toile, a contemporary fabric from Schumacher, is based on a plate-printed textile made in Jouy-en-Josas, France, about 1804. It exhibits the continuing interest in ancient civilizations that characterized the eighteenth century.*

The copperplate-printed fabric valance, **LEFT,** *is trimmed with strips from another copperplate print. Inspired by an antique valance with double scallop,* **RIGHT,** *this interpretation is made in a woven linen check with trim in a smaller check. The scalloped edge adds a dimension of interest to a plain geometric design.*

Dressing the bed not only provided warmth, but also privacy, especially in inns like the Raleigh Tavern, **ABOVE,** where bedrooms opened onto each other. Travelers who could not count on a comfortable bed could at least carry their own: The folding field bed, **RIGHT,** was developed for military service. In the simplest treatments, curtains and testers slid over the frame in a few minutes, as with the striped, **OPPOSITE, ABOVE,** and checked, **OPPOSITE, BELOW LEFT.** Trunks like this one, **OPPOSITE, BELOW RIGHT,** with its decorative pattern of nail heads, could hold all the traveler required for weeks on the road.

PRECEDING PAGES The richness of brocaded silks, reserved for ball gowns, were made by French Huguenot weavers, who introduced their sophisticated trade to England in the late 1600s. These examples show the richness of color and pattern that was available in the eighteenth century.

The bedstead itself might be tall- or short-posted, of fine mahogany or simple pine, a folding field bed or an elaborately corniced Chippendale-inspired monumental creation, depending on the wealth of the owner and the importance of the occupant. Means determined the making up of the bed as well. Simple beds had a straw-stuffed mattress resting on strung rope, with a pile of blankets; more elaborate equipage began with either strung cord and a hide on top, or a "sacking bottom," a square of linen lashed to pegs that could be tightened. Then came a horsehair mattress, a feather bed, sheets, plain or finished with lace, and woolen blankets. There might be a long sausagelike bolster, and feather pillows to support the half-supine posture thought to be the most healthful at the time. And an elabo-

rate counterpane topped the whole confection, like those in inventories mentioned as "a crimson satin quilt" or a quilt "worked by his mother." Fithian writes of one of his charges: "Evening, at Miss Prissy's Request I drew for her some Flowers on Linen which she is going to imbroider, for a various Counterpane."

The real play of pattern, and the taste for luxury and eye toward fashion that underlay it, came in the hangings for the bed and, occasionally, matching fabrics at the window and on chair upholstery. Curator of Textiles Linda Baumgarten's research has found that a fine bed was an expensive proposition that might have required seventy yards of fabric. A handsome bed furnishing might be made of less expensive "Virginia cloth,"

The simplest bedchambers, like these at Wetherburn's Tavern, show the low-post beds, **OPPOSITE** and **ABOVE**, that fit under the eaves, with home-woven striped and checked blankets. The easy chair, by the fire, **BELOW**, kept drafts at bay with its "wings"; the checked slipcover, which could also be woven at home, was typical for such chairs. The handsome dressing stand, **RIGHT**, holds the delft "basin and bottle" that sufficed for washing.

In the Peyton Randolph House, a ruched white valance tops an all-white bed, **LEFT**. A detail of the brass fireplace grate, introduced in the mid- to late eighteenth century for burning coal, **BELOW,** shows off its fine engraving, beaded edge, and tall finial—almost the only fancy-work in the room.

homespun and dyed and woven, a popular choice during the nonimportation period preceding the Revolution, and used by the leading patriot Peyton Randolph. The selection might have included a fine imported wool or a printed chintz all the way from India, or one of the patterns printed in England from engraved copperplates that became prevalent in mid-century. Virginia summers made a necessity of silk gauze or muslin mosquito curtains.

It was a privileged person who could command a dressing table, a small table whose drawers could hold the pins and ribbons and pots of pomade that a fine lady of fashion might want to have at her command. Often the dressing table was covered with a snowy fall of muslin, called a "toilette," a name that in Virginia was transformed to "twilight." On top stood a small looking glass and per-haps some silver boxes and bottles, for a dressing table set was a favorite gift of a husband to a bride. Although a man might also make use of this dressing table, he was likely to have a shaving stand nearby, with "a basin and a bottle" for servants to fill with hot water each morning as the couple drew the bed curtains and rose to meet the day.

WINDOW TREATMENTS

Only very late in the eighteenth century did draping windows in a length of fabric become customary; expense, fashion, practicality, even the climate in Virginia dictated that most windows depended on their shutters to temper the weather, provide privacy, and keep an unused room in its customary protective darkness. Curtains were most likely found in a bedchamber, where privacy and blocking the light were most the issue, though a parlor might occasionally have a pretty festoon blind at the window, drawn up with a flourish by a pulley and cord. Dining rooms were rarely curtained; keeping expensive fabric clean in these circumstances was too difficult. And preservation of material was always a concern, with curtains removed in the summer, for instance, when bright sunshine might fade and damage fine goods. The simplest treatment was a length of fabric shirred on a rod or nailed to the top of a window frame, tucked behind a nail in the daylight. • Venetian blinds may seem a surprisingly modern choice, but they were actually commonplace. Handsome and practical, they were admired (as reported in the *Virginia Gazette* in 1770 by a "house-carpenter") as the "newest invented Venetian sun blinds for windows, that move to any position so as to give different lights, they screen from the scorching rays of the sun, draw up as a curtain, prevent being overlooked, give a cool refreshing air in hot weather, and are the greatest preservatives of furniture of any thing of the kind ever invented." Or a housekeeper could look for a fabric blind, called a "spring blind" or "spring curtain," and very similar to our own shades, made of brown linen or green worsted and hung by a spring-controlled roller.

When windows were left without curtains, as they often were in eighteenth-century Williamsburg, hardware and colored "lines" for drapery curtains were a finely wrought detail, **LEFT. RIGHT** *The upstairs reception hall of the Governor's Palace, seen by many visitors, would have been an ideal place for a lavish display of fabric like these red damask curtains that nearly sweep the floor and frame the deep casement.*

The most elegant means of keeping out light and cold was a pair of shutters built into the window casement, LEFT, *as at the George Wyeth House. The curtains were hung at the bed instead of the window. If the house was clapboard and not brick, shutters were attached to the outside of the house. At the St. George Tucker House,* RIGHT, *a simple valance is enough to add a touch of grace without the expense of a full window treatment.*

CONTEMPORARY INTERPRETATIONS

JUST AS WE DO TODAY, EIGHTEENTH-CENTURY

husbands and wives turned to the bedchamber for peace and privacy. In the busiest of households, we try to preserve this intimate space as a sanctuary. Here is where we find that still center to collect ourselves, where a comfortable chair by the window is just the place to settle down with a book (perhaps in the sort of wing chair designed to protect our forebears from drafty air, but that now serves to support the lolling head of a napper). A small table can serve as a writing desk, a place for an informal meal, a display area for our favorite collection. We share their interest in little luxuries, in creature comforts, in making our bedrooms a special place. We've come to know the best bedrooms are thoroughly individual, filled with tranquillity, places to store up the treasure of time, as well as possessions.

No more blessed with a luxury of space or time than our ancestors, we can borrow their own bedroom elements to furnish our private moments. But we have different needs, and the infinite adaptability of eighteenth-century designs serves us as well. The delight of a dressing table is not for those who prefer the bright lights and shelves of a bathroom, but a small table with drawers could be drawn next to the bed to hold books, a lamp, and a

In a small black and white room set under the eaves, **BOTTOM**, the bold check of the rug is repeated, in reduced scale, in slipcovers and bed skirts. The tea set before a fire, **OPPOSITE**, and creamware plates along the mantelshelf, **RIGHT**, recall the occasional eighteenth-century custom of entertaining in the bedchamber. A small closet, **BELOW**, becomes a charming dressing room, with a dressing table, mirror, and slipper chair.

clock, or stand by a window for a writing desk. A tall breakfront bookcase might fill a wall, holding novels, notes, and writing instruments—and the television and computer. And a mirror is still a must-have, perhaps a japanned looking glass that bears a second glance for its own handsome frame. A wing chair doesn't take up much room, but its comfortable depths could be just the place to sink into at the end of a day, or draw a child onto your lap for a story and a hug.

We own so much more than the original Williamsburg inhabitants that the strictures of storage in a time before closets seem similar to our own. The beautiful chests of drawers, designs as well proportioned as a Georgian house, are the

BELOW A tall-post bed spells romance and comfort, especially when heaped with pillows and a comforter, like this one from *Williamsburg*. The bedspread is one of the most popular reproductions ever created by Colonial Williamsburg; Crown Crafts; first reproduced in 1972, this simple all cotton matelassé double-woven textile has served American bedrooms, even, as on the armchair, as a slipcover. Baker's rococo sofa is drawn close to the fire. Under the window, the Baker reproduction of a British chest made between 1740 and 1760 features a pull-out shelf for writing. A period bedroom in the Brush-Everard House, **OPPOSITE, ABOVE,** is warmed by the Kurdish carpet made by Karastan to resemble eighteenth-century Persian rugs. Antique delft bowl and bottle call attention to the blue painted woodwork, **OPPOSITE, BELOW**.

beginning, for them and for us, though we are less accustomed to the draw-out shelves that were once so useful for the clothing that was typically folded away. A Baker reproduction chest in the Colonial Williamsburg collection, in mahogany with bright brass pulls, is particularly useful in contemporary homes due to its small size, which lets it sit next to a chair as a side table, or occupy a corner of a bedroom next to the bed. The original detail that the eighteenth century required is just as useful in our own: At the top is a pull-out shelf that in the original would have held a candlestick, a traveling desk, or the bowl and pitcher for shaving. Today it extends the surface to hold a book or a breakfast tray.

For most purposes built-in closets with coat hangers serve our needs better than pegs and shelves, but the eighteenth-century love of boxes for storage can find a place again, the perfect container in which to stash a sewing project or the tax forms, makeup brushes or keys. A simple trunk

and the cold, but the need for romance and intimacy remains—here is the bed that is the perfect centerpiece to daily living and nightly peace. These days, just as in the eighteenth century, the choice of hangings and trimmings can set the tone for a bedroom, formal in its silk damask, a cheerful period piece in toile, afloat in a cloud of white muslin. Choose a quilt that's been treasured for years, or opt for a matelassé coverlet. The Colonial Williamsburg reproduction version has been beloved by three generations. Old and new make particularly happy companions in the bedroom, like a mound of pillows trimmed in old lace; collectors of antique linens know they take on an extra interest when displayed in this way.

Surveying all the different choices in hanging a bed, from the Chinese Chippendale peaked cornice to the simple flurry of white cotton in abundance, may inspire a whole room theme; choosing

used for traveling, round bandboxes, a tea chest—all these are attractive hideaways. Stacked in a corner of the bedroom or hiding jewelry on a chest top, such containers retain their usefulness. And a fresh eye can adapt old colonial forms, like a blanket chest or the telescope case Colonial Williamsburg reproduces, to hold all the detritus that seems to drift through a household, such as out-of-season bed linens.

One item of the eighteenth-century bedchamber that still sets hearts going today is the monumental four-poster bed festooned with swags and draperies from head to foot. We no longer have to pull our bed curtains tight against the noise

Athena toile by Schumacher inspired the classical French bed treatment, **OPPOSITE**, against the Powell House Red paint. A simple William and Mary diamond-check slipcover with a graceful cut is on the Norfolk side chair, **ABOVE** and **RIGHT**. The chair partners Baker's Middle Colonies dressing table, with the sharply turned legs and stretcher that distinguish its inspiration as late baroque.

a tall-post bed with curtains will make this a major element in the room. Once these hangings were all that stood between the occupants and a frosty winter night; now we can add wonderful fabrics at our will, building a bedroom full of comfort and coziness that goes beyond the temperature. Here, again, the attention to detail is what makes the difference between ordinary and exciting.

The variety of fabric and wallpaper schemes in the bedroom has widened; the taste for sweet pastels in the bedroom can be replaced with some of the bold effects now found in the new colors of Williamsburg. The Wythe House bedroom that is keyed by a punchy purple, from the boldly striped wallpaper to the copperplate documentary print to the bed surround of Wilton

The householder of the eighteenth century would rarely have lavished a fine paper on an upstairs bedroom in this way, **OPPOSITE,** where gold wraps the ceiling angles to bring a unified beauty to this small space. But a colonial would surely have appreciated saving the snippets of wallpaper to trim storage boxes, **ABOVE,** (top to bottom) Solomon's Seal, Brunswick Resist, and Brewster Floral Stripe, and **BELOW,** (top to bottom) Botanical Chintz, Chinese Flowers, Botanical Toss, and Lotus Damask. A bedroom is a good home for a desk, too, like the generously sized partners' desk, **LEFT;** with drawers on both sides, the desk serves two easily.

carpeting, is a room with real presence, as comfortable by day as evening, when the deep purple must have seemed as warm as the curtains. Or the russet red of the neoclassical Athena toile shown on pages 90 and 91, a logical choice for a living or dining room, makes for a rich and formal and thoroughly adult bedroom, comfortable for work in the daytime, yet restful at night.

At the bedroom window, we have some of the same practical concerns as well; adopting and adapting eighteenth-century window treatments can provide privacy or retain warmth in our own energy-conscious times. Now that fabric is available to all, we can ask for the window curtains that sweep the floor, more typical of late-eighteenth-century designs, or for the more common eighteenth-century taste for matching curtains, bed hangings, and upholstery for a unified whole. The handsome wooden Venetian blinds in Williamsburg might inspire a reappreciation of this old form, once memories of clattering metal splats are forgotten. A valance and short swag of fabric at each side implies curtains without intruding on the decor of a simply designed room. Interior shutters—a staple of colonial modern architecture—can seldom be accommodated by thin modern walls, but can obviate the need for any other window treatments when they are present.

With furniture that serves many purposes and a color scheme that works by day and night, the bedchamber becomes a place for all times.

DINING ROOMS, KITCHENS, *and* PANTRIES

3

We had an elegant dinner; Beef & Greens; roast-Pig, fine boil'd Rock-Fish, Pudding, Cheese &c—Drink: good Porter-Beer, Cyder, Rum, & Brandy Toddy. The Virginians are so kind one can scarce know how to dispense with, or indeed accept their kindness shown in such a variety of instances.

—PHILIP VICKERS FITHIAN, APRIL 3, 1774

When Peyton Randolph, wealthy and prominent, inherited his father's house in 1737, he soon drew up plans for a grand new chamber, a large dining room he filled with glittering looking glasses, fine furniture, china, and silver imported from London. By midcentury, such a room devoted to eating well and entertaining lavishly was found much more commonly in houses built in Williamsburg. Randolph was one of the colony's elite, but even when the well-off and rising businessman James Geddy constructed his house in the 1760s, he made the dining room the largest room on the first floor. At fifteen feet three inches by twenty-one feet five inches, and treated, with the parlor, to carefully worked out trim, it was an imposing chamber. A built-in cupboard with an arched top and decoratively shaped shelves allowed him to display his best possessions, and the broad walls were probably papered above a wainscot for a room that would impress the most lofty and exacting of visitors.

OPPOSITE In the Raleigh Tavern, as in many elite houses, a cupboard, or "buffet," holds fine china, both to display it and for ease of use. The interior of this one is, as was common, painted a vivid red-orange. The creamware tureen transfer printed with exotic birds, **RIGHT**, was inspired by a 1760s fragment from an archaeological dig of the Palace.

In a society that loved its pleasures, dinner, served around two in the afternoon, was a well-observed social ceremony, with the best from the smokehouse and the river and the field dressed prettily and laid on china that was figured to set it off well. Cookbooks of the day counseled the housewife to set her table in an orderly manner, with generally two courses offered, the first an

assortment of meats with vegetables for trimmings, the next a pretty display of a variety of sweets for dessert. Serving dishes and bowls were placed in a formal pattern on the table balancing large and small platters. Such meals, with a collection of glasses for the various wines, were a sophisticated simulacrum of grand English living, and a contrast to what was common among the poor or their own ancestors of just two generations before, when few owned more than a spoon and a trencher of pewter or wood for meals that were endless reconfigurations of native corn and stew, often taken seated on a chest or stool, since chairs were rare.

ABOVE At Bassett Hall, the onetime home of Mr. and Mrs. John D. Rockefeller Jr., a demilune table holds a crystal and gilt girandole.
RIGHT The main feature of the dining room is wainscoting, which both covers and adorns the fireplace wall. A narrow shelf can be used for display, as here, for small urns of mercury glass. The portraits are from Abby Aldrich Rockefeller's folk art collection.

tions was placed on a long table set out under the candles' glow with a fine display of silver.

Thus the dining room became another showplace for both manners and material possessions. Even the dining room was not exempt from multipurpose use, however, with many families using this chamber as a drawing room, too. A handsome table, certainly, could be put into place, often one that could be extended by either raising drop leaves or joining side tables to the end when more people were expected. More small tables for the servants to serve from were placed against the walls, with a side table or sideboard that might be topped in marble to guard against damage from spills or heat. Sets of chairs, perhaps in mahogany, were ranged along the walls. Floorcloths were common, rugs rarer, and curtains rarely appeared, since it was difficult to keep them clean. There might be a bottle case, a lead-lined box to hold cooled wine bottles, and a built-in cupboard, occasionally open above, to store or display the fine china in use. The walls often were the place to show off more of the family's collections, like the

Breakfast and supper were more informal gatherings, the first a family meal that centered around the ham and hot breads of various sorts that are still a Virginia pride, while supper was a simple repast served before bedtime, perhaps some cold meats, bread and butter, and a sweet, or, as Fithian once enjoyed, "a bowl of hot green tea and some tarts." (Colonel Landon Carter had his complaints about his family's ways at table, however, in a tone we all might recognize: "I never knew the like of my family for finding fault. At the same time they will not mend things when they might if they could. Every[one] speak well of my table but they who constantly live at it. If the meat is very fine, it is not done says one, altho Perhaps nobody eat heartier of it. . . . If the Sallad is fine, the melted butter it is mixed up with is rank altho every mouthfull of sallad is devoured . . . and so the good folk go on disparaging and devouring.") The grandest of parties were the suppers served after a ball, when a vast array of tempta-

twenty-four pictures of English racehorses framed in gilt that John Tayloe kept in his plantation house dining room.

As the company paraded into the dining room and took their places in ease and expectation, they knew that everything for comfort and ceremony was at hand, and the afternoon would pass happily according to custom, in "the methodical nicety which is the essence of true elegance" advised by Mrs. Mary Randolph, the eighteenth-century author of *The Virginia Housewife.*

Williamsburg boasted many taverns (King's Arms, **OPPOSITE, ABOVE;** Christiana Campbell's, **LEFT;** Raleigh, **BELOW**), and meals and meetings were often taken there rather than at home. Chairs in such establishments were likely to be an odd assortment of styles, assembled for convenience. Tables were small, and could be rearranged for larger parties. The reproduction china used at the Williamsburg taverns, **OPPOSITE, BELOW,** and the salt-glazed jugs and plates, **BELOW LEFT,** are reproduced from pottery shards that were found when these sites were excavated.

KITCHENS

A colonial kitchen was more a matter of utility than charm, a room full of activity from the beginning of the day as everything from the daily bread to supper's tarts was produced by the cook and her assistants. The kitchens were independent structures of brick or weatherboarding, located away from the house to keep the risk of fire at a minimum and to distance the family from the smells and smoke of producing the meals. "All their Drudgeries of Cookery, Washing, Dairies, &c. are perform'd in Offices detacht from the Dwelling-Houses, which by this means are kept more cool and Sweet," wrote Robert Beverley at the time. In Williamsburg, these small structures are found behind the main house, simple one-room buildings often with a loft

The cook at the Palace, expected to present impressive meals in formal style, could command a battery of equipment that allowed for many cooking techniques and decorative touches. **OPPOSITE** Open shelves held copper pots, crockery, pantry boxes for herbs, bottles, pewter chargers, and pie tins. **ABOVE** For a spring dinner, ice cream, tinted green with spinach juice, might have been molded in the pewter forms.

OVERLEAF To reduce the danger of fire to the main house—and to remove the noisome heat, sights, and smells of cooking from refined senses—the kitchen of the Governor's Palace was built as a separate outbuilding. Here, the emphasis was on admitting light and air so that toiling near the large fireplace would be less onerous. The result is an open work space that would please many cooks today.

CHINA

Much of what we know about eighteenth-century domestic life is due to disasters—the daily cracks and crashes that sent plates and cups and platters off to the dustheap. The excavated wells and privies of Williamsburg are full of broken bits of the past, clues to what graced the tables of the humble and the mighty. Chinawares, imported from England, along with other table appointments made there and in Germany, Italy, Holland, and China itself, were much in demand, and there are examples here from almost every pottery and porcelain used at the time. One advertisement at midcentury enumerates more than a hundred forms for sale, china bowls and chocolate cups, butter tubs and cauliflower stands, Dutch jugs and pepper castors, punch strainers and "delf" bottles, and "figures for ornament," from sailors to squirrels. Even a humble tradesman had a good porcelain or pottery teapot and cups or creamware plates. • Most prevalent at the beginning of the century was the cheerful delftware, painted often in blue with charming freehand motifs that may resemble Chinese patterns, like a pagoda, or more whimsical themes, like a peacock with flowing tail. Thousands of fragments here testify to the popularity of this lead-glazed pottery. The sturdier white salt-glazed stoneware became more popular by the second quarter of the century, with its crisp incised decoration and shiny glaze. Josiah Wedgwood, ever the experimenter, had developed creamy Queen's Ware at his Staffordshire factory by the 1760s, and found a ready market in Williamsburg for styles plain or shaped and colored to resemble pineapples, cauliflowers, and pears.

Nearly every type of china and pottery that could be had in Europe could also be imported to Colonial Williamsburg—for a price. Colonists loved creamware, now available in reproductions based on eighteenth-century designs, LEFT. *Tin-glazed pottery plates,* RIGHT, *displayed at the DeWitt Wallace Gallery in Williamsburg, mingle Chinese and English influences on blue-and-white ware.*

above where provisions could be stored or a slave find a bed.

These simple, usually good-size rooms were likely to be floored in brick or dirt so a spark from the fireplace could do no harm. It was important to plan a high ceiling and wide windows so breezes would help ventilation in the busy work space. Walls and ceiling in all but the most well-off households were rough, with beams exposed. Plastered or not, the walls and every inch of surface were whitewashed frequently in the constant battle to keep the smoke-filled kitchen clean. Shelves and a dresser, a long narrow table on which food could be prepared, lined the walls. Often a central table provided another work surface and was scrubbed hard throughout the day.

Cooks stored their equipment between use, so there was ample storage space in cupboards, chests, and shelves. The ambitious could call on nearly as much cooking equipment as we do. The Palace's cooks numbered tart pans and coffee canisters, chafing dishes, and a fish kettle among their *batterie de cuisine,* as well as such specialized

OPPOSITE In the Governor's Palace kitchen, whitewash and open shelves helped the staff maintain cleanliness. Red and green canisters with tight-fitting lids preserve freshness; on the bottom shelf a sugar loaf waits to be used. **ABOVE** Cloth-covered crocks stored preserved goods. **BELOW** Copper pots of every size stood ready to serve dozens—or hundreds—of guests.

dessert wares as jelly glasses and fancier cut-glass "cream basons" for a handsome presentation of their culinary efforts.

An enormous fireplace was the center of activity with, as the century progressed, a built-in oven at its side, covered with a cast-iron door. Spits turned the day's roast, skillets and frying pans on legs stood on the hearth, and a chimney bar or a crane could hold iron pots and cauldrons over the flame. Although the plenty of the Virginia countryside and the smokehouse, the wine cellar, and the dairy were near at hand, there can be little doubt that this was a room where hard labor occurred, in an atmosphere of bustle and smoke, where slaves, indentured servants, and, perhaps, a hired cook carried out the lady of the house's daily orders for the menu. It seems a miracle that such things as prettily trimmed towering jelly molds on crystal platters or puff pastry tarts filled with quince appeared, to be carried in state across the yard into the dining room.

A housewife was expected to run this kitchen in a well-ordered way, though as the middle class grew, this labor was taken on by servants and slaves. Still, she was in command, the

many keys to such things as tea canisters and sugar cupboard at her side. And even well-off women were intimately involved with the supervision of the running of the estate; Colonel Byrd writes of surprising a planter's wife at the smokehouse engaged in her duties in informal dress; clearly embarrassed, she blushed and dashed away.

A model wife had her "receipt books," imported from London, to inspire her, or, when Williamsburg printer William Parks began to reprint Mrs. Smith's *The Compleat Housewife; or, Accomplished Gentlewoman's Companion* in 1742, she could purchase a book made in and for Virginia, edited, it promised, with "Recipes, the Ingredients or Materials for which, are to be had in this Country." Or she could compile her own, or receive one from her mother: There is a manuscript volume of recipes compiled and written out by Frances Parke Custis of the well-established Williamsburg family, a little book that came later to Martha Washington, her daughter-in-law, which is a beautiful example of both penmanship and cooking ambition.

In the kitchen of Wetherburn's Tavern, **LEFT**, humble vessels are the rule. A large unglazed earthenware cask, **ABOVE**, is typical of those used to ship oil from Spain to the colonies. A baker's "dresser," **OPPOSITE**, holds many items familiar to us today—wooden bowls and boxes, stoneware jars and bottles, a flour sifter, and a rolling pin. The slipware trencher was commonplace then; a treasure now.

{DETAILS}

SETTEES

One of the most versatile pieces of furniture, the settee first appeared in the seventeenth century, but became popular in the next century, spawning countless variations, usually with upholstered seat and back, and sometimes with padded arms as well. Because of its small size—even a three-seater is often a foot shorter than the average modern sofa—and light weight, it can be tucked into corners, moved close to the fire, or posted at the end of a bed. Its open feeling—in contrast to the heavy look of an upholstered-down-to-the-floor sofa—makes it perfectly suited to smaller spaces. In addition it has the virtue of being able to change the feeling of a room from formal to relaxed, depending on the pattern of the fabric used in the upholstery. To demonstrate, the Williamsburg federal period reproduction settee is shown here three ways: with its upholstery and two different slipcovers. Although the settee's basic lines remain the same, the room seems to shift moods. As in colonial times, it is possible to remake our living rooms simply by putting the upholstery in "summer dress"—thereby saving the expensive fabrics during the most active season by protecting them with washable covers.

A classic shape like this settee lends itself easily to a change of mood with a change of slipcover. A formal piece, it retains a sense of occasion in yellow Randolph Stripe, OPPOSITE, against the sunny yellow walls, while it has a much more casual air when dressed in Greenhow Stripe, LEFT, to match the curtains. And Carolina, RIGHT, a blue toile, calls dramatic attention to this corner of the room.

burnished surfaces, metal scrubbed through the years, glass polished with a cloth. Contemporary kitchens often adopt the open shelving the early kitchens knew, where creamware and storage jars in stoneware are on display, easy to reach and part of the decor as well. And the dark tones of Williamsburg colors—the deep greens and dull reds—often make a peaceful backdrop to a kitchen that has its influences in the eighteenth century. The bar in the Raleigh Tavern, open shelved, has more to suggest to us about a place for kitchen preparations that could accommodate modern sensibilities, too.

Certainly the kitchen table, where mixing bowls rested and carrots lost their tops, seems to us the perfect center to a kitchen made for

Chelsea Bird dinnerware, **ABOVE LEFT**, based on plates made between 1758 and 1769 at the Chelsea Porcelain Manufactory, is part of the elegant setting in the dining room, **LEFT**. The round table, inspired by an early-nineteenth-century original, is paired to a reproduction of a chair made about 1795 and elaborately inlaid with foliage, fans, and corner beads. Sparkling glassware, **ABOVE**, with decanter, wine rinser, and stemmed glasses, all *Williamsburg* reproductions, add to the splendor of the setting. The same table, **OPPOSITE, ABOVE**, looks much more relaxed surrounded by reproductions of an wing chair found in Virginia, made about 1800. **OPPOSITE, BELOW** Reproduction creamware matches the casual mood.

living in. Reproduction tables that recapture that golden tone of old wood make the perfect backdrop to an evening meal, for we would, as did the middling sorts in Williamsburg, seat ourselves at its scrub top, comfortable in the warmth, the activity, the focus for the family that the modern kitchen provides.

If we've widened the uses and the appeal of the kitchen, we've also narrowed our definition of the dining room—and lost some of the usefulness and warmth of the room that the eighteenth century knew. Often the dining room was a family's main gathering place, with a fire left there all day to warm the chamber for meals, as well

as provide a pleasant place to write or visit with friends after that early-afternoon dinner. Many of us, these days, don't enjoy the carefully decorated room except at Thanksgiving or another family feast.

But adopting some of the original Williamsburg furniture placements, and adapting some of our own notions of comfort, can make a room that is an integral part of the day. There were often desks or secretaries in dining rooms, with a drop top that could be raised to hide the business of work, and, perhaps, drawers beneath that might hold important household goods. A drop-leaf table could be moved into position when needed, or, wheeled on castors, its leaves down, be taken to another room for supper. And sets of chairs, sometimes

This dining room, **ABOVE**, recalls the colonial habit of pulling chairs from all around the house for a meal; for us, combining different seating—a small sofa, an upholstered chair—with traditional side chairs at the table seems like a new idea. But, with the repetition of the Schumacher Leaf Arabesque on the love seat and curtains, the room retains a sense of unity. Creamware, **RIGHT**, is now, as then, one of the most popular dinnerware services in Williamsburg. This reproduction, like the original, is made by Wedgwood. **OPPOSITE** A display of reproductions of the Duke of Gloucester's table service, commissioned originally in 1770, lights up a dining room corner.

A contemporary kitchen, **LEFT,** borrows inspiration from the past in its simplicity and paint color, Red Lion Inn Green from Martin Senour. Delft apothecary jars, once used for medicinal herbs, **BELOW** and **OPPOSITE, ABOVE,** are perfect hiding places for kitchen essentials like spices or sugar. **OPPOSITE, BELOW** Mottahedeh's Imperial Blue soup plate, an accurate copy of the original, is perfect in a formal setting with sterling silver and crystal.

numbered on the back as an aid to inventory, could travel all over the house, like our folding chairs. A corner cupboard is a place for display and storage, and clears the way for the shuffling of chairs.

Contemporary households could make good use of such an adaptable room, including a desk, a drop-leaf table, upholstered chairs, as the daily place for work and relaxation, with the potential to be a formal dining room when needed. Put the dining table in the center, bring in the chairs, fold up the desk, light the candles, and all the welcome of the evening is there.

Certainly, as we set out the three-tined forks and the rat-tail

knives, the lengths of damask napkins and the English china, we'd feel kinship with any colonial hostess, proud of her table setting. She would be serving a much more elaborate meal than our own, and the first course would be waiting, arranged in a symmetrical design on the table, when guests entered the room. This course, full of meat and vegetable preparations, would be removed, along with the tablecloth, and the table laid again with dessert and more elaborate displays, such as little glass buckets filled with nuts and candied fruit, or jellies in glasses arranged on a stack of salvers, precedents to our own wish to set a beautiful table for friends and family. A colonial hostess might have

chosen to make an elaborate centerpiece as a welcome to her guests, and the choices of china and silver accessories in a wealthy home provided a full range from the charming to the magnificent.

Common in the eighteenth century, a floorcloth might be the beginning of a design scheme today. Practical, yet with vivid graphics that set a mood, a floorcloth is easily made at home and stands up well if prepared correctly. Contemporary decorators would probably include the curtains the colonials avoided; we can clean our cloth

The table in the gazebo is set for a summer's afternoon with stemmed glasses and a pewter strawberry dish, all *Williamsburg* reproductions, and side chairs have been turned out with an array of fanciful slipcovers. What was once tradition is now trend—the slipcover that was used to protect the seat can be the occasion for a decorative flourish as dressy as a ball gown, like the carefully cut Tissu Fleuri cover, **ABOVE,** that echoes the shape of the Norfolk chair.

more easily, and curtains drawn at night bring a feeling of intimacy to the dining table. Though side chairs, armed and armless, are the traditional choice to circle the table, upholstered chairs with low backs can be comfortable, and a handsome adjunct to wooden tabletops, encouraging long evenings, long talks, and relaxation—and can be moved to bracket the fireplace the next day.

We echo the previous centuries in our love of candlelight, but favor better-lit rooms; candles on the table are a special moment for most of us, but there is no reason that family dinner could not become a candlelit occasion. Lighting a dining room completely with candlelight, from a

A bow-back D. R. Dimes Windsor chair can take on many personalities: **ABOVE** A box-pleated skirt made from Edinburgh Check; a long, full skirt in a Greenhow Stripe from Schumacher, **BELOW. RIGHT** A short pleated skirt of Pomegranate Resist on a Queen Anne–style chair and a Diamond Ikat on a Maryland Rococo side chair.

hanging chandelier to sconces on the walls, protected with glass shades, makes a warm glowing space that is part of the romance of an evening. Wired to serve as lamps, candlesticks and sconces create different lighting effects all over the house. Centering a simple stick on a side table will give a gentle light to a dark corner, while a multibranched chandelier, either dangling with glass prisms or a simple tin construction, will effectively illuminate a room.

HOME *and* GARDEN 4

Here . . . they build with brick, but most commonly with timber . . . cased with feather-edged plank, painted with white lead and oil, covered with shingles of cedar, etc. tarred over at first; with a passage generally through the middle of the house for an airdraught in summer. Thus their houses are lasting, dry, and warm in winter, and cool in summer; especially if there be windows enough to draw the air. Thus they dwell comfortably, genteelly, pleasantly, and plentifully in this delightful, healthful, and (I hope) thriving city of Williamsburg.

—HUGH JONES, *PRESENT STATE OF VIRGINIA*, 1724

By Hugh Jones's time, Williamsburg was growing to its full size: Fences were erected to outline the plots of land, small and large houses were built by those intent on making a presence in the new capital, whether by constructing an ambitious house that would announce their position, or a smaller shop or tavern where a newcomer might make a fortune. From the first plans, Williamsburg was intended as a town of substance; stipulations demanded that houses be set back six feet from the lot lines, and that a house had to be at least twenty by thirty feet in dimension. And the town must have rung to hammer blows and shouts as roof beams were lifted into place and windows set in walls. Working either with an undertaker—builder—or a series of tradesmen—bricklayers, carpenters—landowners shaped their dreams.

Most built in wood, as Jones observed; brick was for the massive public buildings—the College, the Palace, the church—that were the pillars of the community. Owners drew on the

The gardens of Williamsburg are one of the town's glories and an inspiration to gardeners everywhere. The Custis Tenement garden, **LEFT,** is planted with annuals like the blue and white larkspur in the foreground. **RIGHT** A colonial revival bench rests on the back porch of the Market Square Tavern.

skills of the craftsmen they employed for architectural ideas, and carpenters had a wide pass-along practical knowledge as well as pattern books to draw on. Gradually, a system of architecture evolved that had English roots but was formed by the demands and the ways of Virginia. Most houses were simple and straightforward, descendants of the simple two-room houses that most settlers considered more than adequate. As Jones observed, the weather dictated that houses be just a room deep, with the central passageway important for both sociability and climate. A deep cellar evolved by midcentury for cool storage, which gave houses a more important look. Taxes on two-story houses encouraged owners to make the most of their attics by pitching the roof steeply, and allowing light and air with dormers. Doors were set off center, and chimneys and fireplaces were on the outer ends of a house, helping to keep the home cool in summer, warm in winter. A growing appreciation of carpentry effects occurred as wealth and knowledge increased; for instance, it is interesting to note

Whether house or outbuilding, the structures of Williamsburg present a rare sense of order and proportion. Climate, fashion, and materials dictated similar solutions to the problem of what to build, while city regulations and a town plan sought to ensure that each was harmoniously sited. Even the dovecote in the Governor's Palace service yard, **RIGHT**, looks like a tiny brick house. The George Pitt House, **TOP**, and Russell House, **ABOVE**, demonstrate typical steeply pitched roofs with dormers for light and air, as does the Bracken Kitchen, **OPPOSITE**.

{DETAILS}

DOORS AND SHUTTERS

Houses in the eighteenth century were shut up tight at night, shutters latched, doors locked. Frame houses most often had their shutters placed on the outside, while brick houses, with thick walls, usually had their shutters mounted on the inside. In Williamsburg, the outer shutters were sometimes louvered to allow a free flow of air when the window was opened. Even the front door could have its own tall louvered outer door that could be left closed in the daytime, which would afford privacy and air circulation and some protection from the busy town streets. • Doors could be simple planks or a solid, well-worked piece made interesting with moldings and painted to match the house. In tenon-and-peg construction, these doors were substantial and required large hinges of iron or brass, as well as an impressive lock. (A ring of keys was always important in the house, as everything from a cupboard to a tea chest could be locked when not in use; these keys jingled along with a woman on her daily rounds.) A visitor's first encounter with a household would be the door knocker, perhaps in brass, like several discovered still in place on doors in the historic area. Transoms brought light into halls with few windows. It was not until after the Revolutionary War that window panes were carried up the sides of doorways as well.

The careful finish devoted to every detail of a house is evident in the Greenhow House, **LEFT.** *Wainscoting surrounds the door and adorns the soffit of the hood, for an effect as fine as any interior. The louvers would allow the interior door to be left open, providing privacy and ventilation.* **RIGHT** *The brass door knocker at the Carter's Grove plantation, installed in the 1920s by Mr. and Mrs. Archibald McCrea, announces the grandeur of the house.*

A fence outlines the yard around the Shields Tavern storehouse, one of many dependencies, or outbuildings, that are scattered to the rear of most buildings in Williamsburg. **OPPOSITE** A stable behind the Ludwell-Paradise House reveals the same attention to detail and finish that prevails throughout much of the town, with its Flemish bond brick and decorative cupola that allowed air to circulate within.

the blocklike protrusions under many eaves, which were a translation of the traditional orders of architecture. These modillions were the wooden descendants of the ancient Greeks' system of stone buildings. But such embellishments appealed to the educated, who were aware of history and intent on showing their erudition and tradition.

These simple houses could grow as families and fortunes demanded; the next, more established generation built on a dining room, perhaps, as Peyton Randolph did when he inherited his father's house. Such houses rambled in response to circumstance. But others, like the Wythe House, built by Richard Taliaferro for his daughter when she married George Wythe, show the other side of Williamsburg architecture, the well-proportioned and carefully modulated graces of Georgian buildings that derived from a builder with a plan. Taliaferro, a planter with a talent for architecture, clearly knew what he was creating: Called a "double pile" because it is two rooms deep, the house is a work of harmony and balance, from central stair hall to gracious upper story, center door, and range of small-paned windows.

RIGHT Elite households like that of George and Elizabeth Wythe were supported by slave-managed workplaces, such as the kitchen, weaving room, and laundry. Most iron elements like this highly decorative lamp bracket, BELOW, were imported from Britain.

The small functional structures behind most Williamsburg houses are now ornamental features of the landscape. The little house, **OPPOSITE**, is the Dr. Barraud House smokehouse, vital for preserving food. Such a utility build-ing would not have merited much decoration; the weathered exterior is a result of the underlying Spanish Brown paint coming through to the surface. In front, the "swept picket fence" boasts "spear point" picket tops. The Alexander Craig House kitchen, **ABOVE**, is, as is typical of Williamsburg kitchens, separated from the main house; the broad chimney attests to the large fireplace within. **ABOVE RIGHT** A privy is prettied with a crape myr-tle and hedge. A row of onions leads to the King's Arms Tavern's privy in the rear garden, **RIGHT**, perhaps an aid to navigation in the dark.

Beyond, between, and around the houses were the gardens of Williamsburg. Spring in Williamsburg then must have been as glorious as it is now, with the town floating in blossoms, the air full of scent and petals and birdsong. Visitors and residents alike feel the desire to walk everywhere, crisscrossing the streets, swinging a gate open to discover what lies blooming beyond the brick walk. Pocket gardens full of boxwood and daisies are tucked behind small houses, and grand schemes run from the rear of the house to the canal. The variety is lavish, from the formal beds planted in colorful harmony to the artless charm of a few tulips crowding against a simple wooden fence. The town itself seems a vast garden, planned and pruned and perfect, its textures and colors part of the harmony of the place.

From the first glimpse, Virginia had been thought an Eden, its shores a tangle of trees and vines and unknown flowers and plants, surely an earthly paradise where anything could grow. "The eyes are ravished with the Beauties of naked Nature," wrote Robert Beverley, an early commen-

Behind the Market Square Tavern, a path of crushed shells leads toward a patch of summer phlox against a picket fence, **TOP**. Ancient deposits of shell, **ABOVE**, were dug out of the ground to be used for walks. Bricks line the path, **RIGHT**, at the Coke-Garrett House, where boxwood hedges add their distinctive scent to the air. **OPPOSITE** Purple chives, a mist of yellow wallflowers, tall foxgloves, calendulas in yellow, and gray artemisia make a subtle planting against formal boxwood hedges in the John Blair House's herb garden. Just beyond is the pyramidal roof of the smokehouse topped by a handsome globe finial.

tator. But for the first colonists, scratching out a place in the wilderness to plant corn and tobacco ·was all that time and energy permitted, though the wealthier could import handsome fruit trees and snippets of box for gardens that had more to do with food than flowers.

But "naked Nature" didn't long suffice, and soon the wealthiest and most educated of the colonists began to cultivate pleasure gardens, both at their plantations and around their Williamsburg houses. Gardening to the eighteenth-century gen-

Post-and-rail paddock fences, **ABOVE**, are still cut by hand. **RIGHT** Simple hand tools like the spade, hand-barrow, besom broom, hoe, edger, garden fork, and winnowing basket have their descendants in our own metal and wood tools, but the eighteenth-century versions are more decorative. **OPPOSITE, LEFT** A bell jar concentrates the early spring sun's rays and protects tender plants from overnight frosts. Humble cabbages fill the Palace vegetable garden, with a privy at the rear, **OPPOSITE, ABOVE**. A wheelbarrow totes a wicker basket filled with branches, **OPPOSITE, BELOW**.

try was more than a hobby or a way to please the eye at home. A garden, when not meant simply as a place where fruit trees and vegetables held sway, was a place to explore scientific interests, to find beauty as well as usefulness, something to share with friends, to express one's theories and to feed ambitions, social and otherwise, and, perhaps, as some colonial gardeners wrote so evocatively, to discover one's self—impulses probably not so far removed from those of contemporary gardeners.

The gardeners with Williamsburg connections with whom we're most familiar are men like Thomas Jefferson and George Wythe, William Byrd II, St. George Tucker, and John Custis, enthusiastic and learned plantsmen who left notes and records that revealed their relationship with the soil. As George Washington wrote, gardening is pleasurable because seeing "the work of ones own hands, fostered by care and attention, rising to maturity in a beautiful display of those advantages

and ornaments which by the Combination of Nature and taste of the projector in the disposal of them is always regaling to the eye."

Women appear only in a glimpse, though surely they loved their gardens, too: A daughter of Williamsburg, Eliza Blow, later sketched out her grandfather Benjamin Waller's beloved garden in order to have it replicated in her own house in Sussex County, Virginia. Her memories were so strong the sketch was used to match the archaeological evidence of his garden discovered later in the restoration—and it did. Philip Fithian gave his typical appreciative account of an afternoon in the garden, where he loved to follow his employer Mrs. Carter for a walk; she seemed to have much to do with the making of it:

LEFT An arbor supports American wisteria and coral honeysuckle in the Bryan House's garden, and more wisteria twines round the porch at the Coke-Garrett House, **ABOVE.** Trimmed boxwood topiaries, **BELOW,** were a favorite colonial device. **OPPOSITE** Near the John Blair Kitchen, the herb garden met the household's culinary and medicinal needs. The classic parterres lined with brick make gardening and harvesting neater and easier.

"After school, I had the honour of taking a walk with Mrs. Carter through the Garden—It is beautiful, & I think uncommon to see at this Season peas all up two & three Inches—We gathered two or three Cowslips in full-Bloom; & as many violets—The English Honey Suckle is all out in green & tender leaves—Mrs. Carter shewed me her Apricot-Grafts; Asparagus Beds &c."

Williamsburg's first prominent garden was that at the College of William and Mary, glimpsed in the 1740s Bodleian Plate, an engraving with views of Williamsburg's public buildings. The College garden was an Italianate and formal arrangement of rows of trimmed green bushes in front of the main building, though there were probably seedbeds and vegetable gardens to the rear. The college gardener remained an important resource for the town throughout the century, advertising such things as seeds for "pease" for sale.

But more personal gardens were encouraged by the plan of the town itself. After he arrived in 1710, Governor Spotswood wrote to his brother in England

FENCES AND GATES

From the very beginnings of the city, a fence was required to be built within six months of the purchase of a town lot, defining a house's property and helping to stop wandering livestock and to preserve the kitchen gardens most households tended. In 1705 the assembly required "every Person having any Lotts or half Acres of Land contiguous to the great Street shall inclose the said Lotts or half Acres with a Wall Pales or Post and Rails." • The stitchery of fences that we see now, a mix of the simple and the fanciful, is similar to the framework of the town that its inhabitants knew; surprisingly, traces of fences were among the first discoveries modern archaeologists made. There were posthole patterns, even bits of wood remaining, and a whole fence post was found near the Anthony Hay cabinet shop. A simple post-and-rail design, it was a practical choice to outline his field. Those in search of fashion might have answered Benjamin Bucktrout's advertisement of 1767, advising he made "all sorts of *Chinese* and *Gothick* paling for gardens and summer houses." Brick or stone walls were rare, though the Palace was ringed with a brick garden wall, topped with broken glass to deter intruders. And brick pillars crowned with handsome stone balls intimated the magnificence to be found within. The elaborate iron gates also announced this was a place of power, one step closer to the Crown. But the gates most visitors to Williamsburg remember are the humbler garden gates, which swing closed behind a wanderer with the weight of an iron ball on a length of chain—ingenuity that still impresses, two centuries later.

The small paddocks and fields in the town limits are one of the pleasures of the Williamsburg town plan. A picket fence like the one, LEFT, *at the King's Arms Tavern, ensured privacy, too. At the St. George Tucker House,* RIGHT, *the garden gate shows a high degree of craftsmanship, with its X-crossings that allow a peep of the garden to show through to the street, and handsome posts.*

A gate bars the path to the graveyard at the Governor's Palace, where Revolutionary War soldiers lie, **LEFT**. This is a "pierced stringer" gate, the vertical members "piercing" the horizontal rail. One would expect such high-style gates around the Governor's house. **RIGHT** A much simpler fence borders a pasture; such fences were easily built with an ax, used both for splitting logs and making the holes in each post where the rails were laid.

The brick garden wall at the Red Lion, where the live oaks grow, **LEFT**, is a rarity; few domestic gardens were enclosed with such an expensive wall. **RIGHT** Graduated pickets make a graceful gate. The ball and chain, a simple mechanism that automatically closes the gate, can be found throughout Williamsburg and is a favorite with visitors to the village.

of his duties, "I am sufficiently amused with planting orchard and gardens." He was determined to make the raw little capital and its new governor's house into a landscape that would replicate the handsome parks and gardens he knew at home, and sought to create pretty vistas and prospects within the plan of the town, according to the period's tastes. In his zeal, he was not beyond removing tree limbs, even houses, to open up a "visto." His plans for completing the Palace were ambitious, involving parkland with roaming deer and a flower garden; terraces, called "falling gardens," at the side; and a canal and fishpond below. The burgesses, watching the public's money fly as the garden grew, demanded that he stop, and turned aside his requests for underwriting such things as an Italian bathhouse by allowing the munificent sum of £1. Still, the public interest in the Governor's projects was enormous, and Hugh Jones, writing his *Present State of Virginia* in 1724, praised the Palace complex: "The Palace, or governor's house, a magnificent structure, finished and beautified with gates, fine gardens, offices, walks, a fine canal, orchards . . ."

The wealthy of Williamsburg, who could buy several town lots and make up a dwelling place of several acres, had the room and the interest to model their

A gardener's first consideration in laying out his plot was form and symmetry; a naturalistic planting of masses of flowers was not the era's ideal of beauty. An orderly garden gave a hint of the orderly universe and the scientific questions that often prompted a gardener's efforts, as well as the quest for a beautiful effect. The arrangement of boxwood hedges with a tailored topiary Yaupon holly in its center, **ABOVE**, recalls European gardens of earlier centuries, when form was at least as important as color. **LEFT** English boxwood fills the parterres of the Governor's Palace ballroom garden, with more Yaupon holly topiary. Benjamin Waller was known for his garden, **OPPOSITE, ABOVE**, and it was replicated from sketches drawn by a descendant. Boxwood parterres are filled with anemones and periwinkle. **OPPOSITE, BELOW** In the Taliaferro-Cole garden, yellow primroses line the turf panels in spring, and the beds are full of bulbs and columbines.

own gardens. "I have a pretty little garden in which I take more satisfaction than in anything in this world and have a collection of tolerable good flowers and greens from England," wrote John Custis in 1725 after seven or eight years of planting the grounds around his house. Intelligent and curious, he was in constant communication with horticulturists like Peter Collinson in England, his "Brothers of the Spade," exchanging seeds and bulbs, and experimenting to see what would grow in Virginia. He ordered striped hollies and yew trees, which he trained as balls or pyramids, and filled his garden with color against the green: Plant lists include lilies, hyacinth, yellow

or vegetable garden was written by Williamsburg resident John Randolph, the king's attorney, who still found time to write a treatise that advised gardeners working in the Virginia climate on how to grow their vegetables. His town house was surrounded by ten acres of land, ample room for experiment.

If Custis's approach to the garden combined an intellectual with an emotional reaction, and Randolph's was purely practical, St. George Tucker, who came to study in Williamsburg from Bermuda in 1771 and then stayed to practice law and teach, made a garden that seemed the center of his life. A friend later described Tucker's feelings for the town: "He calls it the terrestrial Paradise, the Seat of all joy and Delight, the Habitation of Angels and the Society of God's chosen people." On his own acres he began an ambitious garden of fruit trees, shrubs, and flowers—he called his wife the Matron of the Green for her efforts—and numbered each bloom in his diary with the eye of the gardener and the heart of the poet he was.

The gardens these men planted were careful creations, a lifework, but most gardens in Williamsburg surely must have been practical patches that belonged to a merchant or a tradesman, a small backyard effort that probably amounted to little more than a fruit tree or a grape arbor,

asphodel, "jessamine," pinks, and evidence of the search for a perfect rose. He worked to domesticate such wild beauties as the dogwood trees that drifted pink and white in the woods, and sent along wildflower seeds and tree saplings to be planted in English experiments; Collinson wrote later of his "pleasure and Delight" in the Virginia imports. Custis raged against ship captains who didn't care for his plants, and the weather that constantly set him back, but his letters suggest the lifelong joy and solace his garden provided; in fact, his portrait shows him at rest, hand on a book entitled *Of the Tulip,* with a bright flower at his side.

Later in the century, the most important nursery in America was established in Williamsburg, serving the demand from planters on their increasingly lavish estates, colonists farther away, and the town's own ambitious gardeners. And the first American book on making a kitchen

The vigorous level of design detail in every kind of structure is one of Williamsburg's enduring traits. Examples include a well house, **ABOVE**, and a smokehouse, **RIGHT**.

with vegetables and herbs and a few flowers planted among them and chickens scratching between the rows. This was a contrast to the wealthy man's garden, a more formally planned arrangement with a framework of dark green and scented boxwood, perhaps formal parterres, espaliered fruit trees, newly imported bulbs from Holland or England. A stitchery of fences joined garden to garden, as we see today.

The current Williamsburg garden is also a reflection of gardening trends popular in the 1930s, when the first restoration efforts were made. John D. Rockefeller Jr. made a priority of the plantings, and Arthur A. Shurcliff was hired to design the gardens in the restored town. One of the founders of Harvard's landscape architecture school, he was a keen researcher of the history of Southern gardens, examining plantation houses and their surviving gardens and discovering original garden designs in archives. At the time, little was known about the layout of the plots in Williamsburg, though ancient boxwood and hollies often gave a ghost outline of past glories. But Shurcliff's imaginative leaps and research in other Southern states resulted in

The gazebo (a word that loosely translates as "I shall see") allowed for outdoor entertaining even during a summer shower. It would be positioned to give the best view of the garden and landscape beyond.

gardens that are extraordinarily beautiful but inaccurate reflections of what went before. His attitude toward gardening budgets was similar to Governor Spotswood's, but Rockefeller underwrote elaborate projects that have become one of the glories of the town, such as the formal gardens of the Palace, including a hill that covered the railroad tracks and a maze that never was.

Newer research, such as archaeological evidence of postholes and even still-green leaves preserved in a well, when matched with documents like maps, tax and insurance records, and letters and diaries, is forming another idea of a Williamsburg garden, perhaps a sparer, less elaborate form than what we've known before. Yet to wander in these gardens is to share the most immediate, most accessible link to those who once walked—and dug and planted—here, to echo St. George Tucker's poem, "On Domestic Happiness": "Be this my Lot, beneath the rural Shade,/Where peace, and comfort, and Contentment dwell."

BENCHES

Many sources were used for the design of Williamsburg's garden benches. Paintings of genteel British gardens are prominent among these sources. They often take furniture styles in whimsical directions, and interpret the turnings, latticework, and overall forms of interior furnishings in new ways. By including a bench or two in their gardens, Williamsburg homeowners created "garden rooms," thereby extending their living spaces by domesticating nature. For the colonial lady of leisure, these benches served as spaces for relaxation and reflection. At Williamsburg today, the benches provide rest for the weary tourist and inspire the home gardener with their elegant lines and variety of forms. • Dozens of different historic area benches illustrate the variety of sources that influenced eighteenth-century joiners and their twentieth-century architectural successors. Ranging from published chinoiserie designs to old North England traditions, these sources have been selectively employed in creating seats that please the eye. • At Williamsburg today, nearly forty styles of benches can be found throughout the historic area gardens, ranging from simple backless forms to carefully detailed pieces. All are produced by the Foundation's millwork shop using joinery techniques, turns, and details known to eighteenth-century craftsmen.

LEFT *The simple lines of a modern bench blend beautifully with the eighteenth-century setting in this private garden. A curved lattice-back bench,* RIGHT, *nestles in the untrimmed corner of a boxwood garden.*

LEFT *Situated to take in all the sights and scents of nature, this bench rests beside a boxwood hedge in the garden behind the Coke-Garrett House.*
RIGHT *Details such as a bow-turned baluster supporting a sawn-board arm repay careful examination.*

A COLONIAL WILLIAMSBURG SAMPLER

CONSERVATION TIPS FROM THE WILLIAMSBURG EXPERTS

Some of our favorite possessions are those made of paper or textiles, whether new or old. Grandmother's wedding dress, a favorite quilt, a collection of love letters, or framed antique prints and maps—all require some special attention to ensure they are in good condition to pass along to the next generation, and to continue to add interest and beauty to our own homes. Proper storage and display and careful handling and, if necessary, repair and cleaning are all part of the challenge in preserving their value.

Environmental Concerns

Light, moisture, temperature, humidity, dust, and pests are all threats to paper and textiles. Controlling an object's contact with these hazards is a constant concern. In most cases, common sense will tell you to keep your heirlooms out of direct light, storing them properly inside the house rather than in an attic, basement, or garage. Keep them away from cigarettes and fireplace smoke, too. Routine pest control is also important, best achieved through good housekeeping, like regular vacuuming and dusting, and a building maintenance program. Mothballs are not recommended as they can be hazardous to humans; a professional pest control company can be your best solution.

Cleaning

Textiles: Keeping a quilt or other flat textile clean is important to its preservation. Using a handheld vacuum on low suction is often the only safe cleaning procedure. Cover the portion of the textile being vacuumed with a fiberglass screen (available at local hardware stores). Be sure to cover the outer edges of the screening with twill tape to avoid snags. Vacuuming not only improves the appearance of a textile, it removes soil, which attracts insects. Silk is an exception, however, and should not be vacuumed because the fibers are not as strong as those of wool, cotton, linen, or blends. Never launder antique textiles in a washing machine. If wet cleaning is necessary, consult a professionally trained conservator.

Paper: For cleaning paper objects, the best method for the non-conservator is careful brushing with a very soft bristled brush around the image area and careful vacuuming to remove loose surface soil. An exception is pastel chalk, charcoal, and pencil images, which should be cleaned only by an experienced conservator. Never brush a pastel. Any paper heirloom should be handled as little as possible with immaculately clean hands. Wear white cotton gloves when handling framed works on paper.

Repair

When considering how to treat an antique that may need repair, decide if your objectives for its future use are in keeping with the type, condition, value, and historic importance of the object. That will determine the nature and extent of your restoration efforts. Proper treatment by a qualified professional specializing in either textiles or paper conservation is always recommended, and the treatment should be as reversible as possible.

Display

Textiles: When hanging textiles such as a quilt or a rug vertically, be sure the pull of its weight does not tear or weaken the fabric. Position the textile at a slight angle to lessen the stress, possibly mounted on a Velcro strip with hand-basted stitches to distribute the weight evenly along an edge. For very fragile or very heavy pieces, a backing may be stitched to the piece to help carry the weight of the object.

Paper: Displaying paper objects requires proper framing, including acid-free hanging and matting (throughout the housing, not just in the immediate layers near the print), proper mounting materials, and filtration of ultraviolet light, either through the frame glass or at the light source. A good framer will help make selections for mounting works on paper.

Storage

Contact with acidic materials is a major reason textiles and papers deteriorate in storage or on display. In many cases the very materials historically used to protect them have done the most harm, like cedar chests, conventional tissue papers, airtight plastic containers, and wooden or cardboard frame backboards. A greater understanding of the effect of acid on textiles and paper has led to the availability of many acid-free products to keep valuables from deteriorating.

Textiles: Store textiles like quilts and coverlets in layers separated by acid-free tissue paper in acid-free boxes or wrapped loosely in clean cotton sheets. Place tissue in sausage-shaped rolls inside fold lines and periodically refold the textiles to prevent permanent creases. Textiles need air circulation and should not be stored in plastic bags, nor should they be stored directly on

wooden storage shelves or cedar-type chests. The acid in the wood can accelerate aging in textiles. While an acid-free box is best, an acid-free tissue paper or cotton sheeting buffer is acceptable, providing you regularly replace or wash the buffering material, which can eventually absorb acid or become dusty. Avoid hanging textiles in storage.

Single layers of fabrics can be rolled, unless they have painted or elaborately embellished surfaces. Roll the textile in the direction of the warp yarns around an acid-free tube, using appropriate acid-free tissue. Roll heavy blankets and rugs on a 4½-inch tube with the pile outward to prevent crushing.

Paper: Store unframed paper objects in acid-free containers with acid-free interleaving packing materials. Use individual protective enclosures for each object within a container. These supplies are available from local paper conservators and preservation material suppliers. Be sure all the components of the container are safe. For example, a box featuring acid-free lining but containing a wooden core will not protect a paper heirloom.

More information about finding a professional conservator is available from the American Institute for Conservation of Historic and Artistic Works , 1717 K street, NW, Suite 301, Washington, D.C. 20006; (202) 452-9545.

How to Care for Silver

Now, as in the eighteenth century, silver objects are prized not only for their beauty, but also for the intrinsic worth of the metal. Usually alloyed with copper for hardness and strength, silver is manufactured in varying degrees of purity. Colonial settlers would have bought silver objects for all sorts of uses—flatware, hollowware, utensils for dining, coins, buckles, buttons, jewelry, mirrors, candlesticks, gun mounts, and many other domestic luxuries.

Silver is sensitive to environmental influences, which cause it to corrode or tarnish. There are several reasons for such deterioration, including moisture, everyday pollutants like sulfur and chlorine in the air, contact with sulfur-containing materials (such as rubber bands or glue), chloride-based plastics (PVCs or plastic wrap), and human perspiration. Those who live by the sea know that salt air causes metals to corrode, as does salt on the dining table. Silver will always tarnish to some extent with regular use, but attention to its care and storage makes it possible to preserve and enjoy silver pieces, both new and old.

TIPS ON CARING FOR SILVER

- Dust silver objects often with soft brushes, since dust attracts moisture and pollutants.
- If you need to wash a silver object, use hot distilled water and a mild detergent. Rinse and thoroughly dry it. (Distilled water has none of the damaging chemicals, like chlorides, found in tap water.)
- Some polishes can be detrimental and can cause wear and even perpetuate corrosion. Commercial antitarnish polishes can leave behind a film that eventually causes discoloration

and streaking. These streaks can be removed only with highly abrasive polishes, which actually remove some of the metal. Commercial polishes can leave damaging residues in nooks and crannies. Seriously tarnished silver pieces require professional restoration. However, to remove light-duty tarnish, use the least abrasive compound possible, such as a precipitated chalk (whiting) mixed with distilled water into a paste. Be sure to remove all residues by rinsing in hot distilled water.

- If you display silver on wood furniture, create "coasters" by cutting circles of Mylar to protect the finish on the tabletop.
- When possible, store silver objects in closed cabinets, drawers, or cases to prevent air from tarnishing them. There are many products designed to keep your silver safe in storage, including silver cloth and silver paper. Available at hardware stores, antiques dealers, or fabric stores, these products absorb harmful corrosive elements, principally sulfur.
- Store silver objects in areas of your home that have stable relative humidity and temperatures. Avoid keeping them in basements and attics or on mantels above operating fireplaces. Also avoid storing silver immediately above or below air vents, since both cold and warm air can cause condensation.
- Minimize the amount of exposure to intense light.

How to Care for Furniture

Bringing a handsome example of antique or reproduction furniture home is only the beginning. To preserve its value and usefulness and prolong its beauty is a challenge, for careful attention is required to ensure that the furniture you love will stand up to the years of daily use and the special problems created by modern homes.

The conservation department of Williamsburg cares for hundreds of pieces of fine antique furniture. Some is kept in the temperature-controlled rooms of the DeWitt Wallace Gallery of Decorative Arts, where temperature, light, and humidity are ideal; other examples are used in the rooms of the restored houses, where conditions can more closely resemble our own homes. These examples of antique furniture are often complex combinations of materials such as wood and leather, paint and natural resins and oils, textiles, bone, ivory, iron, and brass, and each element requires a different sort of attention. Still, the department's experience with these historic examples is equally applicable to contemporary furniture reproductions, though modern furniture is often protected with finishes that are more resilient than a 200-year-old surface.

The chief enemies of furniture are extreme fluctuations in temperature and relative humidity, overexposure to light, and dust. If you're foresighted, you can protect your furniture and prevent the accumulating damage that will occur if these problems go unchecked.

Most important is maintaining a moderate environment of temperatures between 60 and 75°F. with a relative humidity of 40 to 60 percent. At home, where personal temperature and humidity comfort ranges may not be the same as those for furniture, it is consistency that is most important. Placing a piece of furniture near a radiator, for instance, or in an unheated space like a garage or attic, where the range of temperature and dampness are uncontrolled, will warp boards and ruin finishes. An inexpensive portable humidifier or dehumidifier can effectively reduce damaging seasonal swings in relative humidity. Without this, the wood will swell and shrink, dry and crack, loosening joints and, perhaps, causing veneers to loosen and lift.

Light is a wonderful addition to our homes, and wide windows are everywhere. But the colonial housewife carefully shut her curtains and closed the shutters when a room was not in use—direct sunlight, over time, can fade a wooden surface and

damage fabric-covered areas. If objects remain for a period of time on the top of a table or chest placed in the sun, you'll even find that shadow shapes remain. Drawing a curtain to protect furniture, or placing a fine piece out of the direct rays of the sun, is essential.

Frequent dusting is also critical, not only to reveal the full beauty of the furniture, but to remove the particles that trap surface moisture and feed damaging molds and insects. Dusting improperly can, however, cause even more problems. Make sure that you are dusting with a soft rag, feather duster, or soft brush attachment to a vacuum cleaner; look for something that won't scratch the surface as you move it over a piece. And take particular care with inlaid or marquetry surfaces not to snag and lift loose edges.

Resist the impulse to spray lemony polish all over your furniture or to pour out pools of wax. Avoid using commercial furniture polishes that contain oils and silicone, as they eventually yellow and are difficult to remove in restoration. Also avoid drying oils (like linseed oil), which darken wood, and petroleum oils (like lemon oil), which attract dust. Good quality paste wax is the safest polish to use, and it provides an effective barrier to liquid spills. You need not wax more than once or twice a year, if you do it carefully. Apply a moderate amount of wax to the piece, then buff it to a shine using a lint-free cotton or linen cloth with a tight weave that won't snag any loose pieces on the surface.

To prevent white rings on furniture tops, place coasters under "sweating" glasses of cold liquid and set pads under hot dishes. A spill is no disaster if it is wiped up immediately to prevent the moisture from getting beyond the finish and into the wood itself.

Finally, move furniture as little as possible to avoid knocking loose small pieces of wood or scuffing surfaces. Pick up chairs by their seat rails rather than by the arms or backs. Lift tables not by their tops, but by their understructure, and carefully lift rather than push case pieces.

With a combination of common sense and special care, your fine furniture should last long enough to be the cherished heirlooms of the next generation and beyond.

❂❂❂❂❂❂❂❂❂❂❂❂❂❂❂❂❂❂❂❂❂❂❂❂❂❂❂

DECORATING IDEAS FROM THE EIGHTEENTH CENTURY

Scholars have spent years researching and re-creating meticulously authentic historic interiors at Colonial Williamsburg. Their accurate treatments of beds and windows, their loose slipcovers, and their dazzling dessert tables can be replicated in your home.

Bed and Window Curtains

The accurately dressed windows and beds in the museums, as well as the references in these essays, are based upon the research of curator of textiles Linda Baumgarten and her colleagues in Williamsburg's curatorial and conservation departments.

In the eighteenth century, bed furnishings were often the single most expensive item in a household, and goods were woven only 18 to 28 inches wide. Textiles are relatively inexpensive today, and twice as wide, so we allow ourselves the luxury of matching patterns when we join seams. Such waste was virtually unknown in colonial America.

When choosing fabric, trim, and design, the first consideration is the room and the overall effect you wish to achieve. Are curtains intended to be the focal point of the room or an understated complement to other furnishings and decoration? To replicate a period interior, choose a documented reproduction, such as a blue Indigo resist, a woven linen check, or a red copperplate print (toile de Jouy). Other aspirations in decorative style allow for wider choices of material and in style and technique of fabrication.

A bold monochromatic printed toile makes a statement, while a crisp white cotton dimity or seersucker suggests a comforting coolness to counter Southern summers. Line a printed toile with a contrasting color for impact: the purple toile in the Governor's Palace is lined with green silk. A soft cherry-red cotton satin lining creates a cheerful glow inside red toile bed curtains. Consider using fabrics in creative ways: think of the decorative possibilities of using horizontal, or "railroad," treatments for valances, or of using the appliqué technique, where textile elements are cut out and sewn onto a base fabric in a decorative manner.

A strongly patterned fabric such as a toile can carry a heavy fringe treatment to edge curtains and valances. The dense green wool fringe on the purple toile at the Governor's Palace (page 63) is a good example. In contrast, an unlined curtain and valance treatment with a strongly shaped valance—such as the green checked bed furniture in the George Wythe House (page 85)—is effectively trimmed with a simple twill or woven checked tape binding.

One of the most graceful eighteenth-century curtain designs is the fluid "drapery" curtain that draws up into a soft swag. This

treatment creates a softer and more dramatic alternative to the static "swag and jabot." Popular from about 1750 to 1780, the "draw-up drapery" style was a favorite with English patrons who used Thomas Chippendale as their interior designer. Chippendale intended the patterns in his book for the upholstery workshop as well as the patron, so he gave instructions and diagrams for the design of the cornices (often fabric covered) and the pulley lath systems that supported bed drapery and window curtains.

These curtains work beautifully in a variety of fabrics. In the dining room of the Governor's Palace they are shown in an unlined springy wool moreen (page 24). An elaborate Indian chintz bed at the Palace is lined with green cotton satin; the curtains are pulled up in double drapery, one of the variations shown in Chippendale's influential 1754 pattern book *The Gentleman and Cabinet-Maker's Director.* If the curtain is lined, the lining fabric needs to be sufficiently decorative—it will show when the curtain is pulled up. Satin weave cotton is appropriate for cottons; a complementary printed fabric can also be effective in more modern treatments.

The windows' proportions along with the scale of the room will determine which curtains will work most effectively. For instance, a pair of narrow windows on one wall might look best if each window gets one curtain, each swagged to the outside, rather than two panels crowded onto each window.

Chippendale shows the "draw-up drapery" with the complete architectural complement of a molded or carved cornice, sometimes covered with fabric matching the curtains, and valances (sometimes buckram stiffened) beneath the cornice at the top of the curtain. The curtains can be mounted to a pulley lath without cornices (as with more contemporary balloon shades), but the effect is not as strong or as architecturally complete. The valance is an option that can stand in place of the cornice, or that can be omitted at more modest windows if a cornice is used.

Whether you make your own pattern and assemble the curtains according to Chippendale's design, or hire an interior decorator or upholstery shop to handle the sewing fabrication, bear in mind a few details: The pulley lath, mounted with angle irons to the inside of the cornice, holds and organizes the lines that raise the curtains. The lines run through a row of rings sewn into the lining side of the curtain, then through pulleys or screw eyes at the outer corner (or corners, depending on whether your window has one or two curtain panels) of the pulley lath. The lines run back down the side of the window to be tied off on "cloak pins" that anchor the curtain in the raised position. For an authentic look, pairs of decorative cast brass or enameled cloak pins should be used for securing the draperies of both bed and window hangings. A modern alternative is to mount pairs of cabinet pulls to the window molding—much more attractive than the conventional window shade anchor. These should be mounted low on the window molding, between the sill and the chair rail.

Each pair of curtains is made of two panels that reach to the floor—the length is very important for creating the proper effect when the curtain is drawn up. The width of each curtain depends upon the desired effect. A sumptuous curtain in silk damask will require many widths of fabric; a slightly austere colonial effect in checked linen will need fewer. Avoid making the panels too skimpy, however, or they will lose some of the soft and rich effect when drawn up. Each panel should be at least twice as wide as the window (measured outside the window frame) before gathering.

If the edge of the curtains is bound with tape that wraps around the edge, outer curtain and lining should be sewn with wrong sides together. Otherwise, right sides should go together and are inverted at the top before gathering into heading. Add trim after turning inside out. Unlike contemporary curtains, this style does not have a return of face fabric on the lining side. Face fabric and lining need to be the same width, or the effect will be ruined when the curtain is drawn up and the decorative lining is revealed in the swagged "tail."

A less complicated way to get an effect similar to a "draw-up drapery" bed or window curtain is by swagging a gathered curtain panel using a button and a tape loop. These curtains could be easily and quickly closed to give the sleeper privacy or to protect from mosquitoes. This treatment was often used on hangings made for portable tent beds (also called field, or camp, beds). Curtains were sewn to the tester, or ceiling, of the bed; the entire unit draped over the bedstead as a tent drapes over its frame. George Hepplewhite illustrated this treatment in his 1787 pattern book *The Cabinet-Maker and Upholsterer's Guide.* White cotton (particularly a ribbed stripe called dimity) was popular for this style of bed treatment, in vogue in the late eighteenth and early nineteenth centuries.

Since portability was a factor for original tent bed hangings used during army campaigns, curtains were seldom lined. Edges were bound with white twill tape or trimmed with cotton fringe. Original military tent bedsteads did not have cornices or valances, but when the fashion was domesticated these more elaborate elements were sometimes added.

Slipcovers

Few slipcovers from the colonial period survive, yet portraits, bills of sale, inventories, and prints tell us of the importance of slipcovers in the household of the time. Conserving precious fabrics on a chair was vital, and a cotton or linen slipcover applied from the first served to protect the original silk or wool damask upholstery. Such slipcovers could be decorative, matching bed and window treatments, and also a seasonal choice, when hot summers made sitting on cool linen or cotton a much more attractive choice. Slipcovers could be easily removed and cleaned, too, so they were made loosely to accommodate shrinkage.

Today we choose a slipcover for many of the same reasons, especially for a chair that will see hard wear. A loose cover can be popped off, sent to the washing machine, and be back on the chair for the next day's use. And we are even more intent on the decorative uses of slipcovers, choosing them to match or contrast with a room's color scheme, and shaping the border or selecting a welting to add variety and interest to a room. Anyone making a slipcover today has the choice of following the eighteenth-century pattern, or adapting authenticity to today's tastes.

Two hundred years ago, chairs were so individual, and upholsterers so accomplished at fitting to particular chairs, that every pattern was unique. Sewers cut as few pieces of fabric as possible, usually beginning with the largest piece—the rear chair back. Instead of creating a finished look with right sides sewn together, seams were sewn on the outside with wrong sides together, then covered and sewn again with decorative tape rather than the more expensive piping. The double stitching added strength and artistically defined the lines of the chair. After each seam, the seamstress tried the slipcover on the chair to measure for cutting the next piece. Outside seams saved time because they eliminated the continual need to turn the fabric right side out when trying it on the chair.

Once the slipcover was fitted, joining techniques varied. The inside back seams were either sewn together without tape or left unsewn. In both cases, they were tucked up into the chair. There were also options for the outside rear. A seamstress might make a seam on one or both sides, or she could sew ties made out of the decorative seam tape to connect the sides to the outside rear. The ties were always made of the decorative tape, not the fabric

of the slipcover. Seamstresses also used tape rather than a hem to edge a slipcover.

Sometimes it is necessary to insert a gusset of fabric to cover the front width of the wings or the face of a curved arm. Scraps of other fabric were often used where they wouldn't show, as under the seat cushion. The side and rear skirts of easy chair slipcovers were never pleated or ruffled, but seat cushions sometimes had a ruffled front skirt.

To make an authentic slipcover, begin at the rear of the chair back. Draping the fabric—or ideally muslin to make a pattern—cut the back to the appropriate size. Cut the inside back next,

then sew it to the rear back piece at the top. Cut side pieces and sew them to the inside and rear back pieces. Cut a piece for the "floor," which goes under the seat cushion, and sew it to the inside back and side pieces. This extends in length down the front of the chair and matches the length of the rear back and sides. Cover the seat cushion loosely, joining it together at the back with ties made from the decorative tape.

The Dessert Table

The hospitality that is part of Virginia's heritage for centuries had its origins in the beginnings of the colony, when the humblest emigrant shared his table with friends and relatives. By the time the grandees had established their plantation houses and town homes, gathering together for a festive meal was a daily ritual. In temper with the times, the dessert course especially became the opportunity for a hostess to show off her creativity, taste, and wealth, with a spread of dainties artfully made and artistically composed to fill the dining table at the end of the meal.

Presenting food in an ordered pattern so that it pleased the eye as well as the palate was a testimony to her sophistication and knowledge. Special occasions brought forth tables that glittered with multitiered glass pyramids full of almonds and colorful marzipan, perhaps shaped to honor the occasion. Small glass pails were filled with candied fruit, and other plates held little cakes and edible centerpieces. Colonial hostesses were not likely to center their tables with a huge bouquet of flowers, as we do; instead fresh flowers might be used to grace a plate, or a small vase might be tucked among the platters. Ornamental porcelain, like the Chelsea figures (see page 109), also might be placed on the table.

A contemporary party that focused on a variety of small desserts and treats would be a festive occasion for us, too, and our own tables can borrow this idea of the table as a stage set, to be trimmed with details. The first step would be a white linen table cloth. For the eighteenth-century hostess, placing the plates in a geometric and regular pattern was important. Ceramic figures or tiny bud vases with a posy or two are then set among the

plates and worked into the overall design. Undoubtedly there would be candles to bring it all to sparkling life, and we could intersperse several sets of tapers among the desserts. Marzipan, Jordan almonds, and silver dragees are all still to be

had, and sugar cookies snipped into shapes, crispy gingerbread, petits fours, and candied fruits are easy to make or to buy to fill an assortment of white or crystal platters.

Besides offering a wide variety of desserts, a hostess would make her table pretty by varying the heights of the serving dishes, building pyramids of food to tempt a guest. Collecting graduated sizes of footed cake plates, preferably in similar patterns, will allow you to build a pyramid to a reasonable height, with cookies or candies placed on each tier. Or several favorite plates can be pierced, a rod inserted, and joined to make a serving platter that matches your dinner set. Sweets or fruit can even be arranged in a cake or cookie tower. Begin with a simple plate for a base, spiraling the cookies as you place them in layers.

To complete the geometric effect, place each platter in rows that cross in the middle of the table, where a pyramid of glass sparkles with tiny tarts, small cakes, and fruit frosted with egg white and sugar. Put small vases of seasonal blossoms in each corner, and four candlesticks where the lines cross. Small glass dishes placed symmetrically within the quadrants might hold love apples, figs, tangerines, and grapes. Light the candles and invite the guests in to savor the beauty, as well as the flavors, as they pick and choose among all the treats.

Colonial hostesses were often happy to bring a bit of nature indoors by copying flowers and birds in sweetmeats and almond paste, coloring the marzipan, called marchpane in colonial Virginia. One idea for a winter table is to create a "snow branch": Select a small branch with a pleasing shape, wash it, and allow it to dry thoroughly. Place the white of an egg into a bowl, then brush the branch with the egg white. Roll the branch in crystallized sugar and "plant" it on top of a cake dusted in powdered sugar. Or place an apple in a bowl, anchor the branch to it, then fill the bowl with "snow cream"—heavy cream whipped with no sugar. The "snow"-dusted branch can be decorated with cookies tied on the ends.

More ideas for an eighteenth-century table can be found in *Entertaining Ideas from Williamsburg* by Susan Hight Rountree, published in 1993 by the Colonial Williamsburg Foundation.

❀❀❀❀❀❀❀❀❀❀❀❀❀❀❀❀❀❀❀❀❀❀❀❀❀❀❀❀❀❀

WILLIAMSBURG PRODUCTS AND RESOURCES

In the years before World War II, the restoration project at Colonial Williamsburg was a tour de force in historic restoration. Local newspapers reported that visitors flocked to the small town in Virginia to see Mr. Rockefeller's houses filled with splendid antiques. The quaint houses and gardens charmed them; the respectful use of space and the simplicity of design used throughout the town inspired them. Almost immediately, the public began to clamor for reproductions of the furniture, dinnerware, and fabrics in order to decorate their homes with the same gracious traditional style they saw in the restored interiors at Colonial Williamsburg. For the first time in history, the revival of an American decorating style was embraced by a broad segment of society.

The requests for reproductions were answered first when Josiah Wedgwood & Sons reproduced Queen's Ware from fragments of earthenware plates and accessories found on the site of the Raleigh Tavern. Three hundred place settings of the dinnerware were ordered so that some might be displayed and others might be used by taverns or sold in the new Craft House retail store, a showplace for reproductions and handicrafts, that opened in 1937 beside the Williamsburg Inn. Beyond Colonial Williamsburg, consumers learned more about the elements of eighteenth-century style from publicity covering the restoration. *House and Garden* devoted an entire issue to Colonial Williamsburg and covered the story in articles on architecture, gardens, paint colors, and decorating style.

From the early years, Colonial Williamsburg chose manufacturers who had a deep appreciation for hand craftsmanship to participate with them in historic trade shops in the restored town. They copied antique furniture, pewter, silver, and linens for the public. More licensed manufacturers joined the program over time, and soon a full line of home furnishing reproductions was developed and offered for sale. By the 1960s, entire suburbs were based on Williamsburg architecture, and houses across the country were decorated with paints, wallpapers, fabrics, and accessories inspired by eighteenth-century sources. About thirty years ago, Colonial Williamsburg took its collection of reproductions on the road, and "*Williamsburg* Shops" were born in department stores nationwide, modeled after the first one at B. Altman on Fifth Avenue in New York City. Although this lifestyle marketing technique is well used today, Colonial Williamsburg's "shop within a shop" retail approach was revolutionary at that time.

For more than sixty years, the reproductions program has remained committed to producing items that reflect the same craftsmanship and quality of design. Through the years customers continue to request classic period designs, and the line continuously expands to include new textiles, wallpapers, bedding, rugs, furniture, brass, pewter, china, crystal, paints, and many other items crafted to take the beauty of the eighteenth century into today's homes.

But the Williamsburg Products Program does more than re-create designs and styles from the eighteenth century. The program perpetuates a respect for quality and traditions that might otherwise be lost in today's fast-paced way of life.

To find out more about Colonial Williamsburg's reproductions, call 800-446-9240 to order a seasonal mail-order catalog. Excerpts from the catalog can be found on Colonial Williamsburg's web site at www.history.org.

In Colonial Williamsburg, Virginia

The Museum Stores Group—Home of the *Williamsburg* Products Program
Craft House at the Williamsburg Inn, 757-229-7749
Design Studio, Craft House at the Williamsburg Inn, 757-229-7503
Craft House on Merchants Square, 757-229-7747

The Historic Area Stores Along Duke of Gloucester Street

Greenhow Store, 757-229-1000, extension 2804
Prentis Store, 757-229-1000, extension 2117
Tarpley's Store, 757-229-1000, extension 2066

P.O. Box 1776
Williamsburg, VA 23187
757-229-1000
www.history.org

Antiques and Accents in Yorktown, Virginia

Swan Tavern Antiques
300 Main Street
Yorktown, VA 23690
757-898-3033

Period Designs
401 Main Street
Yorktown, VA 23690
757-886-9482

Nancy Thomas Studio Gallery
145 Ballard Street
Yorktown, VA 23690
757-898-3665

Williamsburg Furniture and Fabric Through Major Designer Showrooms Nationwide

Baker Knapp and Tubbs
800-59-BAKER
www.bakerfurniture.com

F. Schumacher and Company
800-556-0040

Licensed Manufacturers of Williamsburg Home Furnishings

Bedding

Crown Crafts, Inc.
1600 Riveredge Parkway, Suite 200
Atlanta, GA 30328
404-644-6300

Faribault Woolen Mill Co.
1500 Second Avenue, NW
Faribault, MN 55021
507-334-6444

Brass and Iron Lighting Fixtures

Virginia Metalcrafters
1010 East Main Street
Waynesboro, VA 22980
540-949-9400

Ceramic Giftware

Charles Sadek Import Co.
125 Beechwood Avenue
New Rochelle, NY 10802
914-633-8090

Crystal and Delft

Eastern Shore Trading Co.
Polks Road Route #1
Princess Anne, MD 21853
410-651-0600

Decorative Porcelain, Dinnerware

Mottahedeh & Co., Inc.
225 Fifth Avenue
New York, NY 10010
212-685-3050

Spode
1265 Glen Avenue
Moorestown, NJ 08057
609-866-2900

Fabric and Wallcoverings

F. Schumacher & Co.
79 Madison Avenue
New York, NY 10016
212-213-7900

Fences and Gates

Walpole Woodworkers, Inc.
767 East Street
Walpole, MA 02081
508-668-2800

Furniture

Baker Furniture Company
1661 Monroe Avenue, NW
Grand Rapids, MI 49505
616-361-7321

Tradition House
237 Ridge Road
Hanover, PA 17331
717-632-5482

Leather

Lackawanna Leather Co.
106 Somerset Drive
Conover, NC 28613
704-322-2015

Lighting Fixtures

Period Lighting Fixtures
River Road
Clarksburg, MA 01247
413-644-7141

Linen and Printed Textiles

Stevens Linen Associates, Inc.
137 Schofield Avenue
Dudley, MA 01571
508-943-0813

Palais Royal, Inc.
1725 Broadway
Charlottesville, VA 22901
804-979-3911

Mirrors

Carvers' Guild
Cannery Row
West Groton, MA 01472
978-448-3063

Friedman Brothers Decorative Arts, Inc.
9015 NW 105 Way
Medley, FL 33178
305-887-3170

Mirror Fair
1495 Third Avenue
New York, NY 10028
212-288-5050

Moldings and Chair Rails

Focal Point, Inc., NMC
3051 Olympia Industrial Drive, SE
Smyrna, GA 30080
404-351-0820

Needlework, Pillows, and Rugs

C&F Enterprises
705 Middleground Boulevard
Newport News, VA 23606
757-873-0358

Michaelian & Kohlberg, Inc.
578 Broadway, 2nd Floor
New York, NY 10012
212-431-9009

Paint

Martin Senour Co., Inc.
15 Midland Building
101 Prospect Avenue
Cleveland, OH 44115
216-566-2000

Stulb's Old Village Paint
500 Stenton Avenue
Plymouth Meeting, PA 19462
610-238-9001

Pottery

Williamsburg Pottery Factory
Route 3, Box 148
Lightfoot, VA 23090
757-564-3326

Prints

The Dietz Press, Inc.
109 East Cary Street
Richmond, VA 23219
804-648-0195

Hedgerow House, Inc.
6401 East Rogers Circle
Suite #3
Boca Raton, FL 33487
407-998-0756

Highland House Publishers
500 North Henry Street
Alexandria, VA 22314
703-683-8282

New York Graphic Society, Ltd.
33 River Road
Cos Cob, CT 06807
203-661-2400

Rugs

Claire Murray
Route 5
Ascutney, VT 05030
802-674-6017

Karastan/Bigelow
712 Henry Street
Eden, NC 27288
910-623-6000

Silver and Pewter

The Kirk Stieff Company
800 Wyman Park Drive
Baltimore, MD 21211-2898
410-368-6000

Tavern China

The Homer Laughlin China Co.
Sixth and Harrison Streets
Newell, WV 26050
304-387-1300

Tiles

Summitville Tiles, Inc.
Summitville, OH 43962
330-223-1511

RESOURCES

For Williamsburg Products throughout the sections of this book

Title page: Carolina Neoclassic Sideboard by Baker Furniture; Governor's Palace Candlestick by Virginia Metalcrafters; Hurricane Shade by Eastern Shore Trading Company; and the Glass Compote are available at the Craft House at the Williamsburg Inn. **Acknowledgments page:** Royal Linen towels by Palais Royale, available at the Craft House at the Williamsburg Inn. **Contents page, top row, center:** Governor's Palace Open Arm Chair by Baker Furniture; Wythe Looking Glass by Friedman Brothers, available at the Craft House at the Williamsburg Inn. **Middle row, right:** English serpentine sofa by Baker Furniture; "Carter's Grove" carpet by Karastan. **Bottom row, left:** New Fashioned Dining Table by Baker Furniture, available at the Craft House at the Williamsburg Inn. **Bottom row, center:** Creamware Pitcher available at Prentis Store on Duke of Gloucester Street, Colonial Williamsburg. **Bottom row, right:** Gaming Board by Virginia Metalcrafters; and Tavern Glass available at the Craft House at the Williamsburg Inn. Black Earthenware Pitcher available at Prentis Store. **Living Rooms and Gathering Places, page 21:** Rococo New Fashioned Sofa Table by Baker Furniture; Governor's Palace Candlestick and Brass Scissors Snuffer by Virginia Metalcrafters; Pewter Cup by Kirk Stieff; Hurricane Shade from Eastern Shore Trading Company, available at the Craft House at the Williamsburg Inn. **40:** Teardrop stemware by Eastern Shore Trading Company; Bayberry candles available at Prentis Store on Duke of Gloucester Street. **41:** Octagonal Base Candlestick and Table Bell by Virginia Metalcrafters, available at the Craft House at the Williamsburg Inn. **49, bottom right:** Similar reproduction tiles from Summitville Tiles, Inc., available at the Craft House at the Williamsburg Inn. **50:** Governor's Palace Candlestick and small strawberry dish by Kirk Stieff; crystal by John Jenkins, available at the Craft House at the Williamsburg Inn. **51, left:** Duke of Gloucester China by Mottahedah; Brass Mid-drip Candlestick and Candle snuffer by Virginia Metalcrafters; Tavern Glass available at the Craft House at the Williamsburg Inn. **Top right:** Queen's Plain china by Wedgwood; Byrd China Table by Baker; Governor's Palace Candlestick by Virginia Metalcrafters; Fireplace accessories by Virginia Metalcrafters, Acanthus Side Chair by Baker Furniture, available at the Craft House at the Williamsburg Inn. **Bottom right:** Window treatments made with Pleasures of the Farm, by Schumacher; New England Easy Chair by Baker Furniture; Serpentine Sofa by Baker Furniture upholstered with Satin Leaf Stripe fabric, by Schumacher; Byrd Tea Table by Baker Furniture; Tea Caddy by Virginia Metalcrafters; Wallcoverings are Baroque Stripe, by Schumacher. Print, *In Full Cry,* available at the Craft House at the Williamsburg Inn. Floral arrangement by Alexandra Randall. **52:** Providence Hall Cane Sofa by Baker Furniture upholstered in Greenhow Stripe, by Schumacher. Fretwork Tray on stand by

Tradition House; Massachusetts Tea Table by Baker Furniture. **53:** Providence Hall Cane Sofa; Massachusetts Tea Table by Baker Furniture; Fretwork Tray on stand by Tradition House. **54:** Palace Warming Room Sconce; Fire Tools; Tea Chest by Virginia Metalcrafters, available at the Craft House at the Williamsburg Inn. **55, top:** Massachusetts Tea Table by Baker; Bell Jar available at the Nancy Thomas Gallery in Yorktown, Virginia. **Bottom:** Telescope Box by Tradition House; William and Mary Coverlet by Crown Craft and Diamond Check blanket by Faribault Woolen Mill. **56, top:** Tavern glasses by Eastern Shore Trading Company; Wooden Gallery Trays by Virginia Metalcrafters; Telescope Box by Tradition House, available at the Craft House at the Williamsburg Inn. **Bottom:** New York Clothespress and Loveseat by Baker Furniture, available at the Craft House at the Williamsburg Inn. **57:** Rococo Loveseat by Baker Furniture upholstered with Tavern Check fabric, by Schumacher, available at the Craft House at the Williamsburg Inn. Rococo New Fashioned Sofa Table by Baker Furniture, Acanthus Backstool upholstered with Randolph Stripe, by Schumacher, and Hurricane Shade by Eastern Shore Trading Company, Governor's Palace Candlestick, Scissor Snuffer, Octoganol Tea Chest, and Gaming Board by Virginia Metalcrafters; pewter cup by Kirk Stieff; and Telescope Box by Tradition House and Tavern Glass, available at the Craft House at the Williamsburg Inn. **58:** Bruton Sconce by Virginia Metalcrafters; Chelsea Bird Plate by Mottahedeh; candlestick by Kirk Stieff; Serpentine Sofa and New England Sideboard Table by Baker Furniture; Sofa upholstery in Randolph Stripe, by Schumacher; Carter's Grove carpet by Karastan, available at the Craft House at the Williamsburg Inn. **59, top left:** Tortoise Mirror, Bassett Hall Chest and Newport Easy Chair by Baker Furniture, upholstered in leather by Lackawanna; candlestick with Globe by Virginia Metalcrafters, available at the Craft House at the Williamsburg Inn. Tiger prints by Period Design, Yorktown, Virginia. **Bottom left:** "Carter's Grove" carpet by Karastan with close up of the Serpentine Sofa by Baker Furniture Company and covered in Schumacher fabric. **Bottom right:** Providence Hall Cane Sofa with the Rococo Silver Chest; Maryland Rococo Chair and Lucas Trunk by Baker Furniture; Brass Spike Lamp by Virginia Metalcrafters; Catesby Prints available at the Craft House at the Williamsburg Inn. **60, left:** Serpentine Sofa by Baker Furniture; upholstered in Floral Damask, by Schumacher. **Right:** Girandole Looking Glass by Friedman Brothers; Pillar and Arch wall covering by Schumacher. **61:** New England Easy Chair by Baker Furniture upholstered in Toile Orientale, by Schumacher, available at the Craft House at the Williamsburg Inn. **75, upper left:** Toile Oriental by Schumacher available at the Craft House at the Williamsburg Inn. **The Bedchamber, page 85, top left:** Window treatment and slipcover Greenhow Stripe by Schumacher; Stacking Tables by Tradition House, Imperial Blue China by Mottahedeh. **86:** Octagonal Coffee Service by Kirk Stieff; Stool by Baker Furniture, upholstered in leather by Lackawanna; Glass Wine Bottle available at Greenhow Store on Duke of Gloucester Street in Colonial Williamsburg. Other items are available at the Craft House at the Williamsburg Inn. Creamware plates available from Period Design, Yorktown, Virginia; Antique Tea Table from Nancy Thomas, Yorktown, Virginia. Floral arrangement by Alexandra Randall. **87, left:** Randolph Mirror by Friedman Brothers; Hurricane Shade by Eastern Shore Trading; Round Base Brass Candlestick by Virginia Metalcrafters; New England Dressing Table by Baker Furniture. **Bottom:** Newport Easy Chair and Commode by Baker Furniture; Iron Lamp by Virginia

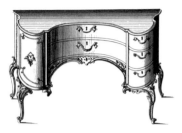

Metalcrafters; coverlets and shams William and Mary by Crown Craft; fabric on the headboards and dust ruffles Williamsburg Check fabric, by Schumacher, available at the Craft House at the Williamsburg Inn. Tea Table available from Nancy Thomas Gallery, Yorktown, Virginia. **88:** Garden Images comforter and William and Mary bedspread by Crown Crafts; Magnolia print by George Ehret, published by New York Graphics; High Post Bed by Baker Furniture; Diamond Check blanket by Faribault Woolen Mill; Queen Anne pewter tea service by Kirk Stieff; Loveseat and Bachelor's Chest by Baker Furniture, Bruton Wall Sconces by Virginia Metalcrafters; Fretwork Tray on stand by Tradition House, available at the Craft House at the Williamsburg Inn. **89, top:** Kurdish carpet by Karastan available at the Craft House at the Williamsburg Inn. **90:** Bedcovering custom designed by the Design Studio at the Craft House at the Williamsburg Inn, Athena Toile fabric, by Schumacher. **91, top:** Raleigh Tavern Chandelier by Virginia Metalcrafters; Norfolk chair by Baker Furniture, with slipcover of William & Mary Diamond by Schumacher. **Bottom:** Middle Colonies dressing table by Baker Furniture; Palace Candlestick Lamp by Virginia Metalcrafters, decanter and goblets by John Jenkins; architectural prints by New York Graphics; available at the Craft House at the Williamsburg Inn. **92, left:** Piedmont Easy Chair by Baker Furniture Company, upholstered in Bronson coverlet from Schumacher; Partner's Desk by Baker Furniture. **Right:** Square and oval boxes covered with a variety of wallpapers from Schumacher; available at the Craft House at the Williamsburg Inn. **93:** William and Mary coverlet and shams by Crown Crafts; bed skirt in Greenhow Stripe and folded blanket from Schumacher; Piedmont Easy Chair by Baker Furniture; available at the Craft House at the Williamsburg Inn; painted chest by Nancy Thomas Gallery, Yorktown, Virginia. **94:** Door locks by Virginia Metalcrafters available at the Craft House at the Williamsburg Inn. **Dining Rooms, Kitchens, and Pantries, page 102, bottom:** King's Arms Tavern dinnerware by Homer Laughlin; Royal Scroll Flatware and Octagonal Candlestick by Kirk Stieff; Hurrican Shade by Eastern Shore Trading Company and Tavern Glass all available at the Craft House at the Williamsburg Inn. **109, bottom left:** Delft Cat by Eastern Shore Trading Company available at the Craft House at the Williamsburg Inn. **110, top left:** Delft Shoe by Eastern Shore Trading Company. **Top right:** Williamsburg Shell Sterling Flatware by Kirk Stieff, Roulette Dinnerware by Historic Design Resources. **Bottom left:** Creamware Pyramid by Great City Traders, all available at the Craft House at the Williamsburg Inn. **111, top left:** Imperial Blue Dinnerware by Mottahedah; Cache Pot by Isis; Sack Bottle by Period Design, all available at the Craft House at the Williamsburg Inn. **113,**

top right: Brown Saltglaze Stoneware available at Greenhow Store on the Duke of Gloucester Street, Colonial Williamsburg. **122, left:** Sofa, slipcovered in Carolina Toile, by Schumacher. **Right:** Sofa slipcovered in Greenhow Stripe, by Schumacher. **123:** Sofa upholstered in Brush-Everard Stripe, by Schumacher. **124, top left:** Chelsea Bird dinnerware by Mottahedah; Williamsburg Shell Sterling flatware by Kirk Stieff; crystal by John Jenkins. **Bottom left:** New Fashioned Dining Table and Norfolk Chairs by Baker; Cellaret by Tradition House, available at the Craft House at the Williamsburg Inn. **Right:** Hurricane Shade by Eastern Shore Trading Company; Swirl-Base candlestick by Virginia Metalcrafters; crystal by John Jenkins. **125, top:** Piedmont Easy Chairs by Baker upholstered with Williamsburg Check by Schumacher; New Fashioned Dining Table and Bassett Hall Chest by Baker; Chandelier by Period Lighting; floral arrangement by Alexandra Randall. **Bottom:** Baluster Stemware by Eastern Shore Trading Company; Queen Ann Sterling flatware by Kirk Stieff; Royal Linens by Palais Royale, available at the Craft House at the Williamsburg Inn; creamware by Period Design, Yorktown, Virginia. **126, top:** Norfolk Side and Arm Chairs by Baker upholstered in Satin Leaf Strip by Schumacher; Governor's Palace Open Arm Chair by Baker upholstered in Antico Damask; Rococo Loveseat by Baker upholstered in Arabesque Leaf; draperies in same fabric; Wythe Mirror by Friedman Brothers; pewter by Kirk Stieff; Airtwist Crystal by Eastern Shore Trading Company. **Bottom:** Queens Plain by Wedgwood; Linens by Palais Royale, available at the Craft House at the Williamsburg Inn. **127:** Duke of Gloucester Dinnerware by Mottahedah, available at the Craft House at the Williamsburg Inn. **128, top left:** Black Pottery and baskets available at Prentis Store, Duke of Gloucester, Colonial Williamsburg; flowers arranged by Alexandra Randall. **Top**

right: Bassett Hall Chest by Baker; handblown glass punch bowl and cups from Period Design, Yorktown, Virginia; candle holder from Nancy Thomas Gallery, Yorktown, Virginia. **Bottom:** Delft Jars by Eastern Shore Trading Company available at the Craft House at the Williamsburg Inn. **129, top:** Delft Apothecary Jar by Eastern Shore Trading Company. **Bottom:** Imperial Blue Dinnerware by Mottahedah; Williamsburg Shell Sterling flatware by Kirk Stieff; Teardrop Stemware by Eastern Shore Trading Company, all available at the Craft House at the Williamsburg Inn. **130, top right:** Tablecloth is a William and Mary coverlet; Kirk Stieff pewter strawberry dish, available at the Craft House at the Williamsburg Inn; black pitcher handthrown by Michele Johnston of Period Design; crystal by Eastern Shore Trading Company; flowers arranged by Alexandra Randall. **Bottom right:** Norfolk Side Chair by Baker Furniture; Tissu Fleuri, by Schumacher. **130–131:** Slipcovers of Schumacher fabric made by the Design Studio at the Craft House at the Williamsburg Inn. **152–153:** Williamsburg Fences and Gates available from Walpole Woodworders; Gate Weight and Chain available from Greenhow Store on Duke of Gloucester Street, Colonial Williamsburg.

Floral arrangements by Alexandra Randall Flowers, St. James, NY 11780, (516) 862-9291.

NOTES

Page 11: ". . . the English America." Hugh Jones, quoted in Jane Carson's *We Were There: Descriptions of Williamsburg 1699–1859* (Colonial Williamsburg Foundation, 1965), 119.

Page 11: "with wholesome springs . . ." Philip Kopper, *Colonial Williamsburg* (Harry N. Abrams, 1986), 28

Page 13: "gardens of the city . . ." Parke Rouse, Jr., *When Williamsburg Woke Up* (Kwik-Kopy Printing, Williamsburg, Va., n.d.), 3.

Page 13: ". . . would be inspired and enriched." George Humphrey Yetter, *Williamsburg Before and After: The Rebirth of Virginia's Colonial Capital* (Colonial Williamsburg Foundation, 1988), 49.

Page 13: ". . . really belong in Williamsburg." *When Williamsburg Woke Up*, 5.

Page 15: For a full discussion of this topic, see *The Colonial Revival in America* by Alan Axelrod (W. W. Norton, 1985).

Page 19: ". . . usual furniture of the hall." Mary Newton Stanard, *Colonial Virginia: Its People and Customs* (Singing Tree Press, 1970), 25.

Page 19: "(W)e took seats in a cool passage where the Company were sitting . . ." Hunter Dickinson Farish, ed. *Journal and Letters of Philip Vickers Fithian, 1773–1774: Plantation Tutor of the Old Dominion*, (Colonial Williamsburg Foundation, 1957), 213.

Page 20 ". . . through which unparalleled vistas open." *When Williamsburg Woke Up*, 6.

Page 23: ". . . better cheer and welcome." *We Were There*, 119.

Page 23: ". . . trailed behind them." *Colonial Virginia*, 146.

Page 23: ". . . a constant tuting." *Ibid.*, 311.

Page 33: ". . . gilt front." *Ibid.*, 310.

Page 39: ". . . newest fashions." *Ibid.*, 89.

Page 43: ". . . a passage of my house." Richard L. Bushman, *The Refinement of America: Persons, Houses, Cities* (Alfred A. Knopf, 1992), 131.

Page 45: ". . . agreeable to the present fashion." *Colonial Virginia*, 87.

Page 59: ". . . Bed to Himself . . ." *Journal and Letters of Philip Vickers Fithian, 1773–1774*, 81.

Page 70: ". . . a pair of fine carved and gilt sconces." *Colonial Virginia*, 87.

Page 70: ". . . put in a bed for her." *Ibid.*, 77.

Page 74: ". . . red check covers." Graham Hood, *The Governor's Palace in Williamsburg* (Colonial Williamsburg Foundation, 1991), 289.

Page 81: ". . . for a various Counterpane." *Journal and Letters of Philip Vickers Fithian, 1773–1774*, 42.

Page 95: ". . . a variety of instances." *Journal and Letters of Philip Vickers Fithian, 1773–1774*, 90.

Page 100: "I was rude, censurable." *Ibid.*, 121.

Page 102: ". . . green tea and some tarts." *Ibid.*, 33.

Page 102: ". . . disparaging and devouring." *Colonial Virginia Cookery*, 8.

Page 103: ". . . true elegance." Mary Randolph, *The Virginia Housewife*, xxi.

Page 105: ". . . cool and Sweet." *Journal and Letters of Philip Vickers Fithian, 1773–1774*, 238.

Page 108: ". . . figures for ornament" Ivor Noël Hume, *Pottery and Porcelain in Colonial Williamsburg's Archaeological Collections* (Colonial Williamsburg Foundation, 1969), 7.

Page 114: A more complete discussion of this and other kitchen topics may be found in *Colonial Virginia Cookery*.

Page 117: ". . . 1 piece of Hogs Lard." *The Governor's Palace in Williamsburg*, 157.

Page 118: ". . . after my decease." From display notes for Colonial Williamsburg exhibition "The Revolution in Taste."

Page 133: ". . . thriving city of Williamsburg." *We Were There*, 10.

Page 146: ". . . Beauties of naked Nature," Peter Martin, *The Pleasure Gardens Virginia* (Princeton University Press, 1991), 16.

Page 151: ". . . always regaling to the eye." *Ibid.*, 144.

Page 151: ". . . Apricot–Grafts; Asparagus Beds &c." *Journal and Letters of Philip Vickers Fithian, 1773–1774*, 78–79.

Page 152: ". . . Post and Rails." Audrey Noël Hume, *Archaeology and the Colonial Gardener* (Colonial Williamsburg Foundation, 1974), 9.

Page 152: ". . . summer houses." *Ibid.*, 13.

Page 154: ". . . orchard and gardens." *The Pleasure Gardens of Virginia*, 52.

Page 154: ". . . offices, walks, a fine canal, orchards . . ." *Ibid.*, 53.

Page 155: ". . . greens from England." *Ibid.*, 58.

Page 156: ". . . God's chosen people." *Ibid.*, 62.

Page 157: ". . . and Contentment dwell." *Ibid.*, 180. For a more complete discussion of colonial gardening, see *The Pleasure Gardens of Virginia* by Peter Martin and *British and American Gardens in the Eighteenth Century*, edited by Robert Maccubbin and Peter Martin (Colonial Williamsburg Foundation, 1984).

BIBLIOGRAPHY

Austin, John C. *British Delft at Williamsburg*. Williamsburg, Va.: Colonial Williamsburg Foundation, 1994.

———. *Chelsea Porcelain at Williamsburg*. Williamsburg, Va.: Colonial Williamsburg Foundation, 1977.

Axelrod, Alan. *The Colonial Revival in America*. New York: W. W. Norton, 1985.

Baumgarten, Linda R. *Eighteenth-Century Clothing at Williamsburg*. Williamsburg, Va.: Colonial Williamsburg Foundation, 1986.

Beard, Geoffrey. *Craftsmen and Interior Decoration in England, 1660–1820*. New York: Holmes & Meier, 1981.

———. *The National Trust Book of the English House Interior*. New York: Viking, in association with the National Trust, 1990.

———. *Upholsterers and Interior Furnishings in England, 1530–1840*. New Haven and London: published for the Bard Graduate Center for Studies in the Decorative Arts by Yale University Press, 1997.

Becker, Robert. *Nancy Lancaster: Her Life, Her World, Her Art*. New York: Alfred A. Knopf, 1996.

Belden, Louise Conway. *Festive Tradition: Table Decoration and Desserts in America, 1650–1900*. New York: W. W. Norton, 1983.

Berkin, Carol. *First Generations: Women in Colonial America*. New York: Hill and Wang, 1996.

Blackford, Bland, Burke Davis, and Patricia A. Hurdle. *Bassett Hall: The Williamsburg Home of Mr. and Mrs. John D. Rockefeller, Jr.* Williamsburg, Va.: Colonial Williamsburg Foundation, 1984.

Brinkley, Kent, and Gordon W. Chappell. *The Gardens of Colonial Williamsburg*. Williamsburg, Va.: Colonial Williamsburg Foundation, 1995.

Brown, Peter. *In Praise of Hot Liquors: The Study of Chocolate, Coffee, and Tea Drinking 1600–1850*. York, Eng.: York Civic Trust, 1995.

Bushman, Richard L. *The Refinement of America: Persons, Houses, Cities*. New York: Alfred A. Knopf, 1992.

Calloway, Stephen, and Elizabeth C. Cromley, eds. *Elements of Style: A Practical Encyclopedia of Interior Architectural Details from 1485 to the Present*. New York: Simon and Schuster, 1991.

Calloway, Stephen, and Stephen Jones. *Style Traditions: Recreating Period Interiors*. New York: Rizzoli, 1990.

Carson, Barbara. *The Governor's Palace: The Williamsburg Residence of Virginia's Royal Governor*. Williamsburg, Va.: Colonial Williamsburg Foundation, 1987.

Carson, Cary, ed. *Becoming Americans: Our Struggle to Be Both Free and Equal*. Williamsburg, Va.: Colonial Williamsburg Foundation, 1998.

Carson, Jane. *We Were There: Descriptions of Williamsburg 1699–1859.* Williamsburg, Va.: Colonial Williamsburg Foundation, 1965.

Chefetz, Sheila. *Antiques for the Table: A Complete Guide to Dining Room Accessories for Collecting and Entertaining*. New York: Viking Studio Books, 1993.

Chippendale, Thomas. *The Gentleman and Cabinet-Maker's Director*. Third ed. London, 1762. Reprint, New York: Dover Publications, 1966.

Clabburn, Pamela. *The National Trust Book of Furnishing Textiles*. New York: Viking Penguin, in association with the British National Trust 1988.

Clarke, Samuel M. *Worcester Porcelain in The Colonial Williamsburg Collection*. Williamsburg, Va.: Colonial Williamsburg Foundation, 1987.

Colonial Williamsburg staff. *Williamsburg Reproductions: The Finest Reproductions of Eighteenth-Century Furnishings*. Williamsburg, Va.: Colonial Williamsburg Foundation, 1989.

Cornforth, John. *Inspiration of the Past: Country House Taste in the Twentieth Century*. Harmondsworth, Eng.: Viking, in association with Country Life, 1984.

Cummings, Abbott Lowell, comp. *Bed Hangings: A Treatise on Fabrics and Styles in the Curtaining of Beds, 1650–1850*, 1961. Reprint, with an introduction by Jane Nylander, Boston: Society for the Preservation of New England Antiquities, 1994.

Davis, John D. *English Silver at Williamsburg*. Williamsburg, Va.: Colonial Williamsburg Foundation, 1976.

DeSamper, Hugh. *Welcome to the Williamsburg Inn*. Williamsburg, Va.: Colonial Williamsburg Foundation, 1997.

Dolmetsch, Joan, ed. *Eighteenth Century Prints in Colonial America: to Educate and Decorate*. Williamsburg, Va.: Colonial Williamsburg Foundation, 1979.

Dutton, Joan Parry. *Plants of Colonial Williamsburg*. Williamsburg, Va.: Colonial Williamsburg Foundation, 1979.

Farish, Hunter Dickinson, ed. *Journal and Letters of Philip Vickers Fithian, 1773–1774: A Plantation Tutor of the Old Dominion*. Third ed. Williamsburg, Va.: Colonial Williamsburg Foundation, 1957.

Foley, Roger, photographer; text by Donna C. Sheppard. *Williamsburg's Glorious Gardens*. Williamsburg, Va.: Colonial Williamsburg Foundation, 1996.

Ford, Thomas K. *The Silversmith in Eighteenth-Century Williamsburg: An Account of His Life & Times and of His Craft*. Williamsburg, Va.: Colonial Williamsburg Foundation, 1976.

Fowler, John, and John Cornforth. *English Decoration in the 18th Century*. London: Barrie & Jenkins, 1974.

Garrett, Elisabeth Donaghy. *At Home: The American Family, 1750–1870*. New York: Harry N. Abrams, 1990.

Garrett, Wendell D. *American Colonial: Puritan Simplicity to Georgian Grace*. New York: Monacelli Press, 1995.

———. *Classic America: The Federal Style and Beyond*. New York: Rizzoli, 1992.

Gere, Charlotte. *Nineteenth-Century Decoration: The Art of the Interior.* New York: Harry N. Abrams, 1989.

Gibbs, Jenny. *Curtains and Draperies: History, Design, Inspiration.* Woodstock, NY: Overlook Press, 1994.

Gilbert, Christopher. *The Life and Work of Thomas Chippendale.* London: Cassell, Ltd., a Studio Vista Book, in association with Christie, Manson & Woods, Ltd., 1978.

Gilbert, Christopher, and Anthony Wells-Cole. *The Fashionable Fire Place, 1660–1840.* Leeds, Eng.: Leeds City Art Galleries, 1985.

Gilliam, Jan Kirsten, and Betty Crowe Leviner. *Upon Going to Housekeeping: Furnishing Williamsburg's Historic Buildings.* Williamsburg, Va.: Colonial Williamsburg Foundation, 1991.

Girouard, Mark. *Life in the English Country House: A Social and Architectural History.* New Haven, Conn.: Yale University Press, 1978.

Glanville, Philippa. *Silver: History and Design.* New York: Harry N. Abrams, 1997.

Goodwin, Rutherford. *A Brief & True Report Concerning Williamsburg in Virginia.* Third ed. Reprint, Richmond, Va.: Dietz Press for Colonial Williamsburg Foundation, 1980.

Gore, Alan, and Ann Gore. *English Interiors: An Illustrated History.* New York: Thames and Hudson, 1991.

Gusler, Wallace B. *Furniture of Williamsburg and Eastern Virginia 1710–1790.* Richmond, Va.: Virginia Museum of Fine Arts, 1979. Reprint, Williamsburg, Va.: Colonial Williamsburg Foundation, 1993.

Harvey, David, and Gregory Brown, eds. *Common People and Their Material World: Free Men and Woman in the Chesapeake, 1700–1830.* Williamsburg, Va.: Colonial Williamsburg Foundation, 1995.

Hepplewhite, George, *The Cabinet-Maker and Upholsterer's Guide.* Third ed. London, 1794. Reprint, New York: Dover Publications, 1969.

Hood, Graham. *The Governor's Palace in Williamsburg: A Cultural Study.* Williamsburg, Va.: Colonial Williamsburg Foundation, 1991.

———. ed. *The Williamsburg Collection of Antique Furnishings.* Williamsburg, Va.: Colonial Williamsburg Foundation, 1973.

Hoskins, Lesley. *The Papered Wall: History, Pattern, Technique.* New York: Harry N. Abrams, 1994.

Hurst, Ronald L., and Jonathan Prown. *Southern Furniture 1680–1830: The Colonial Williamsburg Collection.* Williamsburg, Va.: Colonial Williamsburg Foundation, in association with Harry N. Abrams, 1997.

Hussey, Christopher. *English Country Houses: Early Georgian 1715–1760.* London: Country Life, 1955. Reprint, Woodbridge, Eng.: Antique Collectors' Club, 1984.

———. *English Country Houses: Mid-Georgian 1760–1800.* London: Country Life, 1955. Reprint, Woodbridge, Eng.: Antique Collectors' Club, 1984.

———. *English Country Houses: Late Georgian 1800–1840.* London: Country Life, 1955. Reprint, Woodbridge, Eng.: Antique Collectors' Club, 1984.

Hyman, John A. *Silver at Williamsburg: Drinking Vessels.* Williamsburg, Va.: Colonial Williamsburg Foundation, 1994.

Jackson-Stops, Gervase, and James Pipkin. *The English Country House: A Grand Tour.* Boston: Little, Brown and Co., a New York Graphic Society Book with the National Gallery of Art, 1985.

Jacobson, Dawn. *Chinoiserie.* London: Phaidon Press, 1993.

Jamerson, Clare. *The Potterton Pictorial Treasury of Curtain and Drapery Designs, 1750–1950.* Yorkshire, Eng.: Potterton Books, 1987.

Kopper, Philip. *Colonial Williamsburg.* New York: Harry N. Abrams, 1986.

Larkin, David, June Sprigg, and James Johnson. *Colonial: Design in the New World.* New York: Stewart, Tabori & Chang, 1988.

Lebsock, Suzanne, and Kym Rice. *"A Share of Honor": Virginia Women 1600–1945.* Richmond, Va.: W. M. Brown & Son for the Virginia Women's Cultural History, 1984.

Lynn, Catherine. *Wallpaper in America From the Seventeenth Century to World War I.* New York: W. W. Norton & Co, 1980.

Maccubbin, Robert P., and Peter Martin, eds. *British and American Gardens in the Eighteenth Century.* Williamsburg, Va.: Colonial Williamsburg Foundation, 1984.

Martin, Peter. *The Pleasure Gardens of Virginia: From Jamestown to Jefferson.* Princeton, N.J.: Princeton University Press, 1991.

Miller, Judith, and Martin Miller. *Period Details: A Sourcebook for House Restoration.* New York: Crown Publishers, 1987.

Montgomery, Florence M. *Textiles in America, 1650–1870.* New York: W. W. Norton & Co., 1984.

Moreland, Francis A. *The Curtain-Maker's Handbook. A Reprint of Practical Decorative Upholstery: Containing Full Instructions for Cutting, Making and Hanging All Kinds of Interior Upholstery, 1890.* Reprint, with an introduction by Martha G. Fales, New York: Dutton, 1979.

Morgan, Edmund S. *Virginians at Home: Family Life in the Eighteenth Century.* Williamsburg, Va.: Colonial Williamsburg Foundation, 1952.

Morley, John. *Regency Design, 1790–1840: Gardens, Buildings, Interiors, Furniture.* New York: Harry N. Abrams, 1993.

Moss, Roger W. *Lighting for Historic Buildings: A Guide to Selecting Reproductions.* Washington, D.C.: Preservation Press, 1988.

———, ed. *Paint in America: The Colors of Historic Buildings.* Washington, D.C.: National Trust for Historic Preservation, 1994.

Noël Hume, Audrey. *Archaeology and the Colonial Gardener.* Williamsburg, Va.: Colonial Williamsburg Foundation, 1974.

Noël Hume, Ivor. *Glass in Colonial Williamsburg's Archaeological Collections.* Williamsburg, Va.: Colonial Williamsburg Foundation, 1969.

———. *James Geddy and Sons; Colonial Craftsmen*. Williamsburg, Va.: Colonial Williamsburg Foundation, 1970.

———. *Pottery and Porcelain in Colonial Williamsburg's Archaeological Collections*. Williamsburg, Va.: Colonial Williamsburg Foundation, 1969.

———. *The Wells of Williamsburg: Colonial Time Capsules*. Williamsburg, Va.: Colonial Williamsburg Foundation, 1969.

———. *Williamsburg Cabinetmakers: The Archaeological Evidence*. Williamsburg, Va.: Colonial Williamsburg Foundation, 1971.

Noetzli, E. *Practical Drapery Cutting*. London, 1906. Reprint, Yorkshire, Eng.: Potterton Books, 1988.

Nylander, Jane. *Fabric For Historic Buildings: A Guide to Selecting Reproduction Fabrics*. Rev. ed. Washington, D.C.: Preservation Press, 1990.

———. *Our Own Snug Fireside: Images of the New England Home 1760–1860*. New York: Alfred A. Knopf, 1993.

Nylander, Richard C. *Wallpapers For Historic Buildings: A Guide to Selecting Reproduction Wallpapers*. Second ed. Washington, D.C.: Preservation Press, 1992.

Nylander, Richard, Elizabeth Redmond, and Penny J.Sander. *Wallpaper in New England*. Boston: Society for the Preservation of New England Antiquities, 1986.

Oliver, Libbey Hodges. *Colonial Williamsburg Decorates for Christmas: Step-by-Step Illustrated Instructions for Christmas Decorations That You Can Make for Your Home*. Williamsburg, Va.: Colonial Williamsburg Foundation, 1981.

Olmert, Michael. *Official Guide to Colonial Williamsburg*. Rev. ed. Williamsburg, Va.: Colonial Williamsburg Foundation, 1997.

Parissien, Steven. *Adam Style*. Washington, D.C.: Preservation Press, 1992.

———. *Palladian Style*. London: Phaidon Press, 1994.

———. *Regency Style*. Washington, D.C.: Preservation Press, 1992.

Paston-Williams, Sara. *The Art of Dining: A History of Cooking and Eating*. London: National Trust Enterprises, 1993.

Praz, Mario. *An Illustrated History of Furnishing from the Renaissance to the 20th Century*. Translated from the Italian by William Weaver. New York: George Braziller, 1964.

Rothstein, Natalie. *The Victoria and Albert Museum's Textile Collection: Woven Textile Designs in Britain from 1750–1850*. London: Victoria and Albert Museum, 1994.

Rountree, Susan Hight. *Christmas Decorations from Williamsburg*. Williamsburg, Va.: Colonial Williamsburg Foundation, 1991.

———. *Entertaining Ideas from Williamsburg*. Williamsburg, Va.: Colonial Williamsburg Foundation, 1993.

Rouse, Parke, Jr. *When Williamsburg Woke Up*. Williamsburg, Va.: Kwik-Copy Printing.

Savage, J. Thomas. *The Charleston Interior*. Greensboro, N.C.: Legacy Publications, 1995.

Schwin, Lawrence, III. *Decorating Old House Interiors: 30 Classic American Styles*. New York: Sterling Publishing, 1994.

Seale, William. *Recreating the Historic House Interior*. Nashville, Tenn.: American Association for State and Local History, 1979.

Sheraton, Thomas. *The Cabinet-Maker and Upholsterer's Drawing-Book*. Third ed. London, 1802. Reprint, edited by Charles F. Montgomery and Wildred Cole. New York: Praeger Publishers, 1970.

Simpson, Mette Tang, and Michael Huntley, eds. *Sotheby's Caring for Antiques: The Complete Guide to Handling, Cleaning, Display and Restoration*. New York: Simon and Schuster, 1993.

Sloan, Annie. *Practical Guide to Decorative Antique Effects: Paints, Waxes, Varnishes*. Pleasantville, N.Y.: Reader's Digest Association, 1995.

Sloan, Annie, and Kate Gwynn. *Color in Decoration*. London: Frances Lincoln, 1990.

Smith, Charles Saumarez. *Eighteenth-Century Decoration: Design and the Domestic Interior in England*. New York: Harry N. Abrams, 1993.

Stanard, Mary Newton. *Colonial Virginia: Its People and Customs*. 1917. Reprint, Detroit, Mich.: Singing Tree Press, 1970.

Stillinger, Elizabeth. *American Antiques: The Hennage Collection*. Williamsburg, Va.: Colonial Williamsburg Foundation, 1990.

Sutcliffe, John. *Decorating Magic*. New York: Pantheon Books, 1992.

Tate, Thad, photographs by Dave Deady. *Williamsburg: A Seasonal Sampler*. Williamsburg, Va.: Colonial Williamsburg Foundation, 1996.

Taylor, Dale. *The Writer's Guide to Everyday Life in Colonial America*. Cincinnati, Ohio: Writer's Digest, 1997.

Tharp, Lars. *Hogarth's China: Hogarth's Paintings and Eighteenth-Century Ceramics*. London: Merrell Holberton, 1997.

Thornton, Peter. *Authentic Decor: The Domestic Interior 1620–1920*. New York: Viking, 1984.

———. *Seventeenth Century Interior Decoration in England, France, and Holland*. New Haven, Conn.: Yale University Press, 1978.

Von Rosenstiel, Helene, and Gail Caskey Winkler. *Floor Coverings for Historic Buildings: A Guide to Selecting Reproductions*. Washington, D.C.: Preservation Press, 1988.

Walklet, John J., Jr., Thomas L. Ford, and Donna C. Sheppard. *A Window on Williamsburg*. Second rev. ed. Williamsburg, Va.: Colonial Williamsburg Foundation, 1983.

Ward-Jackson, Peter. *English Furniture Designs of the Eighteenth Century*. London: Victoria and Albert Museum, 1984.

Wells-Cole, Anthony. *Historic Paper Hangings from Temple Newsam and Other English Houses*. Leeds, Eng.: Leeds City Art Galleries, 1983.

Wenger, Mark R. *Carter's Grove: The Story of a Virginia Plantation*. Williamsburg, Va.: Colonial Williamsburg Foundation, 1994.

Wharton, Edith, and Ogden Codman, Jr. *The Decoration of Houses*, 1902. Reprint, New York: W. W. Norton & Co., 1978.

White, Elizabeth, comp. *Pictorial Dictionary of British Eighteenth-Century Furniture Design: The Printed Sources*. Woodbridge, Eng.: Antique Collectors' Club, 1990.

Whiffen, Marcus. *The Eighteenth-Century Houses of Williamsburg: A Study of Architecture and Building in the Colonial Capital of Virginia*. Rev. ed. Williamsburg, Va.: Colonial Williamsburg Foundation, 1984.

Yetter, George Humphrey. *Williamsburg Before and After: The Rebirth of Virginia's Colonial Capital*. Williamsburg, Va.: Colonial Williamsburg Foundation, 1988.

INDEX

René Gardi   Indigenous African Architecture

René Gardi

Indigenous African Architecture

English translation by Sigrid MacRae

VAN NOSTRAND REINHOLD COMPANY
NEW YORK CINCINNATI TORONTO LONDON MELBOURNE

Graphic design   Hans Thoni, Grafiker ASG/SWB, Bern
Photographs   René Gardi, 12 by Bernhard Gardi
Typesetting   Filmset in Helvetica by
                   Jolly & Barber Ltd., Rugby, England
Gravure   Prolith AG, Bern
Offset printing   Büchler & Co AG, Wabern

Swiss edition copyright © 1973 by René Gardi, 3004 Bern

Van Nostrand Reinhold Company Regional Offices:
New York Cincinnati Chicago Millbrae Dallas

Van Nostrand Reinhold Company International Offices:
London Toronto Melbourne

Library of Congress Catalog Card Number 74-1605
ISBN 0-442-22574-1

Published by Van Nostrand Reinhold Company
A Division of Litton Educational Publishing, Inc.
450 West 33rd Street, New York, N.Y. 10001

16 15 14 13 12 11 10 9 8 7 6 5 4 3 2 1

Library of Congress Cataloging in Publication Data

Gardi, René.
    Indigenous African architecture.

    Translation of Auch im Lehmhaus lässt sich's leben.
    1. Dwellings – Africa, West.   I. Title.
GT377.W4G3713   301.5'4'0966   74-1605
ISBN 0-442-22574-1

Contents

Indigenous African Architecture

The many-gabled labyrinths of a mountain peasant home, the castles of the Somba and Dogon, the two-storied mud houses of the citizenry of Sudanese towns, the minarets of their mosques – high as towers but built without cement or reinforced concrete – are just as much a reality in West Africa as are the skyscrapers, bank palaces, warehouses, and factories in large cities on the north Atlantic. On the last page of my book on African crafts is a sentence that reads: "This book contains a number of photographs that it will no longer be possible to take in a few years. Despite the steadfastness and obstinacy of many craftsmen, and their resistance to innovation, one day tradition will succumb to technology." This is, of course, also true for traditional building, though I am of the opinion that old and new will co-exist much longer there than with the crafts. Since poverty forces many to build for themselves, and because tribal thinking and living together in the old patriarchal modes of the expanded family is, in many areas, hardly changed, the dissolution is proceeding very slowly. The transition from a self-sufficient, purely agrarian economy into a commercial one with a monetary basis, the transformation of peasants into wage-earners, the resulting flight from the land and increasing industrialization – modest though it still may be in West Africa – naturally changes living patterns and thus building forms as well.

But this book will report on traditional building and traditional life. Housing is shaped by life-styles, by needs, and, of course, by possibilities. Having bedrooms under a roof is important, but so are all those things that mean comfortable living to a West African – the yard in front of the house, the interior courtyards, little walls to sit against, roof terraces and open verandas under an awning, and resting places for the old people under a nearby tree.

Each house is a portrait of its owner. The architectural forms are as

Ceiling beams are supported by forked posts.

various as the innumerable tribes, and the creative energy and beauty of West African vernacular architecture is astounding. Naturally we will discuss building techniques, roof construction, and floor plans, but we will devote more time to the builders, the owners of the farms and their families. I believe that the main theme of this book is living. If man is to feel comfortable, he must live in security. He can retain his individuality and inner freedom only if there is somewhere he can call home. He is never lost as long as he can still go home. Real living is not achieved by means of technology, but by humaneness. Everyone is shaped by the life-style of their family, and growing up as the son of an independent peasant on a farm is not the same as growing up as the child of a frequently unemployed, poorly paid unskilled laborer under the hot, corrugated tin roof of a barracks at the outskirts of an African city.

A mud hut can be habitable too. Some will find this assertion shockingly reactionary, but others who deal with ecological problems have been warning us for a long time against uncontrolled production and the persistent temptations to consumerism. There is uneasiness in our part of the world; we know that the quality of life does not depend on material goods. Perhaps for that very reason, we should not be in such a rush to destroy the old orders in the African hinterlands. Though, of course, things are not in order there either. Things are not in order anywhere where men, and not gods, live together. In Africa too there have always been the poor and disenfranchised, enslaved by the strong. But I do not believe that a radical upheaval of all its social and economic structures in the name of progress would really banish injustice from the world. I do not believe that man in the concrete wilderness of the city lives a more fulfilled life than the peasant who sacrifices to his ancestors. We know that brutality and crime are on the rise in rich and soulless cities. And somehow it all seems to be related to having a "home." I encountered countless backward Africans who lived happier, more contented and meaningful lives than many a malcontent assembly-line worker – whether on the production line or writing letters in an office. The one lives in a mud hut he has built for himself with the help of his sons and friends, while the other can find no happiness in his pile carpets or tiled bathrooms because he no longer sees any meaning to his life.

The Somba (Dahomey) have their storage on the roof.

The Mat-Tents of the Aïr-Tuaregs

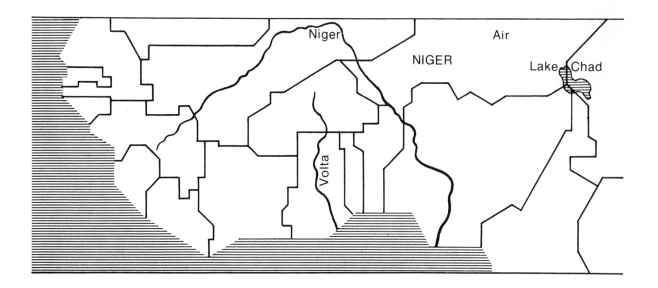

In our part of the world, we are hardly aware of the fact that on the southern edge of the Sahara and in the Sahel, in a belt 8,000 kilometers (4,970 miles) long, stretching straight across Africa from the Atlantic to Somalia, more than six million people lead a nomadic or semi-nomadic life. Sahel is what the geographers call the arid plains with short, irregular rainy seasons adjacent to the pure deserts of the Sahara. It should be added that precipitation in this area is only 150 to 300 millimeters (5 to 12 inches) a year. This is insufficient for planting without irrigation. Thus the people who inhabit this region are forced into a nomadic existence; as flock herders they are dependent on wells and pasturelands, and so these people, almost the last of the truly independent who until very recently hardly bothered about national borders, who are unruly and almost ungovernable, are in fact the slaves of their flocks.

I have found the following definition of nomadism: "Constant mobility, depending on precipitation, with impermanent tent dwellings." That sounds rather dry, and not particularly nice, but it states the essentials. In the Sahara itself, migrations of more than 1,000 kilometers (about 622 miles) are not at all unusual, while in the Sahel the rhythmic, seasonal migrations usually extend no more than 200 kilometers (125 miles) in one direction or another.

The Tuaregs used to raise only camels, aside from sheep and goats, but in the Sahel they too went over to keeping cattle. Under normal conditions, a square kilometer (about one-half square mile) of arid plain supports only twelve head of cattle. Nomads, in general, are troublesome to governments. They are reluctant to send their boys to school, and for the girls they find instruction completely unnecessary. Collecting taxes from them is difficult, and they resist all attempts to persuade them to settle down.

The nomadic tent makes it particularly clear that a "house" is a portrait

A round, Aïr-Tuareg mat-tent
(Niger).

11

Doum-palm leaves provide the material for weaving mats. Its fruit is hard as stone and almost useless.

Palm leaves that have been reduced to fibers are woven into bands as wide as a hand and then sewn into a large spiral.

of the life-style of a people. The "house" reflects not only the needs, but the realities. The people love roomy tents, but they are impractical if they are too heavy, since they have to be transported on the backs of animals. Pitching the tent should not be too time-consuming, since it is nice to have a roof over your head soon after arriving at a new spot. The tent must provide shade, protection from the sun and from the cold of the nights. The tents of the Tuaregs have met these requirements most excellently. The Ahaggars, the Tuaregs of the Hoggar, like their neighbors the Iforas and the Ajjer-Tuaregs, have low, almost flat tents that can withstand any sandstorm. The roof consists of a material that is always at their disposal: it is an enormous cover of goatskin, dyed a ravishingly beautiful red with vegetable dyes. The side walls are carefully woven mats, decorated with small ornaments, and can be rolled up or down according to need. During the day, when it is quite hot, the wind is allowed to play through the tent. If the wind is too strong, the side wall is rolled down, and at night the tent is closed all around with the mats. The custom of using tent poles decorated with carvings is unfortunately gradually disappearing.

The ordinary vacation tents we are familiar with are of little use in the Sahara or Sahel; they are useful for staying overnight, but never for living in, since they are hot as an oven during the day.

Up to page 15, the pictures in this chapter illustrate the mat-tents of a Tuareg tribe that lives in the Aïr Mountains in the northeastern Niger Republic. These round houses, set up in the sand in less than two hours, are light and clean on the inside, and more comfortable to live in than many of the clay huts of permanent city dwellers. Here too, ventilation is provided by rolling the side walls up or down, and it never gets as hot under their roofs as it does under the impregnated canvas ones of our tents.

The present-day inhabitants of the Aïr call themselves Tuaregs. The word signifies a race of Berbers of Hamitic origin. But very few of them are racially pure, that is – light-skinned. When we speak of Tuaregs, we should really always establish beforehand whether we mean an anthropologically pure race, or simply all those peoples who live like Tuaregs, who have adopted their language and customs and manners and who, like them, dress in dark, indigo-blue robes.

This is not so important for us here. In this chapter I want only to show the mat-tent, and to demonstrate that it is a splendid adaptation to the environment. In the Aïr, there is enough wood to allow for long tent-poles, and the doum palm, whose leaf fibers are used for weaving the mats, is common. It is found principally in narrow wooded strips like galleries that run along the riverbeds. Here, riverbeds are not called "wadis" as in the north, but rather "koris."

◄
First this woman sets up the bed and drives in carved, forked branches – they take care of clothes and blankets. Then flexible poles are set in, bound together, and covered with mats.

►
It is light and cosy inside the tent. An infant lies in the hanging cradle.

14

Aïr Mountains: the transition to a settled existence. The stable ribs still resemble the mobile mat-tents; the mud house contains supplies.

Oasis in the Aïr, with houses of settled "Busu," former slaves of the Tuareg.

Straw Houses of Cattle-Raisers

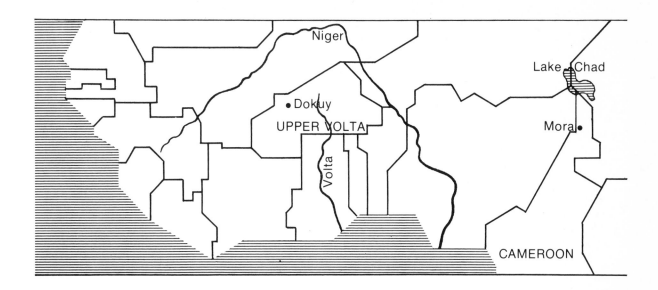

To the south of the Tuaregs live other tribes who are almost exclusively occupied with cattle-raising. They are the Fulbe or Fulani, the Fula or Fulanke, the Fellata or Peulh. They are all the same people, with ever-changing names applied to them by neighboring peoples. They usually refer to themselves as Fulbe, a name that implies the notion of "light-skinned." They occupy a vast area; they are at home in the entire western and central Sudan, from Dakar to Chad, in a broad belt more than 3,500 kilometers (2,000 miles) long. They are citizens of thirteen different states. The Peulh or Fulbe are among the most beautiful people in Africa. The purebreds have conspicuously light skin, and often decidedly aristocratic figures: slender, sinuous, of a graceful physical build with narrow hips, oval faces with fine features.

There is much controversy about their origins and extraction, and the literature constantly yields new and contradictory statements. According to earlier writers, they came from Ethiopia, according to others, from Somalia. Still others believe that the Peulh were originally of Semitic descent, and recent writers find "proof" that points to Egyptian origins. Others propose the Caucasus. The only thing that seems certain is that the incursions into the countries of the Sudan began in Senegal barely a thousand years ago.

Now we must distinguish between the city-dwellers and the cattle-raisers. The former have settled down, become tradesmen and crafts-men, while the others still avoid urban centers and are often on the move with their large herds. Their conversation revolves around one subject, and the proverb runs: "The animals are more important than father or mother." The ownership of cattle is a symbol of power and dignity; for a genuine Peulh, the almost mystical importance of the herd ranks much higher than its actual economic value. These cattle-raisers don't want to have anything to do with agriculture. It should be recalled

Peulh (western Upper Volta). "Tester bed" in a large round house. A supporting beam is seen in the foreground.

19

that in West Africa agriculture and cattle-raising are never pursued by the same people. Especially in the arid regions of the Sudan, flock-herding demands a nomadic existence which rules out agriculture. But this nomadic existence has long since evolved into very different forms. There are the pure nomads without any fixed settlements, and their shelters are correspondingly simple. There are transitional forms, semi-permanently settled; naturally this allows for much better living conditions, but the permanent clay house is still shunned.

In the photographs on the following pages, I would like to show the farm of a Fulbe family in the Upper Volta. In a lovely landscape of gentle hills with many old trees, not unlike an immense park, lies the scatter settlement of Dokuy, about 35 kilometers (22 miles) northwest of the town of Nouna. The chief, an old gentleman with a pointed beard, gave us a very friendly reception, complimented me from a reclining chair, looked at my photographs, and listened to my request. I asked him for permission to photograph his houses and measure them.

The old Peulh, Idrissa Sangare, has three wives and, in spite of this, only seven children. One of his sons is married, but I did not meet him, since he was out with his herds, about 200 kilometers (125 miles) to the south. Other relatives and farmhands were not about either, but also out with the herds. At the present moment, Dokuy is the center for the clan, and

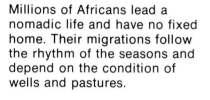

Millions of Africans lead a nomadic life and have no fixed home. Their migrations follow the rhythm of the seasons and depend on the condition of wells and pastures.

probably will be for several years while the herds are moved south and then northward again with the rhythm of the seasons. But the houses here are still not permanent. There are four enormous round houses with walls of woven millet straw, and double grass roofs. The doorways are small and prettily decorated with braided work. The interiors are extremely clean and neat with a hard, almost cement-like dirt floor. To the right is the kitchen, to the left a large double bed (color photograph, page 18). It is raised up on red-fired clay pedestals about 12 centimeters (5 inches) high. On top of this are placed nine round beams which are covered with several layers of matting about 10 centimeters (4 inches) thick. Wooden supports make a sort of tester bed with a canopy and side walls. The foot can be closed off by rolling down mats, and the head is against the house wall. All around are numerous "canaris" – earthenware jars – and above them, two rows of calabashes.

◄
Large round house of a Peulh family, with woven straw walls and a double roof (Upper Volta).

►
Interior of a Peulh house near Malanville on the Niger (Dahomey). The woman is sitting on the bed; the calabashes contain supplies.

23

Pictures of the house on page 22. The calabashes held together by a net on the parents' bed contain cash, jewelry, and identification papers. In case of fire, the net is rescued first.

The three rounded knobs on the lids of each of the jars provide a solid base for the rounded calabashes. Among the Peulh, calabashes are usually dyed white and they are never decorated with burned-in patterns as they are among other peoples, but here, a few were still ornamented with rather reticent patterns in ochre.

We were curious to discover what was stored in these vessels. In one of the houses the earthenware jars contained millet, peanuts, baobab tree leaves; a fourth was empty, and the next one contained two foot rings. The next was empty, the next contained millet, four contained cotton, then there was another empty; the next contained grass seeds for making bread, then rice, then three more containing millet. The calabashes in the middle row were all empty while the small ones on top contained: sugar, tree bark for stomachaches, pods for making sauces, sewing things, and various odds and ends.

Some of the Shoa-Arabs live south of Lake Chad in large straw houses. Here, too, there is a "house within a house"; the parents' bedroom. The kitchen has a protective mud wall.

The inhabitants of the straw house pictured here are not Fulbe, but Shoa-Arabs. They call themselves Arabs, although they are very dark because of inevitable racial interbreeding. Due to waves of immigration from Arabia, via Upper Egypt, through the course of centuries, a variety of heterogeneous peoples evolved who now inhabit a region extending out over Lake Chad. The Shoa-Arabs of whom we are speaking here regard what was formerly Bornuland and Kanem, and the northern Cameroon to about Mora, as their home. They are semi-nomadic cattle-raisers. As the picture below demonstrates, their straw houses with rather disorderly grass roofs are large enough to provide space for a so-called "sleeping house." I found this house-within-a-house quite delightful. It is clean and very prettily arranged, and might be compared to a canopy bed that sleeps numerous people. The rest of the area under the large grass roof is somewhat less clean, since this space is shared with the young domestic animals which are shut in there at night.

The hearth is particularly noteworthy. It is secured by a high rear wall and two lower side walls of clay. This an indication of the transition toward permanent settlements. Nomads usually simply set their cooking pots on three stones. These have been replaced here by a prettily decorated clay cone. These photographs were taken at the northern edge of the Mandara mountains in north Cameroon.

Walls and Roofs of Straw

A somewhat indiscreet gentleman peering through the woven millet-straw wall of a shady verandah. In the background are bedsteads.

The African in the wilds builds with the materials at his disposal – whatever nature presents him with in his environment. He doesn't pay for it, and never transports it over long distances. Building his house requires diligence and hard work, but no capital. This book shows many of the possibilities in house-building, and yet they are only a small selection. This demonstrates that life-styles are not merely a technological problem, but are dictated principally by the character of the house's inhabitant, who does not think in terms of aesthetic or geometric forms, but simply of cultural and practical function. Houses are the purest reflections of life-styles.

On the other hand, house forms also vary with the building materials available. A jungle builder builds with slender staves, bamboo, palm-leaf ribs, and boards – completely differently from the inhabitant of a treeless arid zone, whose environment might provide him with clay, but not even with stone. This is, of course, self-evident, and houses of different building materials are just as varied as the landscapes they occupy.

Here and there in this book my readers will find photographs of woven articles. I would like to note especially the mat tents of the Tuaregs and the artful dividing walls in the Cameroon grasslands house, such as the one being made on page 40. In the lake-dwellings, the walls are made of palm ribs; in Hausa and Fulbe villages there are narrow alleys between woven fences as high as a man is tall. Mud walls are covered with woven mats to protect them from the driving tropical rains. Woven mats are used as house doors and to sleep under. Where wooden boards are lacking, table legs are covered with mats to make a surface. Roofs are sometimes woven, and the picture on page 169 shows a granary like a gigantic basket. Dividing, or interior, walls too are often made of woven materials.

Things are somewhat easier for jungle builders than for the inhabitants of the grasslands. There is a great variety of plants at their disposal for braiding and twisting the ropes and cords used extensively in house-building and roof construction. The barks of lianas is beaten, the pliable fibers of the rattan palm are used; bamboo is split, as are the leaf sheaths of the raffia palm, three times as tall as a man. Cocopalm fibers are also usable. In the savannah, various types of grass are utilized, or the bark is peeled from the baobab tree and beaten into fibers that make a very durable rope.

The man below is demonstrating how mats and walls can be made simply by bending stiff stalks of millet straw and sticking them together. The fences at the left, separating farms, are made of such millet-straw mats. Neither nails nor wire are used in building a roof, so a solid building material is required, and since as a rule, building is done only

◄
In the savannah they like to mark the boundaries of their "concessions" with millet-straw walls as high as a man. In the center, a baobab tree.

►
Thick millet stalks are stuck, criss-cross, into one another, and bent or broken off at the edges of the mats.

toward the end of the dry season (during which planting is out of the question), there is plenty of time beforehand to twist grass into ropes. This is the job of the men and boys.

The amusing picture below shows two things: that prefabrication is not a recent invention, and that house-building is a community enterprise. In many areas a roof is built ahead of time, and then set on mud walls later. In markets I have often seen complete granary roofs being offered for sale. When a buyer was found, it was very funny to see the roof walking away on eight or ten legs. But the men here did more than just carry the roof to the building site. The community participates in the building. The houseowner musters his relatives, villagers, and friends, and they all help. When the work is done, the owner slaughters a chicken, or a goat if he has it, and there is a feast. Later, he will reciprocate, and in his turn help build another's house.

◄
Bimleru, Atlantica Mountains, Cameroon. A prefabricated roof. It is not rainproof this way, for the grass sheathing is still missing.

►
Mabas, Mandara Mountains, Cameroon. Here the situation is reversed; the millet straw of the roofs is held on with woven lids.

The House of the Cameroon Grasslands

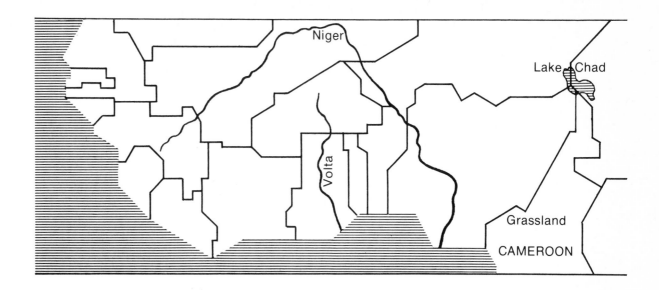

I know of no landscape in West Africa more romantic and lovely than the Cameroon grasslands. Hills with deep depressions and high ridges open out into pastureland. It is a densely populated region with scatter settlements and clustered villages, the houses bedded down in the lush vegetation of gardens and banana groves.

The western Cameroon, where a large part of the grasslands lies, was under English rule for a period of about forty years after the German dominion. A referendum under the supervision of the United Nations in February, 1961, did not bring about the anticipated annexation with Nigeria. The great majority voted for Cameroon. The result was the Republic of Cameroon, and there are now two official government languages aside from the countless African dialects and languages. In western Cameroon the children learn English in school, while elsewhere they learn French.

The inhabitants of the grasslands belong to the Bantu group of peoples. The anthropologist will be most familiar with the Bamileke, but there are also the Bali, the Bamende, the Tikar, and numerous others, all of the same extraction and culture. They are peasant peoples, capable tradesmen, and they also distinguish themselves by the very high quality of their arts and crafts. Their masks, ancestor figures, stools, carved house posts, and the sculptures in their chieftains' houses are very well known. The beautiful bronze work, magnificent red-fired clay pipes, and very fine pottery from this region are also familiar.

The most common type of grasslands house has a square floor plan, about 5 meters (5½ yards) square. Above this is a high pyramid with a very dense grass roof. Among the Bamileke, older types of construction demanding considerable know-how are to be found. The roof over the square house is like a gigantic egg placed on top of it, with its large end cut off. The walls are constructed in the following manner: fairly slender

Landscape in Ndop, western Cameroon grasslands. The house is erected on a square plan. In the foreground is a manioc field.

Bali, western Cameroon grasslands. The men's costumes of this region are famous. Here, a chieftain's notable.

posts are set along the outside of the ground plan at intervals of about half a pace. A second row of posts is then set into the ground, just inside the first square. This smaller square marks the interior surface of the wall. Staves from the raffia palm are bound horizontally to the inner and outer rows of posts, tied on with liana cords at intervals of about 30 centimeters (12 inches). The resulting framework is then filled up with lumps of clay or mud. Usually only round houses are built in the absence of brick, since the corners of a rectangular one would be too weak if only clay is used. But this trick with the framework allows for the construction of a solid rectangular house. (See photograph on following page, below.) The very thick grass roofs survive several rainy seasons, but have to be beaten flat from time to time.

A small village with grassland hills behind it. The village almost disappears between mango trees and banana groves.

Grasslands house. A lattice of raffia palm-leaf ribs is used for building the roof. Bundles of grass are then tucked into this and beaten down firmly.
A wooden framework is used in building the side walls.

The raffia palm thrives in swampy areas. The leaf sheaths, a meter (yard) long, are easily split, and are an ideal, multi-purpose building material.

◄
Door jambs and sills at house entrances are ornamented with carvings characteristic of the grasslands. It is an art that is gradually disappearing.

►
Chief's house in Bafut. The palace stands on a platform of basalt columns. The slender staves were formerly decorated with carvings.

Present-Day Lake-Dwellings

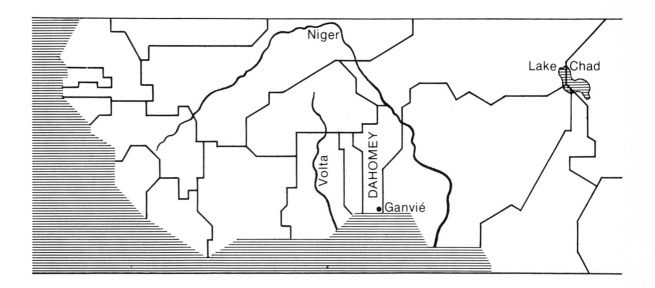

Ganvié is situated on the northwestern shore of Lake Nokwé in southern Dahomey. It is a lake-dwelling village of roughly ten thousand inhabitants that can be reached only by water. Even within the large settlement, all the streets are water and the only means of transportation is the pirogue. The population is part of the large group of Fon peoples.

Two rivers running almost parallel through a broad valley, the So and the Ovémé, carry water out of the north. Lake Nokwé is connected with the lagoons of Porto Novo, and together they cover an area of more than 150 square kilometers (55 square miles). Broad sandbanks with luxuriant cocopalms seal the lagoon off from the Atlantic. In the later summer and fall the rivers are at high water and at this time the water level in the lagoon also rises and there is an increase in its sweet water content. During the dry season when the water is low, the platforms on which the houses are built are about 1½ to 2 meters (5 to 7 feet) above water level. The village boys swimming in the area can touch bottom everywhere. But at high water the situation is different. Then the fishermen can bring their pirogues right up to the door of the house. The inhabitants of Ganvié are highly specialized. They live solely by fishing and trading smoked fish. They leave the cultivation of the banks of the lagoon to others. Their large village is not set into a swamp or marshy area, but is far out in the lagoon, on the open water. This is in keeping with a popular notion about lake-dwellings, but one that is a misconception about the ancient ones. According to recent research, the latter were refuges built along the shores that were in water only at particular times. In Ganvié, however, it is impossible to walk home, even during the dry season. It is interesting to note here that the residents of Ganvié have only been living on the water since the middle of the last century.

At present, the village seems to be developing into a tourist attraction.

Painted house in the lake-dwellers' village of Ganvié, south Dahomey. Colored decoration is the rare exception rather than the rule here.

45

This is entirely understandable, since it is both interesting and romantic to encounter a viable lake-dwelling culture. But a rushed tourist, hurriedly passing through on an afternoon's excursion in a comfortable motorboat, is hardly aware of how impoverished life is there. The fish catches are diminishing, the same primitive fishing methods are used, and there is no commercialization to meet modern demands. There are no freezing plants or canning factories. The fish are still smoked lightly over dangerous open fires in the huts, in a fashion that preserves them for a few weeks only. Already in its short history, Ganvié has had several large fires.

Blue smoke creeps through the roof made of leaves that has aged to a weatherbeaten gray. There, in front of her larger wooden smoker hung over the hearth, stands my neighbor Zossa, the housewife. She stands, perspiring, constantly turning each fish from one side to the other. The

wood charcoal fire is burning in a large, clay-lined basket, which also serves as her stove. Aside from two chests for storing farinaceous products, her lightly built house contains no furniture. The floor serves for seating, and two pretty mats are spread out on it to sleep on. Clothes are hung along the walls, or come to rest in a disorderly pile together with some blankets in a corner.

The piles bearing the platforms and forming the corner posts of the houses are made of durable tree trunks, rammed deep into the lake bottom. Palm-leaf ribs and split bamboo are also important building materials, and they are held together by plant fibers of all sorts. A thick grass roof (rarely one of palm leaves) affords protection from the rain and sun. The heat – up to 35° C. (95° F.) in February, and about 22° C. (72° F.) in August – is less of a hardship than the almost constant high humidity of this tropical zone only 6 degrees north of the equator. The

Lagoon fishing near Ganvié. Branches stuck into the bottom create artificial hiding places for the fish. On specific days, these are surrounded by nets, and the branches are then removed. Thus the prey is surrounded, and caught.

◄
The houses rest on platforms.
Their main supporting beams,
good-sized trunks, go through
the platform and into the lake
bottom.

▶
At the end of the dry season,
the water is only knee-deep in
places. When the lagoons fill
up during the rains, the water
reaches the platforms.

◄
A basket thickly painted with clay replaces the cooking hearth. These primitive and dangerous fireplaces serve for all the cooking.

◄
A pig stall on a small artificial island beneath the lake-dwelling.

►
All traffic is water-borne. Note the bent roof-beam of the house that is still just a skeleton.

poles around which the side walls of the houses are constructed are only loosely aligned, thus guaranteeing good ventilation. This is essential when living on the water. The floor is not made of boards joined solidly together, but of palm-leaf ribs. These round ribs, polished smooth by bare feet, are not completely straight, and small gaps result, making it difficult to set up a table but practical in other ways. Rubbish and refuse not thrown out the window fall through them into the water and so, despite the lack of a broom, these one-room houses always look clean and livable.

Anything edible that falls into the water is cleaned up by the pigs – black pigs with yellow stripes on the torso and long snouts. Before my brief stay at Ganvié I had no idea what good swimmers pigs were. They frisk about in the water, grunting, and swim with remarkable litheness, like beavers, through the jumble of piles under the houses.

Crowing roosters awakened us in the morning. Chickens were cackling, pigeons cooing, and small red and white ducks were nattering and cleaning their feathers. They were part of the picture – but I had not been prepared to find pigs, chickens, and roosters, and even an occasional goat in a lake-dwelling.

There is still no better way of kneading clay for house-building.

Building with Clay

Actually it is amazing that in all the countries of the Sudan there is hardly any building with fired brick. Sun-dried mud brick is the customary building material everywhere, even in the cities. Apparently fired brick was used here and there in previous centuries, but somehow the art of firing was lost. Fired brick is now to be found only in ruined villages such as one in the Hombori mountains, on the miserable road between Mopti and Gao, where André Rouch found walls of this material.

These days, well-prepared mud or clay is still used extensively in building. Argillaceous clay is heavily diluted with water in pits, and then kneaded underfoot. It should be very grainy; a mixture of greasy clay and sandy laterite soil is the best. Apparently, an admixture of chopped straw, hay, or cow manure serves not only as a binding medium, but the microorganisms contained in them also effect the release of certain chemical and biological processes that promote hardening. I have seen ground rubble from ruins being added to the mixture, and soil from termite mounds, containing a sticky slime from the insects, is also commonly added. Good clay for building must be stored, allowed to rest and to "ripen" before water is added again and it is kneaded once more.

The next two pages show that in building with clay, hands are virtually the only building tool. These builders use their hands with admirable dexterity, and it is said that one can have the right "feel" only with the hands. I think that every picture shows the dedication with which the mason works. Balls of clay are thrown up to him; he presses them into rolls, joins, smoothes, and sees to it that no fissures develop. Construction is always done during the dry season, days with a drying wind, or days designated as particularly auspicious by the oracle being preferred. In some areas, days of full moon are avoided, in others, days of new moon. One dare not build while one's wife is pregnant, and there are many rules and laws to be obeyed. And everyone helps. It is delightful to

No tool is more sensitive than the fingers, no implement better adapted than the human hand. The clay yields to its pressure as willingly in building as it does in potting.

54

House-building among the Massa on the Logone. The clay rolls are laid together obliquely.

Layer-building by means of overlapping among the Lobi. The pegs (far left) serve to anchor the next, superimposed layer.

watch the clay balls being thrown up to the mason, and to see the children carry the damp lumps of clay to the building site on their heads. Oh, Africa is an old-fashioned country! There, the children still help with the work at home. Among us, the fathers have been working in their gardens alone for some time, and do not dare ask their children to help in their spare time. They have been persuaded that severe psychic damage must surely result from such frustrations. But among us, where child labor in factories has fortunately been forbidden, our sheltered offspring go to construction sites or shops during their vacations to earn money, in order to find self-fulfillment roaring around on motorcycles while still of school age.

This Labi farm shows clearly how the individual layers of clay are joined together by rolls and overlapping (northern Ghana, northern Ivory Coast). The new layer is set on the lower one like a cone, and the thickness of the wall tapers off toward the top. On the interior, these walls are smoothed, polished with boards, and finally color-glazed with plant juice.

In the customary rectangular-shaped buildings of Sudan villages, dried brick has long since replaced clay. With brick building, the corners are much more sturdy. Hand-formed bricks are hardly ever seen any more and usually – as can be seen at the left – a wooden frame is used as a

mold. The material used to fill it hardly differs from the usual mud or clay. The strength of the African sun takes care of the rest. Building with brick also has the advantage that the bricks can be prepared months in advance. In the photograph below, I find the spectacle of the three builders particularly amusing. There they sit, amid the bustle of the workers, well-to-do gentlemen who could really be dispensed with, peacefully, day after day, watching the progress and overseeing the work. These, then, are specialists at work. An entrepreneur has received a contract and accepted it, and the people really doing the work here are very poorly paid wage-earners and unskilled laborers.

◄
While previously bricks were made by hand, the method shown at the left is now common almost everywhere.

►
A building site in Mopti (Mali). The builders are seated in the background, to watch. In rectangular buildings, only bricks guarantee fairly stable corners.

Structuring the surface.
Left: Clay mortar with embedded courses of stone. Wall of flat, hand-made bricks. Corn cob pattern.
Right: Lines drawn with a piece of wood.
In the last two examples, a cement mortar was used. A strip of metal, bent to a hairpin shape, was drawn across the surface in such a way that the parallel lines were made simultaneously.

Matakam Farms

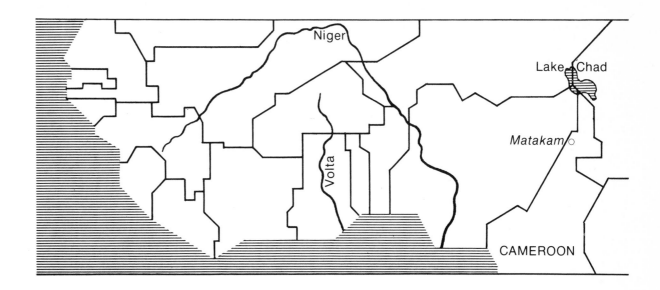

In the Mandara Mountains (northern Cameroon), in a landscape of granite ruins at whose core stand bizarre volcanic chimneys (kapsiki), shut away from the rest of the world and even today out of touch with the Mohammedan valley peoples, there live a number of heathen mountain tribes. Once they emigrated from the east, and apparently, in the course of several centuries, they withdrew ever further into the mountains, harassed by slave-drives, Bornu wars in Chad, and the intrusions of powerful Fulbe groups. In the linguistic usage of northern Cameroon, these people are called Kirdi. This is not an ethnological concept, but rather a curseword that the Islamic Fulbe use to designate them. It means "people without faith," and "the godless," and also implies what we would call backwardness. Thus, the Kirdi are "those who stayed behind," they are considered barely civilized.

I have known several groups of them for more than twenty years, and on my last trip, in 1972, I discovered that aside from the roads the changes were minimal. Hurried tourists do not like strenuous hikes and they seldom get themselves lost in the mountains, so everything has stayed the way it was. High up on Ziver and Upai, I found almost the same conditions that existed twenty years ago. Sacrifices to ancestors and spirits are still a matter of course, and there are still bones set among the stones at entrances to houses to protect them. The mountain Kirdi are headstrong, proud, and obstinate, and they are unreceptive to foreign influences. They do not recognize any authority except that of their ancestors and the spirits that people nature. Of them, I know the Matakam the best, and, madman that I am, I have returned to the Mandara Mountains seven times since I first made my way through one of their farms in 1952. I came to know the black Hephaistos who still understands the art of transforming powdered magnetite into malleable iron. The Matakam are afraid of plains and plateau regions, so the farms

A Matakam compound hidden among the rocks (north Cameroon). The weathered gray roofs are barely distinguishable from the boulders.

are situated on the mountainsides, and the Mandara Mountains are densely populated. In those areas, a population of sixty people per square kilometer is remarkably high (about 155 people per square mile). The individual farms nestle in the depressions, stand high on a jut of rock, or up on the highest ridges, and there is always a respectable distance between them.

Because of the density of the population, arable soil is at a premium, and these peasants have learned how to take advantage of every opportunity and produce maximum yield in minimum space. The color photograph on pages 70–71 shows the ingenious terracing – the work of generations – whose walls follow the elevation contours. These are carefully maintained, for during the rainy season, they prevent soil erosion.

These cultivated terraces must be tended constantly, their walls ceaselessly repaired. Manure from the domestic animals is taken out to

A dwelling in the Matakam compound is covered with the usual raftered roof. The walls are thickly set with stones, and sometimes plastered over.

these fields, often scarcely the size of a table. This method of cultivation helps explain the scatter-settlement pattern and the absence of villages; each farm stands in the middle of the fields it cultivates.

It is in precisely such backward areas as these that especially good examples of traditional vernacular architecture are to be found. Here everyone is still perfectly capable of being his own construction engineer. If someone gets married, he builds his own house – literally. He builds himself a farm with the help of his friends and relatives. A young Matakam marries at about twenty-eight, for only then is he considered to have attained his majority. At this time, the Babgay (the father of the gay, or farm) gives him his share of the land. Thus, a new farm goes up in the vicinity of the parental one, and the young man himself becomes a Babgay.

His farm is not built for eternity. It changes with the course of the years.

Houses containing storehouses are provided with an ingenious clay roof that is then covered with millet straw.

When his family expands, when he acquires new animals, and when new storehouses are required, he builds additions. Later, perhaps, one of the roofs will be allowed to collapse. It may also be that if illness plagues the inhabitants of a farm, they abandon it and build anew at another site. The young man builds his house as he thinks it ought to be, to live in it comfortably.

The photograph and the accompanying plan show the farm of a Matakam smith in Djinglia. The covered entry, (1) on the plan, is cropped at the left edge of the photograph, and the house where the women do their potting, (3), is missing entirely. Smiths occupy a special position among the Matakam, as do their womenfolk, who are the midwives, and who alone are allowed to do potting. This farm, as is the custom, has only one entrance (into house 2 and then through the first courtyard). This entrance is low, and one must stoop to slip through it. It is well secured against demons. The jawbones of sacrificial animals, and even polished stone axes, are stuck into the stones for protection (see photograph on page 68). Thus we enter the house of the Babgay, the *paterfamilias* (house 2). This is the central, crucial house that must be passed through in order to enter or leave the compound. There is no other way, and the teenage daughter cannot come home late on a Saturday night "scot free." The huts are arranged more or less in a

House and corresponding floor plan of a compound in Djinglia, Mandara Mountains, Cameroon.

circle, touching each other. Where they do not, a wall is built between them to separate them. The Mamgay, first wife of the master of the house, lives in number 6. The houses in which the women sleep are called hudoks. Houses 6, 10, and 11 are hudoks. The children of school age live in houses 5 and 7, which are called kalaks. Smaller children live in their mother's house.

In our example, these hudok and kalak houses also contain storage towers or granaries, though this is not usually the case. Usually the storehouses are uninhabited. They are called whuzeps. Number 8 is a large whuzep with two storage bins. The soul-jar is also hidden there (see small circle behind storage bins). This is the residence of the dead father of the master of the house, and is called a vray (see page 118, top). We were the first to bring some of these vray into our museums. Next to this large storage house is the kitchen, in number 9. Just try finding your way from the kitchen through the labyrinth of the compound and out into the open! Incidentally, it is worth mentioning that among the Matakam, only the Babgay has the right to climb up into the millet-storage places, while other storages places, containing beans, peanuts, and other fruits of the field, are managed by the women. Houses 13 and 14 are called kudumbok, and the goats, sheep, and the ram are kept there. House 12, the kudumlde, is a stall for the young steer that will be

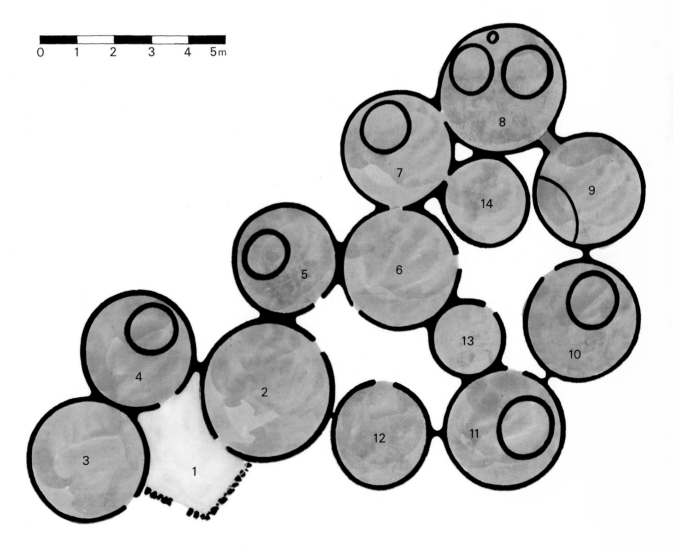

◄
The Matakam are fond of erecting a shady verandah of layered stones and a roof of straw mats by the entrance to their house.

►
A many-gabled Matakam compound. Each house has its significance, and its name. Only one entrance leads into this labyrinth.

►►
Terracing like that in the Mandara Mountains is not found anywhere else in Africa. It is the patient work of generations.

slaughtered for a cult feast. Only number 4 is left, and it provides storage for all sorts of miscellaneous things, wood charcoal among them, since here the man of the house is a smith. The workshop, or smithy, is about 200 meters (650 feet) from the compound.

The foundation walls are of stone held together with a great deal of mud or clay. These stones are uncut, but there is a large selection available. On top of this is carefully set a ring of stones that allow the wind to waft through, so that the interior will not become damp or musty. Only then is the roof set on. Here I would like to ask the reader to turn to pages 64–65. Two compounds are a-building. On the left a raftered roof is going up, as is done with living quarters and stalls. But in the case of the whuzep, or house with storage bins, an ingenious clay cone is constructed. In the picture on page 65, the work has already progressed considerably. The usual millet-straw roof will then be put over this cone. This particular protective structure over the storehouses is a specialty among the Matakam and a few of their immediate neighbors.

The peasants replace their roofs every year, shortly before the onset of the rainy season. They tear down the wild gray straw that has been disheveled by the wind and replace it with new golden yellow mats. Going through the countryside, one can hardly see how densely populated it is; the weathered roofs are almost the same color as the rocks.

Millet is a staple for the Matakam. It is sown in April or May and harvested in October or November.

Muktele Mountain Farms

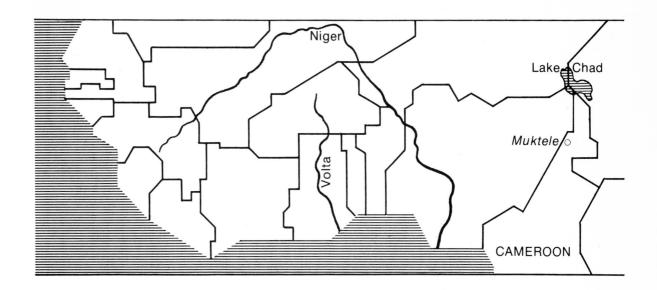

An African peasant is comfortable only when the house he lives in is, in its basic form and details, as much like the one he was familiar with as a child as possible. A son builds his own farm near his father's, and naturally it will closely resemble it, for he sees no need to improve upon it – indeed it would never occur to him.

This tenacious traditionalism is not a characteristic that leads directly to progress; but clinging to old patterns, to what seems to be the tried and true, does provide people with a certain comfortable security. They are not "insecure"; they are not inculcated with the notion that everything is false and untrustworthy these days. So they actually live without doubt, and we might say that "whoever lives without doubts, doubtless lives happily." Naturally this does not mean that in such circumstances the world is in order, that there are no desperately needed improvements to be made, or that there is neither want nor injustice. But it is easier to understand the difficulties that development consultants encounter if one is aware of this proud notion that whatever *is*, is right. Occasionally it seems very difficult to understand the African and to comprehend his philosophy of life, and sometimes what appears to us to be poverty is simply a frugality that has become alien and incomprehensible to us. As we have said, the peasant is comfortable only when he can live as he was accustomed to living as a child. That is why tribes who have left their territories and resettled far from their homeland have built their new houses in the old style. They took their houses with them, so to speak, and did not adopt the building styles of their new neighbors. Since black Africa does not have a documented past, historians are constantly looking for other ways to reconstruct early African migrations, and architectural building styles provide one such way.

The Muktele are neighbors of the Matakam, and they too live in the Mandara Mountains, but they are significantly smaller in number.

Young Muktele girl potting in front of a house wall protected by millet stalks.

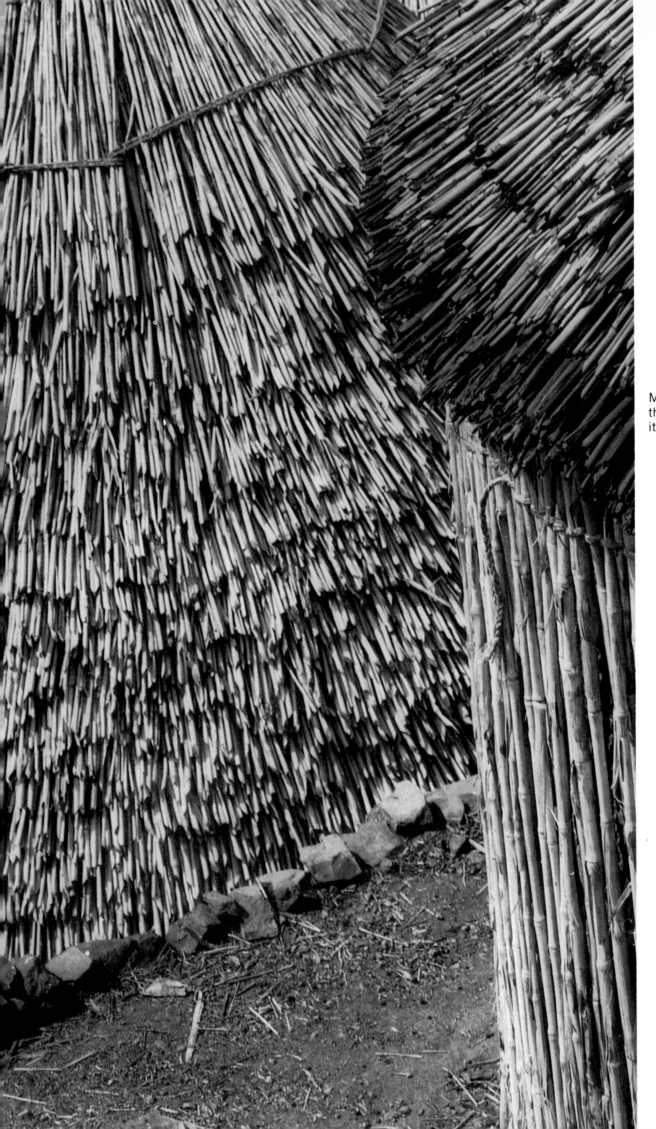

Millet stalks are used to cover the house, and also to protect its mud walls.

While the Matakan, or Mafa as they call themselves, are about seventy thousand strong, the Muktele number three thousand at the most. In life-style and behavior they differ from the Matakam only in minor details, and like them, they live as a rather unruly mountain people in remote scatter settlements. They too terrace their fields, and like so many other mountain tribes, they have a fear of the dangerous plains in their blood. For centuries, stronger peoples threatened them; plunderers and slave-drivers often came on horseback, so even today, they feel they are safer up on the steep slopes.

With the exception of the large compound shown on pages 88–89, the following pages all show the same dwelling compound. It is situated in a remote valley, near Taka Mokolo, and it belongs to the farmer Djabai. It is interesting because of its location on the slope and because there are eighteen steps between house 1 and the kitchen house marked 5. The

Like the Matakam, the Mofu, Gemschek, Potokwo, and others, the Muktele belong to the mountain Kirdi. There are no established villages, but small scatter settlements on terraced slopes.

difference in elevation between house 11 and the bottom level is at least 6 meters (20 feet). In comparing the photograph and the plan, the fact that the photograph shows more roof peaks than the plan is somewhat distracting. But this is because there is a second compound behind Djabai's.

The father lives a few steps down in house 1. It is the largest of the houses, with a diameter of just about 4 meters (13 feet). The passageways are low and narrow. A number of steps lead down a dark passage to house 2, where the first wife, Vadai, lives. Actually her house used to be house 4, at the lower left, but a magician's oracle prophesied a severe illness for her if she continued to sleep there. Now Devdagou, a daughter of the third wife, is housed there. Evidently, she need not fear the evil spirit. At a lower level still is house 3, which is empty. Clambering down still more steps, we arrive at a covered courtyard with storage towers (6).

A Muktele house on a slope. The photograph shows more roofs than are indicated on the plan because there is another compound in the background.

78

Number 7 marks a chicken house; numbers 4 and 5 are living quarters and the kitchens, which close the compound off to the outside. Where the houses are not abutting, entry is blocked by high walls. At the present time, Djabai has three wives; a fourth ran away. She lived in house 10, higher up. To comfort himself, Djabai has now fitted this out as a kitchen for brewing millet beer. House 11 contains supplies. A son died in house 13, and since this was thought to bring bad luck, it was abandoned and is now falling into disrepair. Fétékoué, the fifteen-year-old student son of Vadai, occupies house 12 on his vacations. He has a real bed, a chair, and a small folding table, and his walls are hung with the usual pictures of girls and boxers that he has found in magazines. He has made himself a door out of boards from crates and fitted it with a padlock. In the whole compound, the student's house is the only one that can be locked.

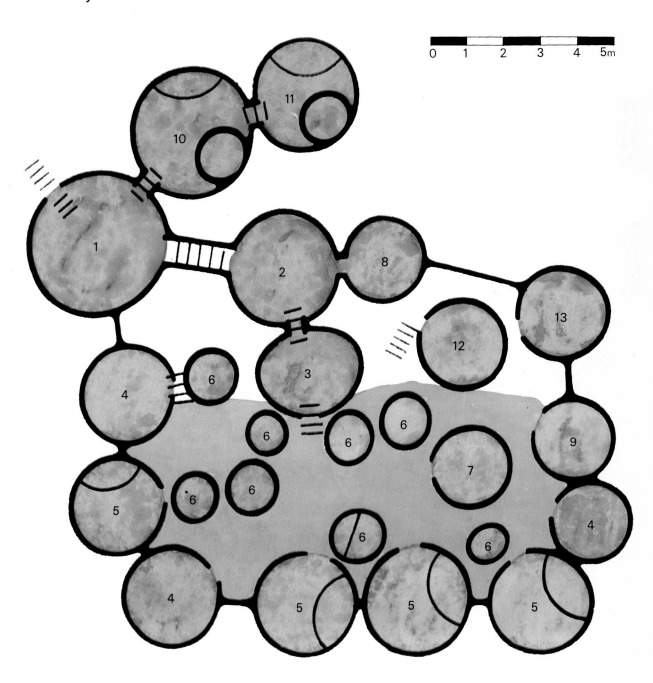

Now if I had not unfortunately changed positions while photographing, it would have been entirely possible to join these two pictures together. It is a view into the master's house. There is little furniture. Djabai is resting on a little bench from where he can see through the open door to the outside, while he's dozing there in the shade. The bench, polished smooth by long use, is not particularly soft, but on cold nights a fire does provide some warmth and comfort. At the left, a narrow passage into the next house is barely visible.

These pictures were taken with artificial lights which naturally creates a somewhat false impression, since actually these houses are never this brightly lighted. If I tripped going down the uneven steps, I could not even see where I was going or what I was bumping into until my eyes had become more or less accustomed to the dimness.

In this Muktele compound too, the master of the house lives right by the

Both pictures show the same room – the father's house. He reclines in his resting place, while his first wife sits on his bed, a narrow board polished smooth by use.

80

entrance, so very little of the day's doings escapes him. After such a brief visit, there are only a few observations to be made on the rearing of their children. There is little scolding or overprotectiveness, and the children have a good deal of freedom. Yet they are given to understand that they are expected to help. Within the family, housekeeping and work in the compound or in the nearby fields is a community enterprise. They live together, and the children are put to work early.

Our crowded apartments are no longer places of production; a family lives a scattered existence, and in many cases the family is nothing more than a consumer association. The father works somewhere, doing something that the children really know nothing about. Now it has been discovered that the labor potential is not being fully utilized, and women are becoming persuaded that it is not enough for them to merely take care of their families and to fulfill one of the most wonderful functions

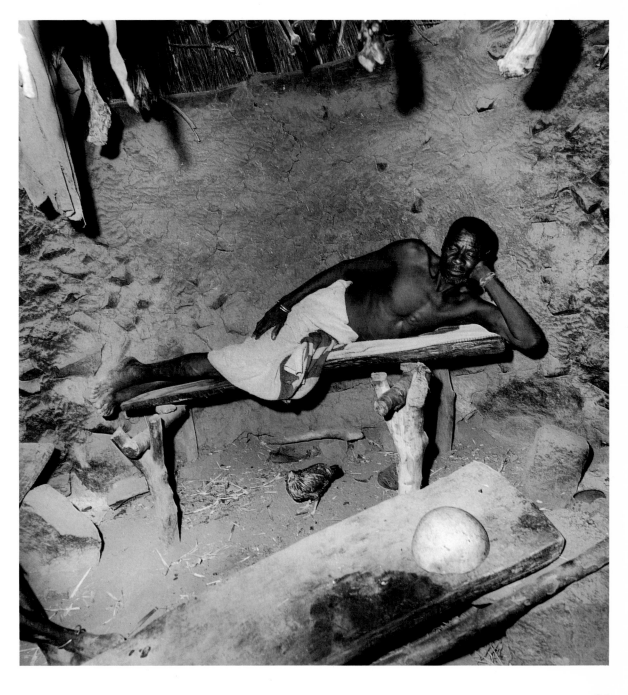

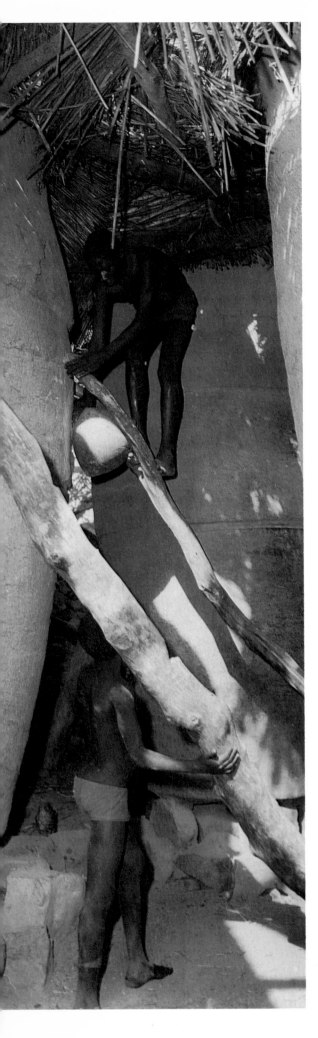

there is – raising their own children. And so they too are harnessed into the work process. They hang a housekey around their children's necks, and are later amazed if there is a crisis of authority. Among the Muktele, at present, there are no juvenile delinquents, possibly because their fathers are real men.

The Muktele use the same building technique as the Matakam: round structures, with no brick, but walls thickly set with stones, and millet-straw roofs. The storehouses are not under one roof as with the Matakam, but rather they stand in a courtyard, each with its own roof. They are mighty towers, subdivided on the inside, as usual. They are immediately distinguishable from the other buildings by the stone bases on which they rest. There is an extremely uncomfortable entrance very high up, as in a gigantic nesting place. The section of the compound where the storehouses stand is shaded on the plan. It is a courtyard with a sun-roof of millet straw, attached just where the roofs of the storage towers begin. Thus their peaks stick out over the top of it. In the compound we show, the sun-roof is very tattered and should have been replaced long ago.

More than a dozen years ago, when I was first staying among the Muktele and their neighbors to the south, the Gemshek, our two town boys from Mokolo were afraid of them. They would hardly leave our side

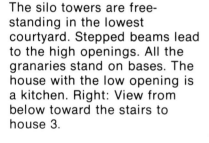

The silo towers are free-standing in the lowest courtyard. Stepped beams lead to the high openings. All the granaries stand on bases. The house with the low opening is a kitchen. Right: View from below toward the stairs to house 3.

Kitchen with a clay block for grinding millet. In the neighboring tower is the bedroom of one of the housewives of the compound. The entrances to these tower-houses are not exactly comfortable.

during the day, and at night they locked themselves in our car while we slept out, usually under a tree. It has yet to be demonstrated that civilization has made great progress among these people. The pictures in this chapter are from my last visit in 1972. There was still no school. One boy from Tala Mokolo attended the Protestant mission's teacher's seminary, and another, Djabai's eldest son Fétékoué, went to school in Mora, coming home only for vacations. These two young Muktele were the first of their people to go to school, the first to learn to read and write. One day soon, of course, they will both turn their backs on their family farms, never again to work the poor soil of those tiny terraced fields with a short-handled hoe. When I was there they were both at home during school holidays, and I had two very young but capable interpreters. Fétékoué took great pride in showing me his house. A folding table, a folding chair, and a bed with a real mattress. These three things alone put worlds between him and his parents and siblings, and since he can read and write and speak French, which no one else understands, he hardly takes any orders from his father any more. Just the reverse – it is the schoolboy who gives orders to his siblings, and even the women. Now he is one of the uprooted.

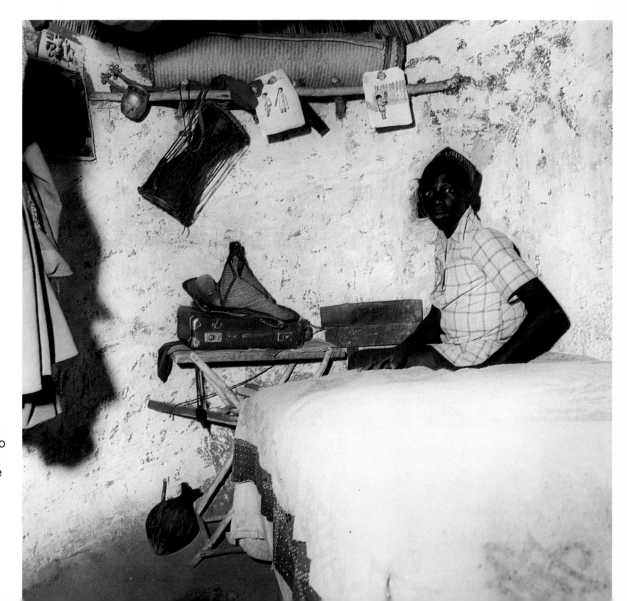

The student's house. He is the only one in the compound who has a table, a chair, and a soft bed. His is also the only house that can be closed with lock and key.

The granite rock-piles of the Mandara Mountains act as catch-basin and the surplus from the rainy season is stored. It is the job of the Muktele women and girls to carry water home from the ingeniously constructed ground-water wells.

▶▶
The "one-family dwelling" of a Muktele chief. A wealthy man with several wives, a swarm of children, and numerous domestic animals needs many such gabled roofs.

Musgum Domes

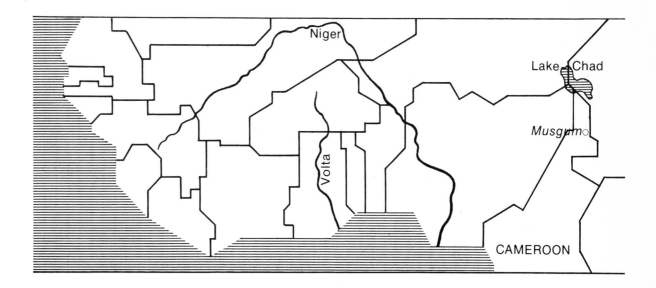

The Musgum, peasants and fishermen, are counted among the plains Kirdi, and live along the river Logone marking the boundary between Cameroon and Chad. Anthropologists have long been aware of the Musgum because of the wonderful little domes they live in, and pictures of these clay houses are to be found in many books on Africa. The profiles of these houses call Gothic forms to mind. At the very top is an opening about the size of a plate. This opening is closed only on rare, rainy days. Because these grayish blue clay domes are built as high as 10 meters (33 feet), the interiors are always several degrees cooler than the outside, even in the hottest weather. The doorways resemble keyholes, being narrow at knee-level and wider at shoulder height. The door frames are sometimes decorated with simple linear patterns.

As beautiful as they are, the reliefs that appear at geometrically regular intervals on the exterior walls, going all the way to the top, are surely not there simply to satisfy a need for ornament. Rather, they also function as reinforcement, and as steps providing easy access to the top when repairs are needed, as after heavy rains. The Musgum house is not built on an armature, and the clay is not supported by any wood. There are no supportive beams on the interior, and no scaffolding is erected for the building. The thin shell of the finished house bears its own weight. Clay is mixed with chopped straw, sticky juices from the acacia may be added, and it is then carefully worked with the feet, until the builder goes to work, with the artistry and skill of a potter.

A Musgum compound is made up of a number of these wonderful conical houses. They are built up in a ring – like a circular wall. The photograph on page 92 (below) shows that the closing wall from one house leads to the next. In the courtyard formed by this ring of houses are the storehouses and chicken houses, and it is here that most of the business of daily life is conducted.

Keyhole-shaped doorway of a Musgum house on the Logone, the river between Chad and Cameroon.

The artful domes of the Musgum are remarkably thin-walled, and support themselves without any built-in wooden framework or central supports.

Actually I have been misleading you by describing the Musgum house and its construction in the present tense. Unfortunately, it must be admitted that it scarcely exists any more. My pictures were taken in 1952. Twenty years later, I again headed north from Yagoua, toward Pouss and a little beyond. This time I no longer saw a single inhabited Musgum dome. Even in 1952, many Musgum had already gone over to building walls in what was probably still the old manner, but only to the height of a man, and then covering them over with a straw roof in the style of their neighbors. The photograph below, dating from the same year, shows this new, simplified, but significantly less original form of building. Perhaps somewhere there is still an inhabited compound.

The dome houses that I saw on my last visit were in Pouss and Yagoua. They had been constructed by the authorities as a tourist attraction, so that the old forms could be remembered. The two gatehouses at the entrance to the animal preserve at Waza are not genuine either, of course, but visitors enjoy them because they are photogenic. The fact that governmental authorities (then French) paid premiums to Musgum who continued to build in the old style, in hopes of preserving this cultural heritage, did little good. Pictures of these magnificent Musgum homes belong in my book, but it should be understood that in reality they are already a thing of the past.

The pictures in this chapter date from 1952! Even at that time, the Musgum had begun building to only half the former height, and topping off with a straw roof.

The Castles of the Somba

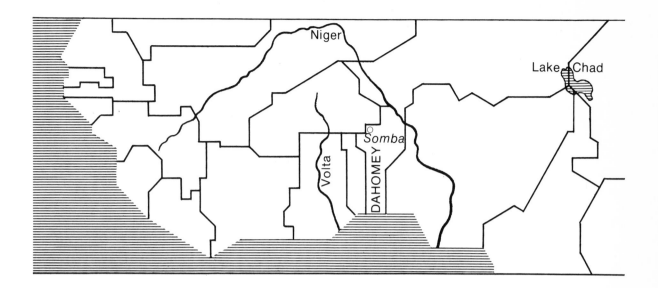

In the Atakora Mountains in northwestern Dahomey, and in neighboring Togo, live a number of old Nigritian peoples who could be called castle-builders. The old forms of these round structures were always covered with flat terraces; the grass-covered conical roofs were probably a much later addition. The pictures on these pages show the castle-like Somba compounds, and the photographs were all taken in the vicinity of Tanguiéta. As with many such groups who are scarcely banded together into larger political entities, there are no villages. The few there are are of recent date, and rather artificial. The Somba always demonstrated their independence by putting up their castles where they pleased, on whatever spot they deemed clever. Just as among the Kirdi in northern Cameroon, scatter settlements grew up, and the distances between one compound and another is rarely less than 150 meters (500 feet).

Until very recently, the Somba were still very much naked children of nature, with a tradition of ungovernability. At one time they were the "problem child" of a French colonial government, and they continue to occupy that position with the government of the young republic. The Somba are said to be unruly, pigheaded, and stubborn as mules. Certain areas they inhabit toward the Togo border are functionally closed to all traffic for months at a time during the rainy season, and naturally such conditions reinforce lack of concern about laws, incomprehensible legislation, and burdensome taxes. Attempts have been made for years to lure the Somba out of the mountains and hills, and to settle them in definite settlements along the roads. Schools, hospitals, and good wells were promised to no avail, so it was followed by a certain amount of arm-twisting. For a time, "modern" building modes were set forth, and the building of the traditional "castles" was proscribed. All to no avail.

A traveler in the Atakora Mountains will still find the beautiful Somba

Somba house, Dahomey. A single entrance, and no windows – small wonder they resemble castles.

Somba castles are built using the technique of unplastered layer-construction. One layer is allowed to dry before the process is continued.

castles, but now the roads are lined with children begging from the tourists at the tops of their lungs. The mountaineer who once went about in dignified nakedness is now dressed in a ragged raincoat, a woman in a lace-edged pink slip – presents from well-meaning foreign ladies' auxiliaries. Their castles, however, stand as always, built of clay layers and without any facing. A layer is put down, allowed to dry, and another applied on top. Plastering is thought unnecessary, and hands are the only tool. The castles consist of individual round houses – towers set up more or less in a circle. Naturally they are closed toward the outside, but toward the inside they are open. Thus, a sort of honeycomb structure results, with a yard in the center. This area is roofed over, but since it is impossible to make such a large clay roof without supports, or to brace it only against the exterior walls, branched posts are used to support cross-beams. Then logs, straw, and stamped clay together produce a solid terrace. The round towers are higher than the roof terrace, and little walls between them create a solid parapet. Steps lead up from the interior of the yard or floor. Just as among the Matakam, there is only one entrance, and it is controlled by the master of the house. Proud, assertive adolescent sons now build their own quarters outside the castle, but this is a recent development. One thing that makes the Somba compounds so delightful is the fact that the round

Round towers set in a circle enclose an interior space resembling a threshing floor. Millet storage is under both of the straw roofs that have simply been set on. In front of the house are sacrificial altars.

towers jut above the roof terrace. At the top, they are storehouses, but they are also fitted out as living quarters for the women and girls. In any case, the entrance to these "bedrooms" is not at all comfortable, since one can get through them only on all fours. During the dry season, cooking is also done up on the roof terrace. The women can live up there, protected and secure, guarded by the men, but not without contact with the outside world. From this lookout, nothing can escape you. You can see which of your neighbors are going to market, and which of them come back drunk. You can see if your neighbor managed to sell all her pots. Maybe a particularly fetching boy goes by, and the girls on the castle terrace all crane their necks to watch him. He wears a straw hat and a pair of homespun pants. Over his left shoulder is a bow, and a cooking pot full of nasty poisoned arrows. And then, being a good neighbor, he stops to ask the girls how things are. "A bo?" he asks. That

◄
The heavy ceiling beams do not rest on top of the walls, but are set on forked posts. In the open tower at the rear, stairs lead to the roof terrace.

►
The entrance to the house is closed only at night with a thick millet-straw mat.

◄
Access to supplies is awkward, but the arrangement for hanging up the "lid," on the other hand, is decidedly clever.

►
Much of the life of the household goes on up on the roof terraces. The housewife sleeps in the little house with the awkward loophole entrance. Notice the light- and airshaft.

means simply "Are you?" and he is answered, "Yes." Or he may ask, "Are you strong?" or better still "Are you happy?" and he is answered, "Yes." And then the confident fellow goes on, and never once turns back.

One day, the Somba castles too will have disappeared. One day it will no longer seem necessary to set up altars before their entrances, or to sacrifice young white chickens there. Under the corrugated tin roofs-to-be, these magical safeguards will have no place; the magician who still predicts the future with his wood will soon be out of work. But for the time being the Somba, at least those off the main roads, still live as before. They are not merely frugal, they are poor, but as yet they have no worries about consumer pressures, neuroses about standards of living and environmental protection. With them, we face the old dilemma once again: how can we help them without destroying the old patterns.

◄ Abandoned compounds quickly fall into ruin. There can be many reasons for changing residences and building anew.

► A jaunty old Somba peasant. He carries a leather whip over his shoulder as a weapon.

102

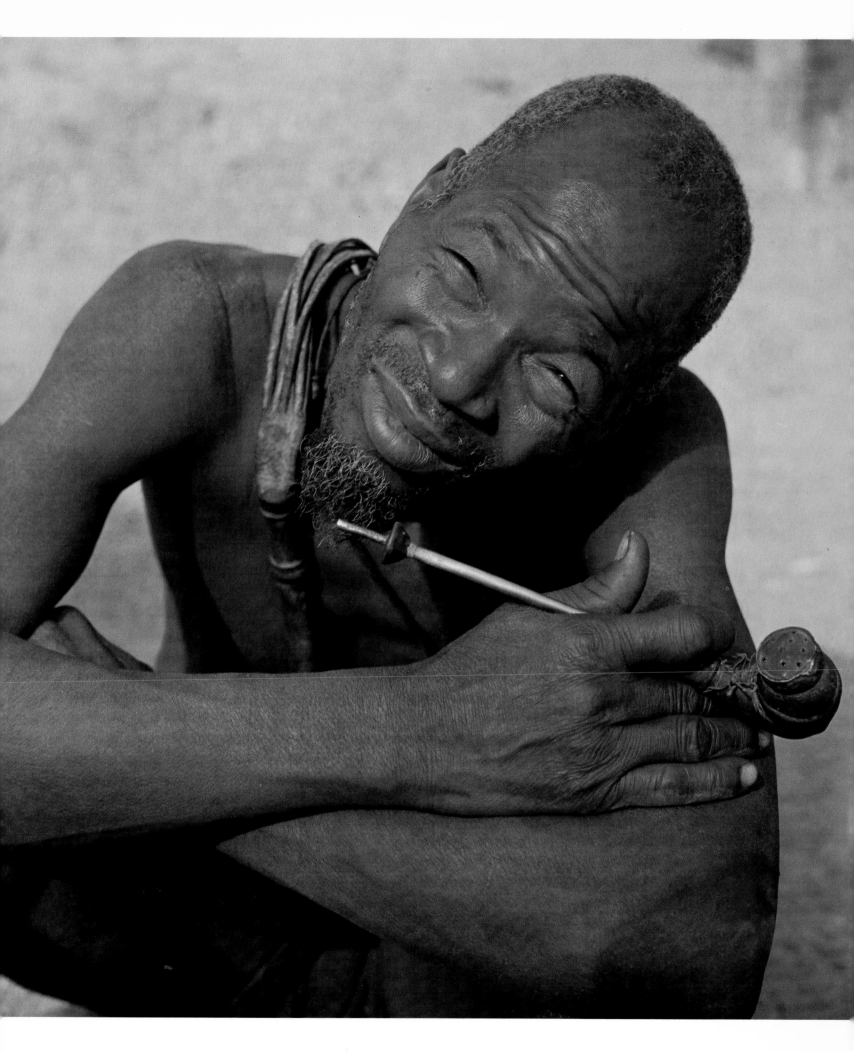

Dogon Cliff-Dwellings

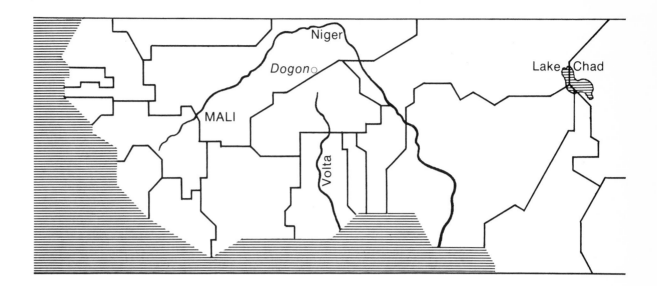

About forty years ago I saw photographs of Dogon villages in a book by Arnold Heim, a widely traveled, original Swiss geologist, whose name is probably not familiar to the younger generation of my readers. In his book *Negro Sahara*, the description of an adventurous trip from the Guinea coast through the central Sudan and the Sahara, in a Citroen – in 1934! – he tells of a short visit to Dogon villages. He calls the inhabitants by a name that was in common usage at that time: Habbé, a term not popular with those to whom it is applied, since like Kirdi, it means "the unbelieving."

The book fascinated me at the time, but of course I had no idea then, as a young student, that like Arnold Heim, I would make a pilgrimage through the same villages. But surely his books must take some of the responsibility for my travel fever. While burrowing through my photographs to find the right ones for this chapter, I discovered a number so similar to the pictures in Heim's book that it stretches the credulity a bit to realize that there is a forty-year time difference. Clearly, the Dogon have preserved their life and building style to a considerable degree, right to the present day.

The land of the Dogon lies in the Republic of Mali, far to the south of the great bend of the River Niger. The nearest town of any significance is Mopti on the Niger, the usual point of departure for trips to the cliffs of Bandiagara. From the north, the approach is through a gentle plateau landscape, to a steep cliff with a drop of 200 to 300 meters (600 to 1,000 feet). This "falaise" extends for almost 200 kilometers (120 miles), running northeast-southwest. Now, when I look up the meaning of "falaise" in my dictionary, I see the definition "cliff," or "coastal cliff." The latter gives the accurate impression, for standing at the top, looking out over a dull, empty plain, with very few trees stretching out below in the haze, is like overlooking a sea. Only later does one discover that there

Dogon granary, with what may be a fertility symbol.

understandable that for years, anthropologists have turned again and again to study the Dogon.

There is an extensive literature on the Dogon. I would recommend above all publications of the late French ethnologist Marcel Griaule, as well as those of his pupil and successor, Mme. Germaine Dieterlen, who has lived with the Dogon repeatedly from 1937 to the present. The two are generally considered the foremost authorities on these people. Three Swiss psychiatrists, Mr. and Mrs. Parin-Mattéy and Fritz Morgenthaler, undertook psychiatric studies among the Dogon, and to conclude this chapter I would like to quote from the book that resulted from their studies, entitled "Whites Think Too Much." This excerpt may help to explain why the Dogon and other peoples of West Africa are so content: "The self-contained nature of this culture is reflected in the words of Dommo, 'Here everyone is content. All are content with things

◄
"Why must water always be carried up rather than down?" asks a tormented girl. "So that you will grow strong," replies her father, reclining in his chair, lighting a fresh pipe.

▶
Dwelling in Sanga, a village on the plateau. The harmonious articulation of the façade is noteworthy. The niches are inhabited by ancestors.

as they are.' With a wide sweep of his hand he indicates the landscape spread out before us. 'If one works well, and can harvest, there is enough to eat. Then there are feasts. One goes to other villages where there is drink, and one talks to the people for a long time, and then one goes home again.' When I asked Dommo why he thought it might be that whites were not usually contented, he had no answer, but he explained to the village chief what I had asked. The chief deliberated for a short time, then Dommo translated his words: 'Whites think too much, and then they do many things. The more they do, the more they think. Then they earn a great deal of money, and when they have money, they worry that it could be lost and they would have no more. Then they think even more, make even more money, and never have enough. And so it is that they are not happy.' The well-being of the culture seems to speak through Dommo's words. In the landscape he surveys, he feels at home.''

◄
This two-story house does not hang on the cliff face, but stands at the top. It represents a relaxed building style – there is no sense of obligation to make straight walls or rectangular corners.

►
A Dogon holy cult site, with traces of millet-porridge offerings.

114

Of Soul Jars and House Altars

Africa is searching for its way into the future. Life-styles are changing, the large coastal cities are getting bigger and bigger, more and more children go to school, and many African nations have well-attended universities. New industries are springing up, factories are being built, the network of roads is constantly expanding and improving, and every big town can be reached by airplane. I would like to point these things out, because they are just as real as all the archaic indigenous things we have spoken of so often previously.

But while in Africa too, faith in progress has begun the deification of technology, the middle ages are still alive in the wide hinterlands. The power of "black magic" is still unbroken. There are dozens of taboos to be followed, and the authority of the old, the heads of houses, and the chieftains is great. The Africans are a deeply religious people. There are rites and ceremonies to be observed in connection with building and daily living. Religious safeguards are required. These begin with the building site, of course. It is impossible to generalize, and there are vast differences between one country and another, one tribe and another. In northern Cameroon, I found that the site for a building was determined with the help of an oracle, consulted by the blacksmith. Elsewhere, the "Lord of the Earth" has jurisdiction in choosing a site. He is the oldest living descendant of the founder of the village. When the building is first begun, sacrifices are already essential; offerings are made of beer, but frequently also of animals. In earlier centuries there were also known to have been human sacrifices at the founding of towns.

These days it is sufficient – and this is progress – to bury all sorts of lucky charms, "grigri," or amulets – a precaution that the Muslims regard as essential. Here and there there are specifications, ritual orders, and proscriptions that must be observed during the building, and afterwards as well. I would like to discuss this a bit. Though it is all very complicated

Altar in a Bobo Fing soothsayer's house, western Upper Volta. The feathers of sacrificed chickens adhere to the four jars. In the foreground: yam tubers.

Matakam soul jars. They are called vray, and are usually hidden in the storehouse. Deceased parents live on in them, among their families.

and confusing, one thing becomes abundantly clear: in traditional building, and with everything that has to do with houses and housing, the essential material necessities are always coupled with ritual and religious concepts. Ceremonies having to do with life and death take place either in or near the house. For many tribes, the dead remain in constant contact with the living. The souls of the dead, furthermore, are residents of the compound. The custom of burying the deceased in the house is also common, and in the Cameroon grassland I knew a friendly and educated school teacher who faithfully set out a small bowl of soup by the fire every day for his dead father.

The two photographs at the left show soul jars like those most characteristic of the Matakam in the Mandara Mountains. The Matakam are convinced that the soul survives the death of the body. They know that the souls of the ancestors go on living in the proximity of their own children, and so they build them a place to live. These jars are usually kept in the whuzep, or storehouse, and they are called vray. The eldest son guards the father's vray, while the mother's is kept by the eldest daughter. Offerings are made to them on particular occasions, and woe to the children who forget. It is rather comforting to imagine that one is not without some influence even after death, that one is provided for in one's children's house, and can still get angry if they behave badly.

Twenty years ago, as I have already mentioned, I was the first European to bring examples of such soul jars into Swiss museums. Naturally they were uninhabited, but the wives of the blacksmiths, who alone among the Matakam have the right to make pottery, understood that my grandmother, too, might like to live in such a house, and so we were able to acquire some vray.

On the next two pages are pictures of Somba house altars. Another type, from the Bobo in Upper Volta, is seen in the color picture on page 116. Altars are for making sacrifices. Sometimes they are inside the house, frequently they are out in front, and there may be a number of them, as there are with the Somba. Sacrifices are essential; they represent a desire for security. In considering an altar, it is important to determine in each place and in each case whether it is an altar to ancestors in general, or for specific important forebears, or if it is an altar for sacrificing to certain deities. The altar is never the embodiment of a deity or ancestors, but rather the place where one remembers them or speaks to them. It is, so to speak, the telephone that allows a connection with transcendental forces. The sacrificer is the medium between the sacred and the profane, and the altar provides the possibility of achieving a connection through sacrifice. Not everyone has the right to sacrifice.

In the picture on page 121, the master of the house is sacrificing a chicken. He is the master of the compound, as well as the eldest member

of a small family group. He is responsible not only for the welfare of the entire clan, but as the priest, for the house altars as well. In many regions, the blacksmith, who knows how to deal with fire, enjoys particular respect, and is the one who leads the sacrifices. In other areas, it may be the medicine man, the magician, priest, soothsayer, or whatever name is used for these old men with great authority.

It is not a simple matter. Sacrifices must ensure not only the favor of the spirits of the ancestors, but they must guard against all manner of evil forces that threaten the compound, that may bring illness, want, and adversity. There are living fellow men who have magical forces at their disposal, who can bring harm and become dangerous when unkindly disposed. They are responsible when animals sicken or small children die after a high fever. As much protection as possible is sought against these witches and warlocks. Examples of protective measures are

Altars in front of a Somba house, northwestern Dahomey. The father of the house is the caretaker, and only he has the right to sacrifice. It should be established to whom sacrifices at various altars are made, whether to a particular deity or an ancestor.

Various safeguards are necessary to ward off evil influences. One favorite place for "fetishes" – though this term is really inadequate – is the roof peak. Above: Among mountain people near Gavva, Nigeria. Below: Among the Fali, north Cameroon.

A second important place is the entrance of the house. Safeguards in the form of stones resembling old axes, bones, parts of plants thought to have magical powers (Matakam).

Left: A ''Doba'' that helps bring blessings and fruitfulness to the fields. Right: A ''straw doll'' is expected to produce the same effects (Atlantica Mountains, Nigeria-Cameroon border).

Pictures from a brewery.
Though difficult to decipher,
the female figures are probably
fertility symbols (Bimleru,
Atlantica Mountains,
Cameroon).

shown on pages 122 through 125. Some locations for these safeguards are preferred to others: access to the house should always be secured, as well as the forecourt. Most important are the entrance to the house, the door sill, the hearth, the storehouse, and the roof-ridge.

The photographs on these two pages show strange decorations on the walls of a small beer brewery in Bimleru in the Atlantica Mountains (north Cameroon). Here they are present not to ward off evil, but actually to lure good spirits. Presumably we are dealing here with some sort of fertility magic, intended to ensure that the beer turns out especially well. Time and again I have seen strange figures and ornaments on the walls of granaries or inside houses. Usually the present inhabitants knew no explanation for their having been put there. They would simply say, "Pour faire beau." The figures are no longer understood; they have been robbed of their significance, and have thus become simply decora-

Soothsaying with certain oracles. One might seek advice on which day to begin building. Above: A crab has touched certain symbols and the resulting changes reveal the future. Below: A soothsayer begins by making a sacrifice of millet beer. Both photographs are from the northern Cameroon.

Above: A small chicken is beaten to death. The position of its legs will give indications about the future (north Cameroon). Below: A Somba soothsayer (Dahomey) beats wood, and from this he "hears" the future.

▶▶
Inside the magic circle of stones that the uninitiated dare not enter, this man questions the oracle by mixing varicolored stones (Mofu, Cameroon).

tion. Now the great puzzle begins. Researchers are looking for the meaning of these symbols. All sorts of things are read into them; there are attempts at explaining them, but very little can be proven. In any case, these wall paintings and reliefs are pretty, and mysterious.

The last pictures have to do with oracles and soothsaying. If someone makes a sacrificial offering, it is because he wants something or asks for something. Since questions are naturally often bound up with wishes, he usually wants some sort of answer as well. It would be nice to know if it is propitious to begin building a house now. It is important to know if the right site has been chosen. Should one begin the planting? On what day would the beer-brewing turn out especially well? There are many reasons for going to a soothsayer. He is a specialist, an old man, a magician. Among the Matakam, it is the blacksmith who knows how to consult the oracle.

There are many kinds of oracles. Here, at the left, a soothsayer from the Mofu tribe is consulting the future with the help of the stone oracle. He will give specific answers to specific questions for anyone seeking advice – for pay naturally – in millet or chickens. The man sits inside a magic double ring that no one else dares enter. He throws different colored stones back and forth on a stone slab, and reads things in them. Sometimes sacrificial chickens can serve as an oracle. The chicken that has just been killed on page 129 reveals the future in the following manner: it is thrown against the ground, and its death throes are anxiously watched. The position of the legs indicates whether or not a wish will be fulfilled. If need be, they do not shy at duping the spirits, and helping along with a little stick if things don't turn out as hoped. I have even seen a second chicken sacrificed when things didn't turn out quite right with the first one.

The crab oracle is also particularly interesting (page 128, top). The shell is filled two-thirds full with sand. Then water is added until there are about 2 centimeters (¾ inch) on top of the sand. Small wooden sticks representing people are stuck in all around. In the middle, all manner of symbols are built up, representing good fortune, wealth, illness, and such. Then a small river crab is put beside it, and a basket is inverted over it all. After about an hour, the soothsayer examines the changes. He notes which "people" have been toppled by the crab, and which symbols are no longer in place, and then he tries to read these signs like a fortune-teller.

I would like to point out that these oracles are always taken very seriously, and anyone who is sometimes disappointed by the fact that progress is not being made by leaps and bounds in Africa should realize that the walls of tradition are high, and very difficult to climb over.

A Gurunsi Extended-Family Compound

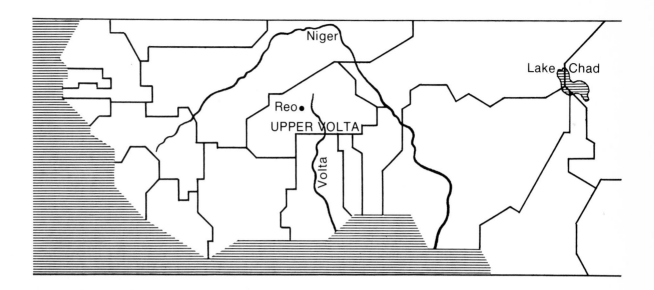

The Republic of Upper Volta, of not quite 300,000 square kilometers (106,000 square miles), and a population of more than four million, occupies much of the principal area of the western Sudan. Its capital, with the splendid sounding name of Ouagadougou, lies at the heart of a large group of Mossi peoples. At one time, Bobodioulasso was the center of government, but that changed with independence. This small country, consisting largely of savannah, lies jammed in between Mali, Niger, Dahomey, Togo, Ghana, and the Ivory Coast. It is twice as heavily populated as the Ivory Coast, and almost seven times as heavily as the Niger Republic. The population consists of a confusing variety of farming peoples with many languages and dialects. The "old races" should be distinguished from the "immigrants." The Gurunsi, with whom we shall be dealing in this chapter, like the Mossi, the Bobo, and Lobi, are among the tribes that have always lived here.

Among the Gurunsi we were presented with the opportunity of reporting on the compound of one extended family that was almost like a hamlet. While we were there, there were about sixty people in residence. Since I imagine that my readers might be curious about the course of one of my typical working days in Africa, I would just like to describe very briefly how we photographed a compound among the northern Gurunsi.

We drove west from Ouagadougou to Reo, the seat of an assistant prefect. It was the first time I had ever been there; I knew no one, had no useful addresses, but I had heard that there were supposed to be some interesting compounds in the area. So we stopped at a little saloon for a bit of orientation. The refrigerator was unfortunately "en panne," so the beer was lukewarm. No matter where you are, something is always coincidentally "en panne" that particular day. But some helpful fellows who were sitting around and let us buy them a beer soon told us that Reo has neither a hotel nor a campground, that the Catholic mission had

Windowless exterior of a large Gurunsi compound with a mighty baobab tree by the entrance.

been there since 1912, and that the house of the "Commandant" was up on the hill. So we drove to the prefect, still called "Commandant" in former French colonies. I explained my intentions to this friendly Mossi, and helped fill in gaps with my "sample book," just as traveling salesmen are fond of doing. My book contains all sorts of official recommendations, big photographs from previous trips, the dustjackets from my earlier books on Africa, and color pages from them. For years, this book has proven to be extremely useful in dealing with officials, customs authorities, and all kinds of people of whom one would like a favor. In Reo too, it had its effect. An empty house was put at our disposal, and every kind of help was promised for the next day. I paid a duty visit to the Father Superior at the Mission, and then discovered in the next few days, much to my astonishment, that despite the presence of a mission in the immediate vicinity for almost sixty years, neighboring compounds

Prettily made façade. The light rectangles are freshly painted at regular intervals; corncobs were pressed into the plaster around them while it was still wet. The plaster accretions below are the result of run-off from the roof terraces.

still had sacrificial altars, protective bones, and indications everywhere of the existence of a powerful ancestor cult. Tenacity is one of the important characteristics of Africans.

The next morning things went well. It had been agreed that a respected man of the area should be our middleman and interpreter. This fellow, Monsieur Maurice, told us, furthermore, that he was a good friend of our intended "victim." So we drove out in back of Reo, first through lovely gardens with onions, leeks, carrots, and tobacco, then out into the country, and soon into dry savannah. After only 12 kilometers (about 8 miles) we had reached our destination, a scatter settlement with the pretty name of Elkulkola. Every compound we drove by seemed to be suited to our purpose, but Monsieur Maurice shook his head, and pointed to a massive baobab, or monkey-bread tree, off in the distance. The baobab, with a trunk that was surely more than 4 meters (13 feet) in circumference, stood right next to a large compound, and was in fact part of it, for in its shade were benches for resting, and it was here that guests were received.

Fortunately, the head of the household was at home. Some of his brothers appeared, and soon we were surrounded by boys and girls, and hosts of small children. Some of the women of the compound mustered enough courage to come out, and people from neighboring compounds also appeared. Then the customary, drawn-out palaver began. Monsieur Maurice addressed a long, complex speech to the chief, with everyone else listening as well. He explained my wishes and intentions, maintaining that the Commandant demanded that we be well received. I managed to create a friendly atmosphere with tobacco, scented soap, and all manner of sweets. The chief earnestly and thoroughly examined my photographs of other compounds in Cameroon, the Ivory Coast, Niger, all results of previous trips. Until now, he had not said anything and none of his expressions revealed what he really thought of this imposition. Then he declared himself willing to help us, and to allow us to photograph and measure at will. Later he hardly bothered about us at all, but there were plenty of other helpers who eagerly ran around with a tape measure, or provided information.

We entered the compound and Monsieur Bationo – that was the chief's name – took us on the rounds. We went from house to house, stepping in here and there, clambering up stepped beams or clay stairs onto roof terraces to get an overall view. Our two guides, Urban and my son Bernhard, made worried faces, for it was their job to make us a floor plan out of all this confusion of living quarters, millet and corn granaries, pigsties, chicken houses, and dovecotes. As is fitting, the head of the house lived in the finest of all the houses. It consisted of two large rectangles built into each other, with solid wooden doors and broad mud steps. No simple stepped beams lead up to the roof terraces here.

The compound is inhabited by the Bationo family. All together, five brothers and the eldest brother's married son make up the extended family. The chief, by the name of Bamoua, has six wives. His brother Nebelbue has four, and another by the name of Niama has three. The other brothers are monogamous, and since the married son is also monogamous, for now, there are sixteen women living in this compound. This corresponds to the number of living quarters on the periphery (see plan on page 139). If you count precisely, you will discover three more that are empty. Thirty-five children live here – only thirty-five in sixteen households. This number is too small of course, but fifty-seven children have died in this compound before the age of two. Naturally, the infant mortality rate is still high in general, but this figure was frightening. Perhaps an epidemic struck this family.

We also counted domestic animals. Two heifers are communal property. That too, is a pitiful number, but the year before a number had fallen victim to an epidemic and had not yet been replaced. Aside from them, there were goats, sheep, a single donkey, a few scrawny dogs, cats, guinea hens, turkeys, and ordinary chickens and pigeons. Eggs are not eaten, incidentally, and the fowl are kept only for meat. Apart from the cows, the domestic animals belonged to the individual men, but we were told that the pigs, of which there were a considerable number, "ne sont pas de la famille." They didn't belong to the family. They belonged to the women, who, in keeping with the patrilinear system that rules here, are also considered strangers. The pig occupies a special position. While every other domestic animal from the heifer to the chicken is suitable for sacrifice, the pig is not worthy of this honor. Presumably this has something to do with the fact that pigs were introduced into this area only much later.

Our compound, then, consists not of a single family, but of a large group, or extended family. As is the custom, it is led by the eldest member of the oldest generation, who wields considerable authority. He is the guardian of the house. He orders new building, divides the living quarters, and disposes the community property. He is the middleman for every conceivable acquisition. He divides the fields and the farm work; he determines when it is time to sow and to harvest. He is also the judge in family quarrels and the religious leader. He takes care of the house altars, and only he has the right to offer sacrifice. All of this functions very well as long as this individual remembers that the community expects a certain demeanor from him, and that he must put himself at the service of this society. His conduct should not be determined by his personal wishes, but demands that he understand priorities and of course, subordination. A young woman who enters into a community like this after her marriage knows that she does not have her husband to herself, but that she is a member of a large community, and that she will have to adapt and fit in to this extended family. On this particular day we worked hard and had an interesting time. The plan of the house kept me busier than I had expected. I was allowed to visit a number of the houses. The cleanliness of the main rooms was immediately conspicuous. The clay or mud floors had all been beaten smooth and hard as cement with wood, and the only thing missing was the wax that we are accustomed to. The walls had been painted with brew from the juice of the néré tree, and rubbed very smooth. In every house was a clay block against one wall where millet was ground to flour (page 144), and the small holy places for ancestor worship were never absent.

Everywhere there were women at some sort of peaceful work. The older girls helped, and everything was done quietly and without any rancor. Nuts from the karité tree were ground to extract a white, slightly sour

Some of the compound's children. There are many cousins, siblings, and half-siblings. In the latter case, they simply say "même père, mais pas la même mère."

vegetable oil from them. Women were grinding corn into flour in mortars, and a specialist was making an immense jar without benefit of a potter's wheel. Baskets were woven, dyes were mixed for painting the house walls. Someone sat in front of the house and wound ropes. Boys were bringing wood to the compound. Bustling activity, and a peaceful sense of community ruled. Only the men did nothing. They sat around, filling their pipes with a stinking tobacco they had planted themselves. True, one was fiddling with a new door for a house, made of millet straw. The doors, incidentally, are all without locks. That, too, will change. In this compound, the children's children will all go to school, will be more enlightened and more knowledgeable than their parents, but they will no longer be able to live without lock and key.

At the right is a plan of this large Gurunsi compound. All along the periphery of this rough circle with a diameter of about 65 meters (213 feet) stand the living quarters of the individual women and their children. The fathers who have a number of wives live now here, now there. The different colors on the plan demarcate one apartment from another. There are, by the way, no passages from one dwelling to another.

House number 2 has three rooms, while house 3, next door, has five. Clearly this varies from one apartment to the next. The foundations of the houses are round, oval like plums, or rectangular with rounded corners. The back walls are naturally windowless and form a closed wall toward the outside, so that from a distance the compound really does look like a low castle. Only three narrow openings, barred at night with thick spars, lead to the outside. They are marked with the number 7. The main entrance is by the great baobab tree (8). The individual living quarters are so boxed up in each other with irregular floor plans that the only way to more or less sort out the confusion is from the rooftops. Away with all fences between houses, away with the divisions – the view should be wide and unhampered, with no divisions between separate families! That is more or less the motto of progressive architects. Oh, how wrong that is. The more people are jammed together, the more the individual requires a little privacy. Here in this large community, each family carefully screens itself off from its neighbors by a little wall (marked by the number 4). This can be seen quite clearly in the photographs on pages 141 and 145. The number 5 on this plan still requires explanation. These walls are somewhat higher than the other separating walls, and as the plan indicates, they are almost closed off completely, with only a narrow entrance. Here, well screened from others' view, is where one washes. Here again, the emphasis is on privacy. Number 1 denotes the large houses that are at the disposal of the compound chief. Wide stairs (9) lead up to large roof terraces provided with a parapet, as are the others. Inside the circle of the living quarters

Large compound inhabited by a number of related families, with a diameter of about 65 meters (213 feet), Gurunsi-North, Upper Volta.

138

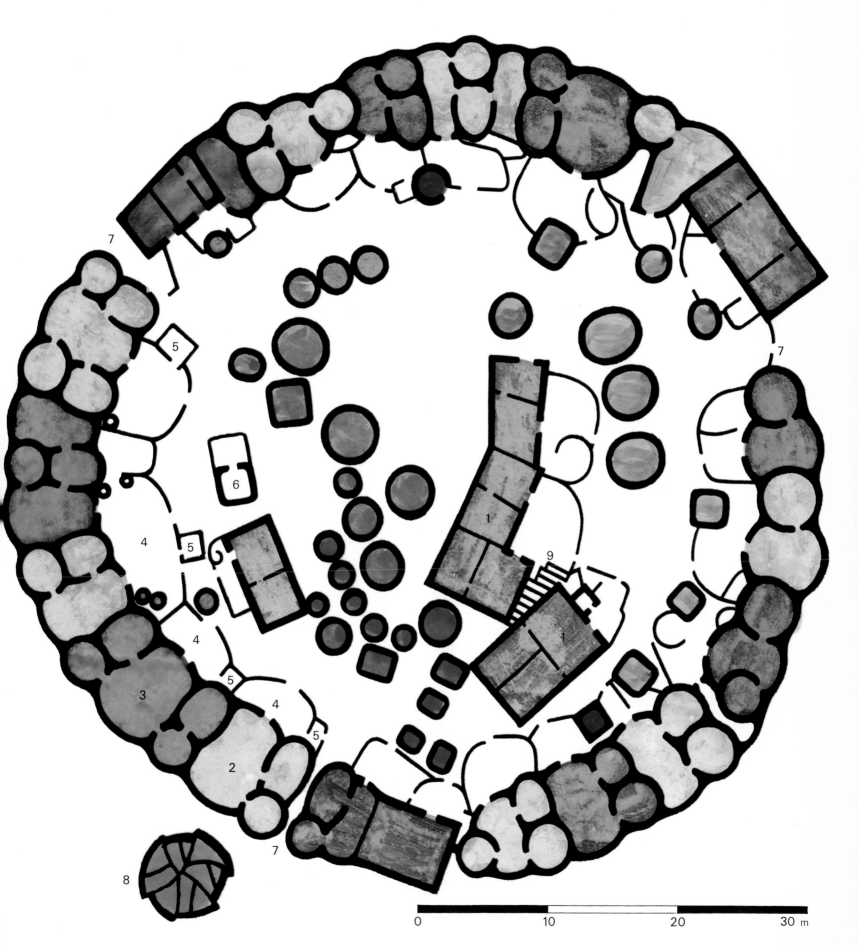

Only from a height does it become clear how the round buildings are built into one another. The roof terrace is very important; it can be a chicken-yard, produce is often dried there, and on hot nights, it becomes a bedroom under the stars.

are the storehouses and stalls. In looking at the pictures in this chapter, it should be recalled that the houses affording protection from rain and at night are not the only area that serves for living. For most of the living is done out-of-doors, and the entire enclosure is a real part of the housing. The courtyards, the little walls for sitting, and roof terraces are all a part, as is everything else within the circle of the walls, as well as the shady area with benches under the baobab tree by the entrance.

Both of the pictures on these pages were taken from the roof terrace of the master of the compound. The classic stepped beam can be seen in both: a tree trunk with a fork at the top so that it can be leaned against a wall without rolling, with notches cut into the wood for steps. This forerunner of the ladder is found all over the world. The door of the house keeps out stray dogs at night. Happily, at least for the present, this remote region still has nothing to fear from thieves.

Each family is screened off by a little wall at the edge of their forecourt. The rounded wall encloses the washing place; there are large water jars, and the wall offers protection from indiscreet observers.

141

Courtyard with screening wall. Beer is brewed in the large jars.

View through the door into the main room, 2 on the plan.

Here is a plan of house 2, next to the main entrance. The photograph at the left gives a view from the courtyard into the main room. The dark shading represents the thickness of the walls. The marked articulation in the first room derives from the supporting beams enclosed in the mud walls visible behind the working man. Freestanding supporting beams are indicated by circles with an X inside, as in number 9. The pale shades represent a sort of platform that also serves as a bench. The jars and pots in the background are clearly standing at a higher level than that of the floor. Room 4 is an unadorned bedroom. Mats are spread out on the floor for sleeping. The small, also windowless room next to it is the kitchen, which is used mainly in the rainy season. The stove is next to number 11, and there are pots, jars, and calabashes along the walls. The small dotted circles indicate particularly large earthenware jars. Drinking water is stored in number 5, but in jar number 7 we found stronger stuff, namely beer. In the photograph at the upper left, the little boy stands next to number 13 on the plan, that is, the beer kitchen. The circles marked with the number 8 denote small domestic stores of millet, corn, and beans, much like those that stand in the courtyard of the pottery maker (color photograph on page 145). The clay block with a stone for grinding millet seen in the photo on page 144 is number 6. And finally, number 12 is especially important. It is the holy offering place for the family, with a little altar which the women and girls may not touch.

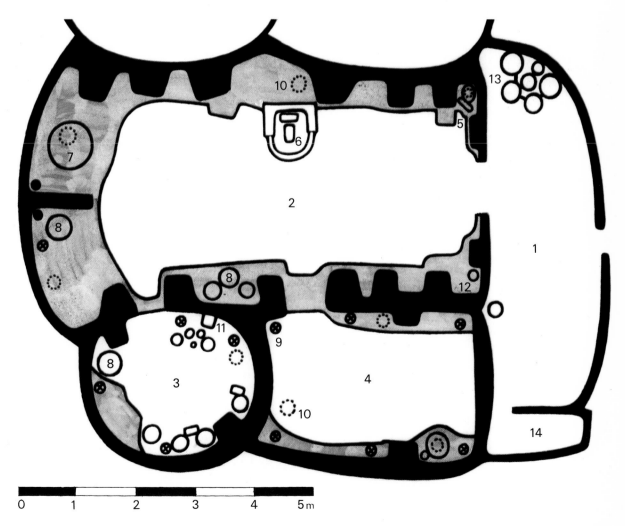

```
0     1     2     3     4     5 m
```

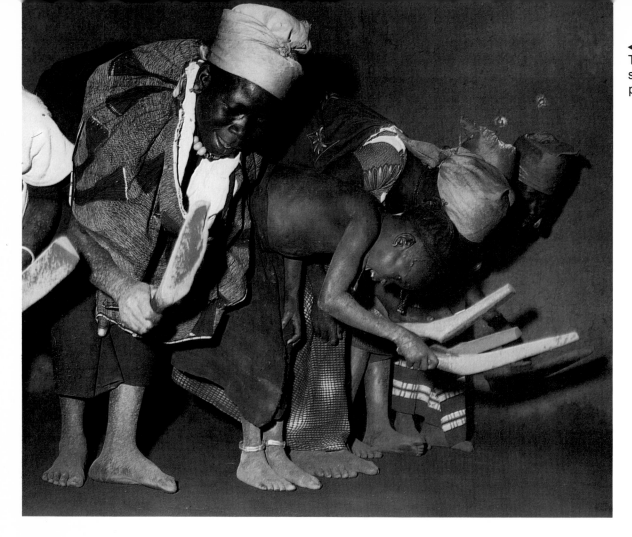

◄
The floor is stamped down and smoothed with wooden paddles. Photograph: B.G.

◄
The housewife grinds millet to flour on this clay block. Like the walls of the room, it has been polished with wood and dyed with plant juices.

►
One of the women of the compound has specialized in potting. Her little granaries are to be found in every dwelling.

The rice is weeded and the beds improved. October through November is the season for harvesting the rice and picking cotton, and the second yam harvest is due. The peasant is constantly busy, and hardly knows an idle time of year. But that is not all. Bananas, tobacco, pepper, and all sorts of vegetables are planted near the villages. Calabashes are made from the woody shells of enormous gourds. The women and children gather the fruits of the karité tree that grows wild, from which they produce butter, with considerable effort. It is an important ingredient in cooking. Most compounds also keep goats, sheep, chickens, guinea hens, ducks, and often pigeons as well.

Rich farmers have a small herd of cows, and this is a big status symbol. But farmers are not shepherds, and so the Peulh are charged with keeping the flocks of the Senufo, in return for which they are given the milk.

◄
A Senufo peasant compound. At the left is a large granary and next to it, a sacrifice place with a roof.

►
Senufo granaries are tall and slender. Oil-bearing fruits are being dried on the mat.

151

Under the grass roof is the karité kitchen. The hard fruit of the karité tree is, by a complicated process, converted into a white oil which plays an important part in cooking. Photograph: B.G.

This is the plan of a compound in the village of Natio Kobadara, near Korhogo. The chief of the "concession" is called Bambalé Coulibary. He is not the eldest here, but his older brother, Katiénété, got too tired, and resigned his position. There is nothing very new to report about the art of building here. It is a community enterprise, with the men building, and the women carrying water to the site. Houses with rectangular floor plans are found next to old round houses, as is often the case in many areas now. The houses are set up more or less in a semi-circle. Since this compound is at the edge of the village, the outside, at least, is closed off against the countryside with walls between the houses.

To give you some idea, let me explain the numbers: 1 through 13 are living quarters, two of which are currently uninhabited. The head of the family community lives in 1, his wives in the round houses numbers 2 and 3. The old chief, Katiénété, lives in 11. The two biggest round houses, 9 and 10, have diameters of about 5 meters (16½ feet). Karité butter is boiled down in the covered kitchen (14). Small huts containing a fetish, or other holy places, are marked by the number 15. Next to the cookhouse (14) and the well (16) stands a mighty mango tree that provides shade. There is also a sun-roof for the animals (17). The triangles denote hearths, and all small unnumbered circles represent storage or granaries.

Senufo peasant family compound in the vicinity of Korhogo, Ivory Coast.

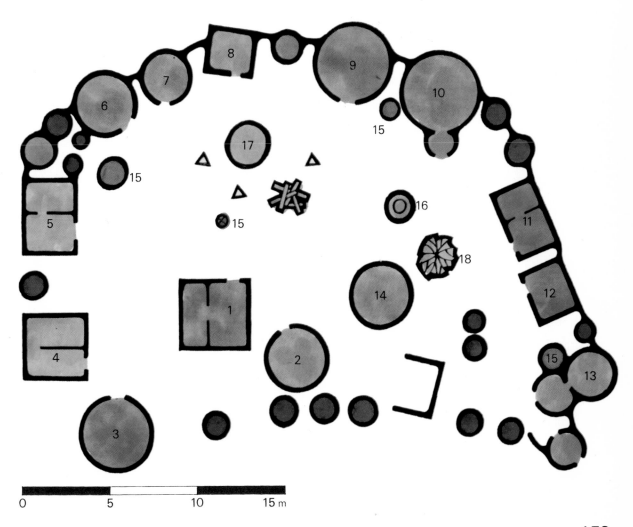

153

While I was pursuing other work, I left my son Bernhard in Natio Kobadara for a week. The plan of the compound is his, and his notes provided the basis for these pages.

Kobadara means "At the Edge of the Water." This refers to a small swamp nearby where rice is planted. Originally the village consisted only of two quarters that are separated by a wide path. Now a third quarter has sprung up, consisting of a number of rectangular houses with tin roofs, and a school. The Natio families live in one of the old quarters, the Sono in the other. According to the interpreter, they differ somewhat in their speech. There is also a sacred grove for each of the quarters, but of the two, the Natio grove is the more important. Possibly this quarter is older.

At present, there are twenty-two people living in the compound I have described, and of these, two are not members of the family. The chief's large rectangular house, the holy place with the spearhead in front, and the large kitchen for making karité butter are noteworthy. The six pigs belong to Katiénété and the chief; the few goats, sheep, and two cows to the entire family. They are tended by Peulh shepherds in return for the milk.

Most of the land still belongs to Katiénété, who, as the oldest, and thus the living ancestor, maintains contact with the dead. Another part of it belongs to the present head of the family, and the small remaining bit to Kolou, the eldest, married son of Naply, the chief's oldest sister, who also lives in the compound. The unmarried men have no right to any land. Such a man assists his father or uncle, and is paid in kind. When Katiénété dies, the land goes to the chief. In this compound then, lives the old Katiénété, whose wife lives elsewhere, then the chief Bambalé with his two wives, and the oldest sister of these two, Naply. She is a widow and lives with her two married daughters, whose husbands live elsewhere. Aside from another, younger sister of the chief, a second, unmarried son of Naply's, there are still another few younger family members who live there.

It is important to explain what is meant by "the wife, or husband, lives elsewhere." Among the Senufo, aside from the customary cohabitation, there is also another, much older, family-oriented form of marriage. The woman remains with her family even after marriage, and thus does not leave her parental compound, works there for her family, and raises her children there. The two marriage partners, separated this way by tradition, visit each other periodically, as interest or necessity dictates. The boys then leave their mother for the father's compound as soon as they are able to take solid food. The girls stay with their mother, even after they have married and borne their own children.

Island Villages on the Niger

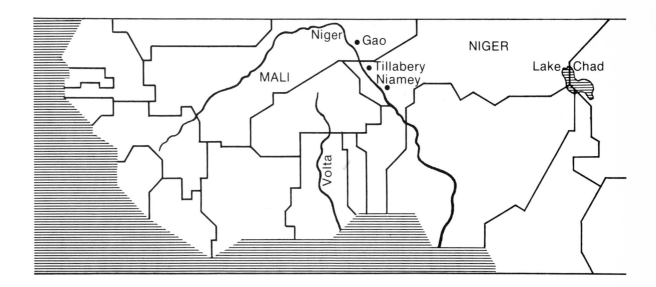

It was more than twenty years ago that I first saw the River Niger. At that time we were coming out of the Sahara, and after the hot, arid wastes of past weeks, it was an unbelievable experience. We clambered up a golden yellow dune and there, unexpectedly, lay the broad band of the Niger with its green edging of swamps and rice fields. We were not the first to have this experience, and this craving for water. Again and again in the past, people had come down upon the river from the north, and it is not at all surprising that the inhabitants, for safety's sake, sought refuge in its islands. A look at the map shows the enormous bend of the Niger that stretches far up into the Sahara. In this chapter we are concerned with an unnavigable stretch, full of rapids, that extends downriver from about the Mali border toward Tillabery, about 70 kilometers (45 miles) west of Niamey, capital of the Niger Republic. This part of the river is dotted with sandy islands that are inhabited by the Sonhrai and Wogo. They are not fishermen, but farmers, who leave their islands by pirogues to reach their fields on the riverbanks. At one time, plundering Ifora-Tuaregs drove them to the islands, and there they stayed. They fish only on the side, though at low water in March and April, fishermen from Nigeria journey for days for the fishing there, and then they trade with the peasants.

In order to get to know these island villages, two companions and I left from Ayorou in a pirogue manned by three natives. We went downstream at a leisurely pace, spending the nights in various villages. The river divided into a number of branches, a veritable confusion of estuaries. It became an obstacle course of countless islands of reeds, red granite cliffs, and narrow passages with eddies and small rapids that low water would surely have revealed as thinly disguised sheer rock. There were birds everywhere, the old familiar ones: crowned cranes, different sorts of herons, crocodile watchers, grayfishers, snake-

In the villages of the Sonhrai region along the Niger, the extraordinary numbers and jarlike shapes of the granaries stand out.

157

necked cormorants, ducks, Sporn geese, and thickets full of weaver-birds. Again and again we encountered other pirogues; here farmers were adeptly wielding their paddles and bringing home their rice, there others were searching the banks for driftwood.

We stopped at every inhabited island, got out of the boat, and were the objects of amazement. It seemed that few tourists had ever strayed there. At the landings there were usually a few doum-palms spreading a bit of shade, and an African river trip can make one extremely receptive to shade. There are no real trees here, so the pirogues along the shore had all been purchased far away in central Nigeria.

We visited Seno and Kendadji, Nantoubey and Savani, among other places, and we discovered that the rectangular mud house is making headway everywhere, but that the hemispherical grass huts so typical of the Sonrhai are also still being built. In all the villages, the large numbers of round granaries were conspicuous. They are gigantic jars, with sticks or stones built in at intervals to allow access to the opening at the top. During the dry season, these "storage pots" do without their removable covers. The prefabricated, conical roofs are put on only after the granaries are completely full.

The village of Nantoubey is situated on a small island. Clay for the production of bricks is found here, in the village square.

In comparison with the people of other regions, the islanders seemed to me to be well-to-do. This is not surprising, since there is never a water shortage at the river, and crop failures due to drought are unlikely. Life in these villages is extremely peaceful! There are no cars, and because the distances are so short, even bicycles are hardly worthwhile. There are small schools on the islands, but there is still no electricity, no mail, and no cafés. The island of Savani has a single solitary donkey, but no unmarried girls. This at least was the lament of a young and single schoolteacher from Niamey who felt like an exile there. We spent the night in his schoolroom, where it was clear that the peasant boys have important things to learn. On the blackboard was a lengthy explanation about rust on iron, and the fact that what was going on was a slow combustion process, though "sans dégager de la lumière." Hardly any girls at all came to school, the teacher explained, and furthermore, it was extremely dangerous to have any dealings with a married woman. "You don't notice anything, and then all of a sudden, you have a harpoon in your back, just like a fish."

These island peasants, who, judging by the number of their granaries, never go hungry, plant the usual millet and peanuts on the river banks, and plant all sorts of vegetables in small island gardens, but they are primarily rice farmers. Terraced rice fields behind dikes are uncommon. They usually plant their rice in the tidal areas of the islands and along the shores, as they have for decades. Thus they are at the mercy of the water level. The men we saw harvesting rice were up to their bellies in water, and the rice stalks were more than a meter (a yard) long. It was not cut

with sickles, but with straight knives. The small sheaves were laid into the water between the water-lilies and then gathered in a pirogue. As the picture at the left shows, only wooden branches are used in threshing, and then – just as in picture books – the women separate the kernels from the chaff with the wind's help.

The picture below shows a threshing place on the shore. The granary is still roofless, and its vase shape is particularly clearly shown here. It stands on bare rock. The two candelabra-like trees in the background are doum-palms. On this island, called Nantoubey, we made a plan of the peasant Almou Doulai's compound. He owned numerous granaries, and while he and his wife Dibo always knew without looking whether one contained millet or rice, I could never discover any difference in their structure.

The little compound – the plan of which follows – belongs to Almou Doulai. He is still very young. Talkative and contented, he cheerfully helped us with the measuring. So far, Dibo had only presented him with one child, a girl named Abibou, who was still an infant. In the same compound lives a younger brother, Ibrahim, with his wife Bibata. This marriage is still childless. The brothers' mother, Hanka, died, but one of the living quarters is inhabited by their father, who is usually "en brousse," which is to say, living somewhere on his fields in a miserable

◄
Peasants threshing rice with extremely primitive flails. Rice has been cultivated along the river for many years.

►
Threshing ground at the river bank. The pronounced vase-shape of the uncovered granary is noteworthy.

hut. Only a very small family lives here, and yet count the granaries. All those marked by the number 5 are millet granaries; 6 denotes rice. But let me go in order. The number 1 denotes the four living quarters. One of these is presently unoccupied, and another is used by the grandfather for staying overnight when he comes home, which leaves two remaining for the young couples. Number 2 marks the cement-like courtyards that are part of each dwelling, as the photograph below shows. On hot nights, the father of the house sets up his bed on this "terrace." The bed is a wooden frame that is stood up by the woven door during the day. The kitchen houses are marked by the number 4, and since there are only two women living here, there are only two kitchens. They are like large rice granaries into which an entrance has been broken in the front. Number 7 is a chicken house. These little houses for the fowl also resemble small granaries. Number 8 is a flat straw roof

One of the many dwellings on the plan. This type of house, traditional among the Sonhrai, is now gradually being replaced, even on the islands, by rectangular mud houses.

supported by four posts. Beneath it lie a number of mats. This is the shaded resting place, and guests and friends are received here. Actually, there is always a place for receiving guests. The pen for the domestic animals is number 3. There is a small cow, a calf, two sheep, and about half a dozen chickens. That is rather modest, but the people living here are very young. Number 9 indicates trees that for the time being are still too small to provide much shade.

On the south side of the small plot there is a wall about chest high, whose counterpart on the north side is deteriorating. Toward the north, that is toward the top of the page, it is barely fifteen paces to the river's edge, where there is a small pirogue that Almou Doulai or his brother use to go to the fields.

There too, right near the water, a small garden has been planted with tobacco and carrots. To help water it, a calabash is hung in a net, and water is sloshed from the river over the garden beds with an adept swing of the net.

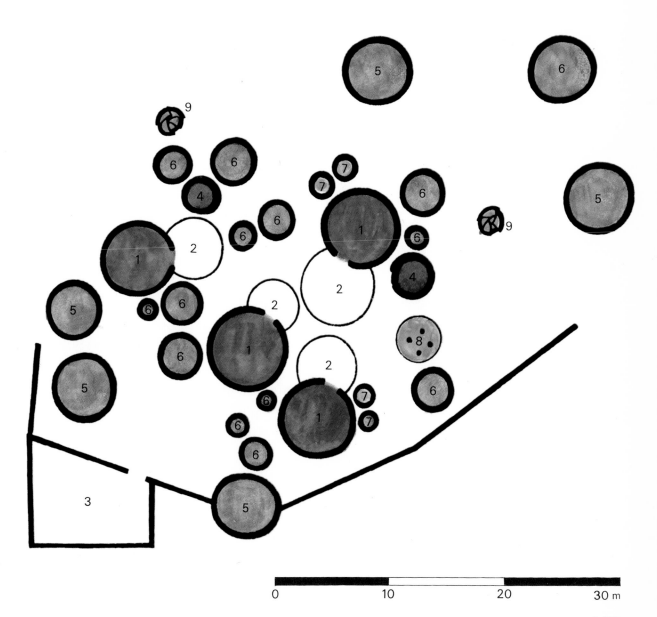

0   10   20   30 m

A Picture-Book of Storehouses

The fruits of the fields are kept in storehouses: millet, corn, beans, rice, and peanuts. In countries with dry seasons that last many months, and during which no planting can be done, these supplies are essential. Seed too, must be preserved and kept secure until it is needed. Storehouses are also fundamental to their owners' prestige. If a man has many large storehouses or granaries, then he must be a rich, and correspondingly influential man. From the outside of course, it is impossible to tell if they are all filled up. The old familiary story! There's no way of telling by looking at it whether or not a fancy car is paid for, either.

It is a pleasure for me to show my readers the variety of storehouses on these few pages. These pictures prove how imaginative the villagers are, and document their creativity. All storehouses stand on stone, or a foundation of posts. A base of wood grating is usually laid down on top of this, in order to guarantee the ventilation necessary to protect the grain from mildew. Usually the storehouses are within the confines of the compound. This can be seen clearly on the plans on pages 139 and 163. Sometimes clusters of granaries are found outside a village. Among the Kirdi in Cameroon, they are hidden away within the houses, and the Somba in northern Dahomey build them at the edges of their roof terraces (color photograph, page 9).

It should be noted that a number of the granaries depicted are still roofless. Roofs are put on only after the granaries are completely full of millet, or with the threat of the very first rains, at the latest. Many ingenious granaries are made using the techniques of ceramics. The walls are sometimes astonishingly thin. In the case of the gigantic pot on page 167, it is hard to believe that it doesn't crack in the dry heat, that it can withstand the pressure of its contents without bursting. Now, there is no longer anyone who dares build such a high granary.

Large corn granary in southern Dahomey. The wind passes through it easily, and the corn is dry before it is brought under the roofs of the houses before the great rains.

Oasis of Fachi in the Tenere desert (Niger). As in earlier times of unrest, the millet granaries of individual families are located within the secure walls of the old castle.

A masterpiece of clay construction: an enormous millet granary, photographed on the Niger, between Gao and Niamey.

◄
A peasant painstakingly storing sheaves of Italian millet.
Photograph: B.G.

►
Upper left: Bobo Oulé, Upper Volta.
Upper right: Musgum, Cameroon.
Center left: Doayo, Cameroon.
Center right: Sonhrai, Niger.
Bottom left: Taneka, Dahomey.
Bottom right: Gurunsi, Upper Volta.

The storehouse was filled too full; the side door did not hold, and is now in need of repair (Bobo Fing). Photographs: B.G.

Protective design on a granary in the vicinity of Nouna, Upper Volta.

172

Resting Places

In any settlement or village, one is almost certain to meet a couple of old gentlemen in front of the compounds, or in some centrally located square, under a shade tree, taking their rest, chatting, perhaps occupying themselves with some small handicraft, or "just plain there." They accept greetings readily, eagerly lift their bright, embroidered caps, but it is up to us, the passers-by, to extend the first greetings. They move closer together, and suggest we take a seat.

Everyone has more time than we do. The old leave the work to the young earlier than we do, and let the poor beleaguered women do much of it. They live quietly, making things comfortable for themselves, and for that reason there are resting places everywhere. They are an important and necessary institution, and as much a part of living as the hearth; both promote well-being. Sometimes, special houses are also put up for the men.

The toguna, or gathering-place of the Dogon men (see following page), is an example. There may be an important meeting now and then, when a serious decision is made, but on most days the men just sit there like anywhere else, under a shade tree. These spots are always positioned so that people going by can be seen or met, and where there is something to watch that can be discussed afterwards. They are never off somewhere in pitiful isolation, as are the people in our institutions for the aged.

An old-folks home? A rural African finds it incomprehensible that in our splendid countries the old people have no place in their children's homes. He cannot believe such horrendous barbarism. Is it really conceivable, he asks, that people can send those who gave them life, who will surely be of assistance as intercessors with the ancestors, away from their children and families, away from where they lived their lives, off to a strange house to be among strangers?

Resting place under a shade tree in the square of a small Bariba village in northern Dahomey.

175

◄

Men's house in a Dogon village. The curious roof is made of dense layers of straw, laid criss-cross.

►

It is good to rest under a shady roof in front of the compound, at the spot affording the best view. The ceramic collar surmounting the stone is the abode of the soul of an uncle who died childless (Matakam, Cameroon).

Imposing façade of a town house in Djenne on the upper Niger (Mali). The windows betray Moorish influence.

Houses in Town

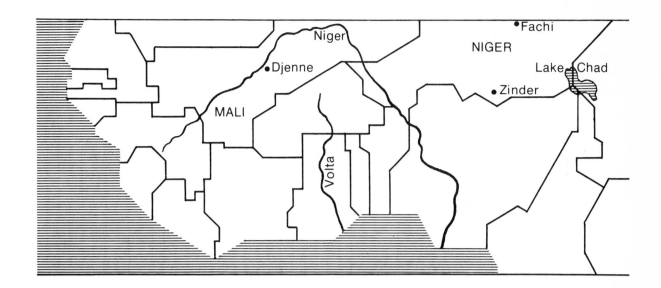

Rows of rectangular terraced houses, narrow lanes between the rows, are typical of Sudan towns. These mud brick houses are plastered with an especially carefully prepared mixture. Their ceilings are made of split palm or sticks of some sort of wood (depending on the region and available material), and supported by forked posts. The roofs have parapets, and the resulting terraces are used for sleeping during the hottest seasons.

No city has ever fascinated me as much as Djenne on the Niger (Mali). Like the neighboring cities of San, Mopti, and even Timbuktu, Djenne was once an important trade center during the period when there was active commerce with Mauretania and Morocco to the north. Traces of that heyday can still be seen today. Many of the houses in Djenne represent a particularly pure form of the so-called Sudan style, and the façades of the houses at the left, or those seen in the view into an alley (page 182), are monumental in their own way. They represent a high point of this clay building technique that is now presented only by mosques.

Characteristic of these elegant two- and three-story town dwellings is the magnificent articulation of their façades. The wooden bearing columns and supporting beams are "built in," and dressed with plaster, but the structure remains visible, and these same verticals function as decorative elements. The clay cones that top off the façades simply underline their monumentality, and the verticals have the effect of making the houses look higher than they really are.

Djenne is situated on an island in the tangled network of branches of the Niger. During the dry season, the town can be reached by a narrow dam, but at high water it is accessible only by water. Even today, it presents the aspect of a well-fortified medieval city with high walls. In the center of the town is the gigantic marketplace, at the edge of which stands the

►►
Even today, Djenne with its high walls presents the aspect of a fortified medieval city.

179

famous mosque of Djenne. Passing from this main square through the alleys extending out to all sides, one discovered much to one's delight that there are still numerous well-maintained middle-class houses to be found. The Moorish influence is unmistakable, and these richly ornamented windows are clearly not derived from black Africa. Note the water-spouts in the picture at the left, red-fired, with clay pipes jutting far out: they drain water off the terraces during the rainy season.

The house shown below is not in Djenne, but in Bandiagara not far away. A wealthy man has built himself this beautiful, three-story house fit for "gentlefolk." Its structural elements are clearly visible, and here the horizontals as well as the verticals have been emphasized. The part of the house shown in the photograph gives some idea of the grand harmony of this façade, though unfortunately the relief patterns on the vertical supporting walls are somewhat eroded.

◄
The stern façades and verticals of the pilasters lend these houses in Djenne the illusion of impressive size.

►
Upper-class house of a Moorish immigrant tradesman in Bandiagara, Mali. The visible structural elements have the effect of planned decoration.

This house belongs to Katche, a dye-master in Zinder, a town in the Niger Republic. Toward the street (see plan below) is an almost unornamented façade with a single entrance. From the street it would be hard to tell if it were the wall of a house, or simply a high wall that, together with façades, closes off the "concession." This is the house of a well-to-do dyer. He lives here with his wife and five married sons who are also members of the dyers' guild. Number 1 is a reception room with reclining chairs. The old gentleman and his wife live in the finest house (2), which can be reached in this labyrinth only by passing through another reception room (13). The sons and their families and many children live in houses 3 (son Ali), 4 (son Sanda), and 5 (son Abdu). The two other sons, Isi and Laudi, live in front toward the street in houses 6 and 7. Three round, covered kitchens are marked by the number 8. Number 10 houses all sorts of supplies, sacks of millet, peanuts, sugar, and the like. Number 9 is a rather large tower granary. Number 11 houses countless pigeons, especially prized when roasted. At the lower right (12) is a covered stall for animals. During the day sheep and goats meander around in the various courtyards. A beautiful riding horse is tied up somewhere in the front courtyard. Hidden, at the upper left, is a pit that serves as the WC. The entire "concession," bounded on three sides by others, is about 25 by 30 meters (82 by 98 feet).

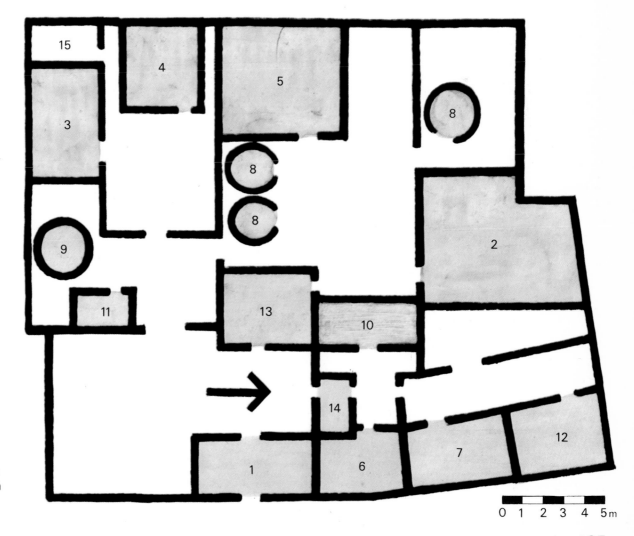

Plan of a Hausa compound in Zinder, Niger. The photograph corresponds to a view through house 14, to the right.

0 1 2 3 4 5m

The remote oasis town of Fachi in the Tenere desert, Niger, is built of salt-mud bricks that offer practically no resistance to rain. The risks this material imposes are accepted since it doesn't rain every year in the Tenere.

By way of contrast to wealthy Djenne, the two pictures on the preceding pages and the color picture at the right show the rather impoverished cityscapes of the town of Fachi, a lost oasis in the Tenere desert (Niger Republic). Fachi, and the neighboring oasis town of Bilma, have the same style of building, and are both inhabited by Kanuri. The towns are not easily reached, more than 600 kilometers (375 miles) from Agades through the Tenere, a desert almost devoid of vegetation – a sea of nothingness – over a badly marked and often almost impossible road.

Both oases, Bilma as well as Fachi, have been known for centuries for their important salt-works, and even today Tuareg caravans still move through the Tenere to trade millet from the south for dates and, above all, for salt. In recent years too, during the winter months, twenty-five thousand camels still move through Fachi to Bilma. Without their salt, both oases would probably have died out long ago. Never in my travels have I felt as lost as I felt there. There are the hot salt-works and the Kanuri who operate them. There are a few miserable gardens, groves of date palms, and, huddled together and lost in the sand, the plain little houses of these oasis towns. The defensive walls of earlier times have fallen into ruin, the big castles are now merely decorative. But for centuries the inhabitants had to protect themselves against plundering hordes of Tubbu from the Tibesti.

View of poor, isolated Fachi, an oasis town inhabited by the Kanuri. Without the profits from the salt-works, this inhospitable place would have been abandoned long ago.

Between Fachi and Bilma lie about 170 kilometers (105 miles) of desert, but both towns are built in the same style and of the same materials. Their flat-roofed houses are jammed close together. Split date-palm trunks are built into the roof terraces. The walls are made of salt-mud bricks manufactured in the salt-works. There are hardly any stones in the vicinity, and no clay, so that material at hand is used for building, though it has the disadvantage of "melting" in the rain. In a strong rain, the salt dissolves and the bricks disintegrate. A brick we placed in a bucket of water fell apart in the space of half an hour. Salt-mud bricks can be used for building only in places where it hardly ever rains, and the Tenere desert, between the Aïr Mountains and the Tibesti Range, is one of the driest regions of the southern Sahara. In Bilma we met school-children who had never, to their knowledge, seen rain. Bilma sometimes has only a few millimeters of precipitation over the course of several years. There are even prayers to protect houses against the rain. In spite of this, there is never a shortage of water in either oasis. It rises up in artesian wells, coming up from unknown faraway sources.

The façades of the houses are plain. In old buildings, the coarse wall surfaces show the traces of rain. Their interiors are like dark caves. Because of sandstorms, doors are small and there are no windows, but the floors are always sprinkled with clean sand, which is never in short supply here, and many families have wonderful thick rugs, brought from Fezzan by the caravans.

▶▶
The splendid palace of the Sultan of Agades.

Ornamenting Façades with Reliefs

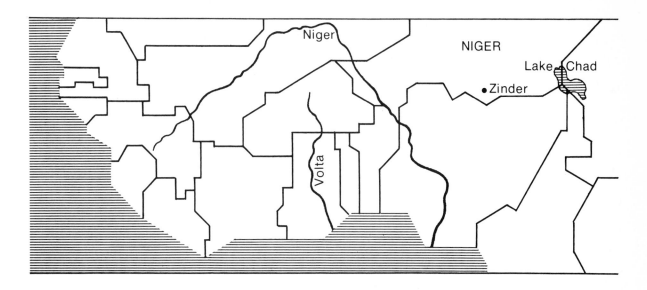

The pictures in this chapter and the next showing the façade decoration of middle-class houses come, for the most part, from the town of Zinder in the Niger Republic. From 1900 to 1930 it was the capital, but was then supplanted by Niamey. Today, Zinder, with its 40,000 inhabitants, is the most important place in Damagaram and all of eastern Niger. Its quarters are inhabited by a mixture of peoples: Beriberi, Libyans, Moors, and Tubbu. There is also a group of settled Tuaregs, but by far the greatest number of Hausa. More than any of the other well-to-do citizens, they love to decorate the street façades of their houses with traditional clay motifs, or sgraffiti. Evidence of similar façade ornament is to be found all over Hausa territory, that is principally in northern Nigeria. A bit outside the modern, lively city, lies the old quarter of Birni. It is, in a manner of speaking, the old city of Zinder, with narrow winding alleyways, and it was once surrounded by high walls. Even today, the Sultan lives in quiet Birni, and there, the old story still has it, a virgin was bricked up near what are now the meager remains of the city wall, as a sacrifice to ensure protection of the city.

Monsieur Delisse, a teacher active in Zinder, has taken the trouble to make up a catalog of all the houses in Zinder that, in his opinion, are especially interesting, and to put them on a city plan. In the process, he found more than six hundred buildings. That is noteworthy, and it seems that now, in certain streets, the tradition-conscious tradesmen, many of whom bear the honorable title of Mallum, bet with one another about who has the most beautiful façade. A richly ornamented façade does wonders for the image, proves that rich people live behind it, and thus is part of being fashionable. It is comforting to notice that this decoration is found not only on old, half-ruined houses, but on new ones as well.

Interlacing arabesques on a house in Zinder, Niger.

The Hausa are basically a conservative people. They wear their old

193

costumes and their beautifully embroidered caps; the old is preserved with pride. Under the influence of Monsieur Senghor, President of Senegal, there is a movement afoot in many parts of West Africa, not just Hausa territories, to make people aware of the value of the old African culture again. The large exhibitions in Dakar and the demonstrations known as "Negritude," are reasserting the old traditions, handiwork, and art that languished so long under strong European influence while mass-produced European articles were extolled over anything native. That kind of nationalism is to be warmly welcomed. Once, at a national celebration in Niamey, the capital of the Niger Republic, I noticed that those in national costume – the richly embroidered boubou – were allowed to sit in the front rows of the reviewing stands to watch the parade, while those dressed in the European style had to find places behind them. It is to this movement then, that we owe the preservation of

Houses in Zinder. The figures at the left are so precise and complete that they seem to have been copied exactly from a pattern. This robs them of their carefree freshness.

the ornamentation of the façades. In Zinder I even had the impression that the custom was experiencing a sort of renaissance.

The pictures here and on the next four pages show façades with half-relief. The areas next to and directly above the house door are particularly richly decorated, as are the window-frames. The ornaments are geometric, often interlaced arabesques of the sort that are classic in the Muslim world.

I wanted very much to discover how these decorations were applied to the walls, but Monsieur Delisse did not know. He was not interested in the craft end of it, but only in the style. European friends told me that it was the work of specialists who sometimes came from Kano after the rains. As is so often the case, I was helped out by chance. In the Zengou quarter I fell to talking with a house-owner whose decorations over his doorway were crumbling. I offered to pay for the repair if he would

Through page 199, motifs from
Zinder. The figures are all
different, but betray the same
style.

198

A center line is drawn in lightly at first, then firmly. Then the mason cuts the edges of the applied rolls of clay.

Sgraffiti

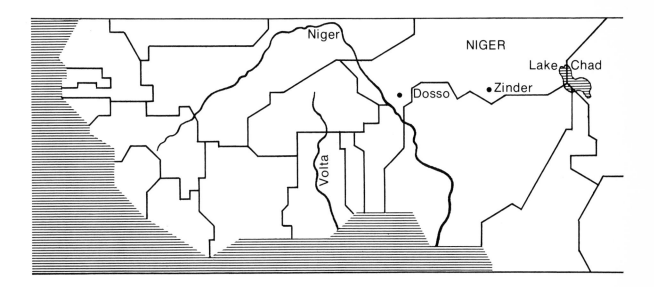

The endpapers of this book show what sort of sgraffiti are going to be described here. It is a very simple method of wall decoration, but the title of this chapter may be misleading, because in real sgraffito work, layers of different colored plaster are laid on top of each other, and patterns are made by scratching away the upper layers. Here in Zinder, ornaments or figures were scratched into a smooth wall while it was still damp, and the patterns resulted from merely roughing up some of the interstices. The smooth parts were painted in chalk white or with color later.

Much to my delight, I found entire house façades that were still decorated in this fashion, particularly in Birni, the old quarter of Zinder. What I maintained earlier about relief decoration is also true of this not entirely bona fide form of sgraffiti: they are to be found on completely new houses, and I had the impression that there was a sort of "landmark preservation" movement under way. True, I didn't like all the motifs. Sometimes attempts had been made to execute them particularly well; they were geometrically perfect. Evidently they had first been drawn up on a plan and then copied precisely on the wall. In these instances, the spontaneity had been lost; the happy ease is gone, and these walls have no soul. Once again the Europeans had steered me wrong; they had told me that no one in Zinder understood this art any more, and that the master masons from Kano had already departed. I didn't set much store by the story, and went on the lookout for a wall to beautify, and a mason for the job.

In the Birni section of Zinder we found a prettily decorated house with sgraffito work, but one of its walls, about 3½ by 3 meters (12 by 10 feet), showed only the weathered surface of the rust-brown mud plaster. Since the owner of the house was taking his ease, legs crossed, on a clay bench out in front of his house, it wasn't difficult to persuade him

The decoration results from the alteration of rough and smooth surfaces.

205

it would do things for his image if that wall looked a bit prettier. So at the right, you see the seated Sallissou with his cat. Once again, the necessary mason was found without any difficulty. Boys were sent out to find him, and within the half-hour I was explaining my intentions to him. I showed him photos from earlier trips, and explained that I absolutely had to show my friends how the beautiful façades in Zinder came into being. I extolled Zinder's artistically-minded citizens, and flattered them, and since we were no longer alone, all the gathering of onlookers who had collected nodded in agreement. The mason pocketed an advance and promised to prepare everything. On the appointed day we went back, rather excited, to see if everything would work out.

And how! Folding chairs had been set up in front of the wall for our comfort. The mason, Abdullai, was waiting with his assistants. There was a pile of sand, a sack of cement beside it, and only the container for water was still empty. Two buckets were purchased from the next water-carrier that went by, with the expectation that I would pay. At eight-thirty, the work began. The weathered wall was first plastered smooth with a thin wash of cement. Then the mason divided the damp wall into a brick pattern with a strip of wood about a meter and a half (5 feet) long, incising the lines with a piece of metal. The wooden strip did not serve as a measuring stick at all. The cross lines were hardly parallel, and the distances between them were irregular. For the time being, everything proceeded in a slow, friendly, and relaxed fashion. Monsieur Sallissou, the house-owner, brought out some roasted nuts, and watched for a while. There was already an audience, and everyone who went by stopped, let himself be filled in, and then agreed that my plan was excellent. On the other hand, they also thought I was a little crazy, since, as they had heard, I was going to pay for something that wouldn't even belong to me.

The division of the surface area and the drawing of the figures was the concern of the mason alone. His assistants were allowed to scratch out the interstices, and to roughen them. The sun rose higher; it got hotter. The cement began to dry, and hardened light areas were already appearing. Now the wall was sprinkled with water, and they began to hurry. And so, pretty soon, the mason, both his assistants, my companion, the house-owner's son, and a few others as well were all scratching away. The mason and I watched to see that nothing went in the wrong places, and shortly after noon the work was finished.

The next day, the painter painted the smooth places white. Everyone examined the work, I wrote a "certificat" for the workers, saying that Ali Haruna, "peintre de 3ᵉ catégorie," and Abdullai, mason in Birni, had restored a wall to my satisfaction. The owner of the house was also satisfied, and was present when I paid the mason his wages, less the advance. I am certain he demanded twice as much as he would have

The fact that Monsieur Sallissou's dress goes so well with the house is coincidental, but the picture does show how much good taste is at his disposal (Zinder, Birni quarter).

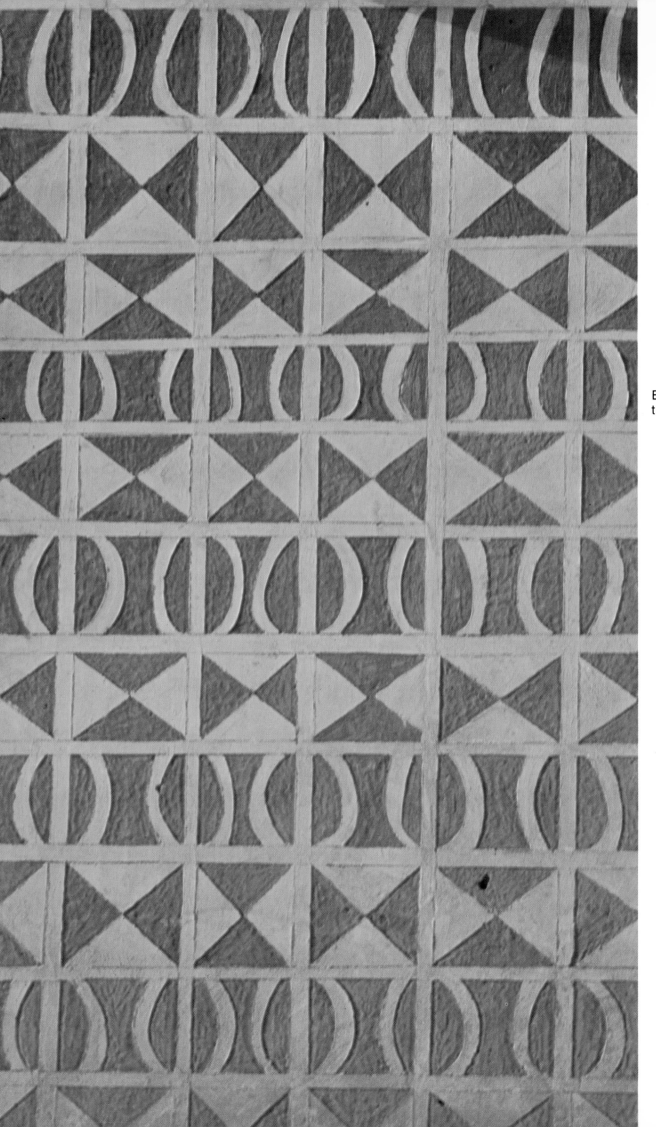

Examples of wall decoration in the Birni quarter of Zinder.

from a local resident, but however that may be, I thought it was cheap. Then I got a surprise. The house-owner, whom I had just presented with a new façade, demanded a fee for allowing me to photograph his house. At that point, I delivered one of my best speeches about gratitude and ingratitude in this world, and everyone who was listening nodded, and the pious Monsieur Sallissou nodded too, and laughed, and replied that it was just as I had said. He forgot completely how shameless he had been but five minutes before. I had reason to be very pleased with my speech, as he disappeared and soon returned with a little present for me. Then he thanked me politely and ceremoniously for his new wall. The cheerfully colored walls on the next pages are from Dosso, a town far to the west on the road to Niamey. It is the façade of a chief's palace. Its exterior gives little indication that there is an audience hall with splendid vaulting within.

◄
The master has drawn the design. The apprentice is only allowed to roughen the surfaces with his little piece of metal.

▶
The following day the painter appears and paints the smooth surfaces a bright color.

210

This decoration with incised figures on the small palace of a chieftain in Dosso (Niger) is of recent date. I found similar flower motifs in Agades.

These pictures are next to each other on a house wall in Maroua, Cameroon.

Wall Paintings

Interior and exterior walls with plastered surfaces are often painted. Examples of this can be found in the chapter on the Gurunsi compound. The façade is painted partly white (page 132) and the walls of the room are glazed dark red with juice from the néré tree (page 144).

Aside from this simple coloration, there are all sorts of other architectural decoration. We have already talked about reliefs and sgraffiti. Mosaics of inlaid stones and cowrie snails, often mistakenly called cowrie shells, are also common. The most common kind of decoration is painted – in three important colors – red, black, and white predominating. The rectangle and the triangle recur most frequently, and spirals or circles are rare. Examples of such ornament can be found in the lake-dwelling house (page 44), and there is also an especially beautiful example in the interior of the house of the great soothsayer (page 116). In the same house I also photographed representations of snakes and crocodiles, and of totemic animals that play a part in religious beliefs. Doorways and the entrances of houses are favored places for decorative painting. It is difficult to pin down the reasons for this. It is regarded as ornament, and the comment one fellow made about the decorations was "Ça fait riche." But surely at one time they were intended to serve a protective function. Thus, even today, these paintings are most commonly found in cult houses or at sacrificial sites.

The color is often applied while the plaster is still wet. Apparently the color sets better this way. Black earth from a swamp or charcoal yields a serviceable black. Burned shells from the river or kaolin supplies white. Certain plant juices or soil containing ochre is used for red. Plant juices are also used as binding media. They are applied with the flat of the hand, with fingers, or with brushes made of chewed woody stalks or bunches of grass.

I must apologize for the fact that the text on serious wall-painting just

The bilingual warning "God sees you, thief" on a house in western Cameroon is ungrammatical but clear.

This giraffe on a house near Kribi (south Cameroon), is about 1½ meters (5 feet) high in the original.

does not want to go with the pictures. It really doesn't, and the photographs here have little or nothing to do with traditional West African architectural decoration. They are all new, but I found this naïve folk art so delightful that I thought it would be a pity to leave these few examples out.

Adages or events familiar to everyone are depicted, and to make sure that everyone will understand, an explanation is added. This is the case with the two color pictures with the hyena and the monkey, or the hunter and the antelope (page 214). Both are by the same painter. Evidently he met with success, because I found both motifs recurring with only slight variations on a number of houses in the town of Maroua (north Cameroon).

Inscriptions on houses are also amusing, and they are a great source of cheer. One (page 216) warns thieves. Another I copied from a doorway in Dahomey reads, "I Ahmed live here. When I sneeze, I sneeze hard. If you don't like it, look the other way." On the wall of a small house was written, "This house belongs to me. It is still small, but the bird builds his nest bit by bit."

The big giraffe on page 217 was in the company of a lion and a rhinoceros on a house in a jungle zone on the Atlantic, where these animals surely never existed.

Wall paintings on a house in Porto Novo, the capital of Dahomey. Neither Africans nor an institute for African languages were able to translate the texts for me later.

Ingenious Vaulting

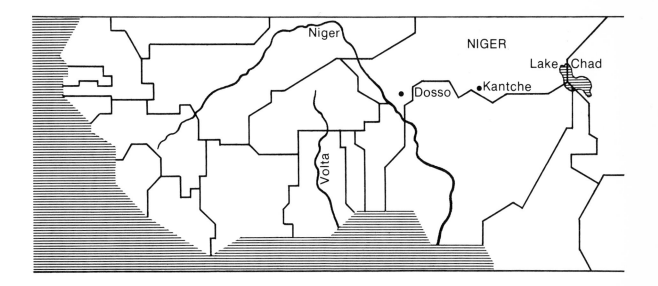

The pictures on the next few pages prove that it is entirely possible to build vaults without cut stone or modern reinforced concrete. The pictures are of sultans' palaces and mosques. In Kantche, a place about 75 kilometers (45 miles) west of Zinder, in a quiet, tree-lined square just off the large marketplace, there is a small sultan's palace beside a mosque that is also interesting. I had a letter of recommendation to the owner of the small palace in my pocket, but unfortunately Monsieur Amadu Isaka, Head of the Canton, and also, as Sultan, the traditional regent, was in Niamey. Naturally I was disappointed, but the friendliness of everyone, including the sultan's family, was very helpful. A steward, the Mallum Ladu Mado, was fetched, and he took us through the house and let me photograph unhampered. The dignified fellow in the flowing gown and an egg-yolk-yellow peaked cap is just coming down the stairs into the reception room in the picture at the left. It is an amazing staircase. The lines and arches intersect in the vaulting, and the penetrations at all the angles create unexpected perspective effects. The audience chamber has a platform for the throne with a very beautiful ceiling above it. Decorated lamp niches are everywhere. The audience chamber of a chief in Dosso was just as impressive with its splendid ceiling vaulting (see following two pages). The many single arches that begin at the floor come together on the ceiling at a central point which is highlighted by a bright enamel bowl. In the mosque of Kantche (page 225) the principle is reversed, and the structure of the baobab tree is imitated. Branches stretch in separate directions from the thick, short trunk to support the roof. The construction principle is simple: flexible branches, slender tree trunks, bundles of faggots are tied together. They make up the skeleton of the vaulting, that is then covered with well-prepared clay. This is a "reinforced concrete" made of wood and clay – a marvelous adaptation to the circumstances.

Entry and stairway in the Sultan's palace at Kantche, about 70 kilometers (45 miles) west of Zinder, Niger.

221

The audience hall in the palace of a chieftain at Dosso (Niger). The columns unite in a very impressive vaulted ceiling, constructed of wood and mud only.

223

The columns narrow at the top and join at a single point marked by a colored enamel bowl.

The baobab tree is imitated here: a short, thick trunk with separating branches to bear the ceiling (Dosso, Niger).

Rows of columns create aisles in mosque interiors. Right: Kantche, Niger. Left: Dosso, Niger.

Mosques, High Points of Sudanese Architecture

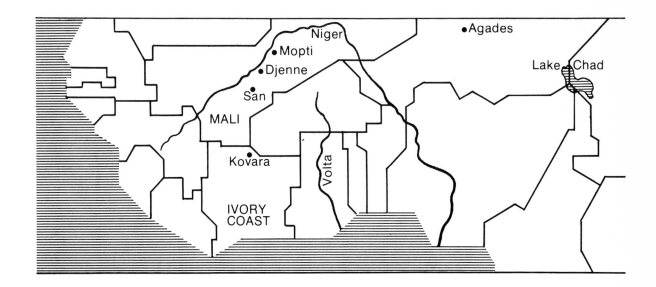

Islam began its swift triumphal march through West Africa in the eleventh century. Because of the Sahara trade, cities and market towns had been in active contact with Arabs and Berbers from the north almost two centuries earlier, and these traders brought with them not only goods, but, with Islam, new ideas as well.

Later "holy wars" that in fact resembled rapacious raids far more than attempts at conversion brought reverses, but in about the thirteenth century many princes converted to Islam, and it came to be regarded as the religion of progressives. The new ideas that it brought with it also changed trading practices. In any case, in all the lands south of the Sahara, Islam spread, and the believers now gather for prayer in an area that extends as far as the natural barrier of the great jungles.

The new faith adapted itself considerably to pre-existing beliefs, and it can hardly be compared with the strict orthodox fundamentals of Arabian Mohammedans. Monteil wrote that Africans "practice Islam without betraying animism." We should clarify here that animism is a religion in which nature is populated with a multitude of spirits who exercise influences on the fates of men. Islam demanded fewer changes in previous customs than Christianity. Polygamy was not forbidden, and no Muslim preacher has ever come out against slavery. The African woman is not veiled, and she is much freer and more self-sufficient than her Arab sister to the north.

Islam is still spreading further to the south. During the colonial period, many professed it for political reasons, as a demonstration of opposition to the Christianity of the colonials. And now there are mosques in all villages and towns, artistic and impressive structures or simple mud huts. In the Koran schools, the children reel off the suras they have learned by rote but do not understand.

Mosques are oriented toward the east, their long axes running

On the roof of a mosque in Nouna, Upper Volta. The muezzin is in contact with the imam, standing in the mihrab below, leading prayer by means of a speaking tube. Photograph: B.G.

north–south. The house of prayer for believers is always divided into a number of aisles by wooden posts or mighty columns that support the ceiling. As impressive as the interiors of large Sudanese mosques are in their simplicity, they cannot compare with the magnificent mosques of the Orient. Mud cannot replace marble, and mats of woven straw are more modest in their effect than bright, thick carpets.

In southern, wooded savannah regions there is considerably more rain than near the bend of the Niger, for example, or in Agades. There, styles have adapted to this fact. Mosques in this area have innumerable pointed and rounded pinnacles. They resemble the points of cones, or eggs. Water runs off them easily and clearly, builders are aware that these forms offer increased resistance to rain.

The two photographs on pages 232 and 233 invite comparison. There is a conspicuous similarity between the termite mound and the village

◀ In the prayer court of the mosque at Meana, a village on the right bank of the Niger between Gao and Niamey.

▶ In the very plain village mosque of Barani, near Nouna, Upper Volta. Photograph: B.G.

Mosque in Bouna, Ivory Coast, and a termite mound. The astounding similarity is not coincidental.

The beautiful little mosque of Boundiali, west of Korhogo in a Senufo region, Ivory Coast. Many of the countless turrets are topped off with ostrich eggs.

An extremely weathered mosque in Dani, a Bobo Oulé village on the Upper Volta-Mali border.

◄
Turrets on a Bobo Fing mosque, Upper Volta, and, below, two sacrificial altars in front of a nearby compound. Since these altars are presumably older than the mosques in Africa, we can assume that Islam absorbed the old forms. Photographs: B.G.

►
The singular, very old mosque at Kouara, north of Ferkesedougou, Ivory Coast. Here, too, are the familiar cone-shapes.

►►
Probably the most beautiful mosque in the western Sudan: the monumental structure with its three minarets dominates the great market square of Djenne, Mali.

mosque, and I think that coincidence can be counted out. There is no mistaking that the termite mound was the model for this style of building. I can support this supposition with further examples.

One of the oldest and most unusual mosques in black Africa is in Kouara, not far from Ferkesedougou in the northern Ivory Coast (page 237). The strict verticals of northern mosques are absent here. The structure consists of many smooth conical points lined up next to each other. They are conspicuously similar to sacrificial altars like those I photographed in numerous Bobo villages in Upper Volta. The similarity between these turrets of a village mosque in Bobo country (page 236) that have nothing to do with the usual minarets, and the two altars in the picture below, in front of the house of a non-believing peasant, is so great that here too we can draw a connection. Islam adapted itself, and even absorbed external elements of its new environment, such as the heathen altar form, into the style of its mosques.

The most beautiful mosques I ever saw – the acme of the clay architecture that developed in Sudan lands – were the famous, monumental mosques of San, Djenne, and Mopti in the Niger Republic, so often reproduced. The mosques represent centers of activity in these cities. All three can stand as representative examples of many other mosques in the upper Niger region between Gao and Senegal.

They are the usual dry-brick structures, using fresh clay as mortar. The plaster is prepared with a care not expended as a rule in building ordinary houses. It is allowed to "ripen," and kneaded again and again, and by the admixture of oil or karité butter, the façades are waterproofed for several years.

Mosques are more carefully maintained than ordinary houses. Houses are not built to last forever, and they are changed often, but mosques last beyond one man's life-span, and often stand in the same spot for centuries. They are overhauled every year. This undertaking, in which large segments of the population participate, always takes place on a particular day, and has a festive character. Unfortunately, we missed the work festival at Djenne by a matter of days.

The most conspicuous elements are the strong verticals of the façades. Countless buttressing beams create a rib effect, and because of this articulation, reference is sometimes made to Sudan Gothic. As a rule, three minaret towers jut out above the front façade. The ceiling of the mosque is supported by many columns, often more than a meter (yard) thick at their base. Wooden trunks are walled up into squares or rounds. In the mosque at Djenne they end in pointed arches, and this enormous room with its aisles once again calls the Gothic to mind.

The interior is illuminated by only a few windows. Rows of bottomless kanari, or clay jars, are built into the great flat roof of the mosque. These serve for ventilation, and on rainy days covers are put over them. The small turrets that result from letting the ribs and support columns protrude over the roof are often topped off with ostrich eggs. They are at once decorative and indicative of Islam's veneration of the ostrich. Another conspicuous element in many mosques is the pieces of wood jutting out of the façades. Usually they protrude in bunches (see page 244). They are so solid that during the annual renovations no scaffolding is required. It is for this reason too, that they are so symmetrically placed, and all sawed off to the same length. Just to give my reader a more precise idea of dimensions, I would like to say that the mosque at San is 50 meters (164 feet) long, 30 meters (98 feet) wide, and 8 meters (26 feet) high to the ceiling.

A minaret of black Africa that Heinrich Barth has made a classic is shown in the photograph on page 246. In 1850, this German scientist was the first visitor to Agades, a city far to the northeast of the Niger

Republic. At one time, Agades was as important a city as Timbuktu, which has always exercised a greater influence on the European imagination. In the sixteenth century Agades had seventy thousand inhabitants, while its population now is set at less than ten percent of that figure. But its famous minaret became a landmark. The present form of the mosque goes back to the fifteenth century, though the tower was considerably restored in the nineteenth century.

This structure, almost 30 meters (98 feet) high, also has protruding wooden sticks, and there are almost invariably a few ravens sitting on them. The tower is more impressive still because the mosque is very plain and low. And the visitor who takes the trouble to make the laborious climb up the extremely narrow stairs to the first platform is rewarded by a magnificent view of Agades, and beyond to the distant Aïr Mountains.

Left: The mosque of Mopti that is now unfortunately hemmed in by modern buildings. Right: The mosque at San. Photograph: B.G. The mosques at San, Djenne, and Mopti, all in the same area in Mali, represent the same style.

◄
Once again, the mosque at Djenne. The emphasis on verticals by means of the three towers and the countless pilasters topped with turrets make references to "Sudanese gothic" tempting.

►
The interior of the mosque at Djenne. Here too the pointed arches are reminiscent of gothic. Photograph: B.G.

About This Book

The reader has surely noticed that the many houses and dwellings shown in this book are inhabited. They are not beautifully tidied up, prettily furnished model rooms that can be seen in many museums, and that are particularly well known in Scandinavia. Real people animate these compounds, prove that they are inhabited, and that we are showing the present day.

Attempts are now being made to change building methods, to make life easier for the inhabitants without altering the functional and very beautiful architecture. Stairs take the place of a stepped beam. The difficult loophole entrances are replaced by openings sized to the human body. Bedsteads fit through them, and there is no need to lay sleeping mats on a bare dirt floor any more. Gradually, even windows are gaining acceptance. Certainly, these are welcome improvements. "New building methods are taken up here and there with a matter-of-factness that would make a professional architect go pale with envy," writes one architect in a German trade journal. Various West African nations have official programs aimed at introducing innovations without endangering the old vernacular architecture too greatly. This is a difficult, and very welcome, undertaking. Study groups are at work. Dedicated European experts come as development consultants, learn the traditional forms, and make recommendations on how the existing materials and feasible building techniques can be used to build more durably. Means are sought to make clay mortar water resistant. Admixtures to make it more solid are tested. Success would be to everyone's advantage, and success seems to be within the realm of the possible.

But the reverse of all this can also be reported. Some governments forbid old building forms. They view them as a proof of backwardness, and, thus, as unworthy of a modern state. Anonymous, vernacular architecture, of which my readers now have some understanding, is

Tabaski festival in Agades. Festively clad women in front of the city's landmark, the minaret of the old mosque, almost 30 meters (98 feet) high.

247

being destroyed out of some misbegotten notion of progress. All too often, the result is as could be expected, dreary little brick houses with hot tin roofs, arranged in incomparably dismal rows, jammed together much too closely at the outskirts of cities.

Even while I was working on my book on West African crafts, plans had been afoot for a number of years to follow it with a sequel on traditional architecture. My photographic files yielded up all sorts of valuable material, but I still found it necessary to make four extended trips for the sole purpose of documenting this book. As usual, there were difficulties with the selection, and I am sure I will be angry later at having chosen the "wrong" photographs from the wealth of material. Experts will discover many gaps, or discover that a building style that is a particular favorite of theirs is missing. But unfortunately, it is impossible to put everything one would like to include into a book that does not even set out to be scholarly. I do hope, however, that my book will bring my readers closer to the African once again. I think respect is due the African, because with limited means, he builds sensibly, functionally, and above all, beautifully.

A door decorated with burned ornament, in Kwa, a Bobo Fing village, Upper Volta.

This book was produced without contributions from anyone. I bore the costs of the expeditions and the original publishing myself. I also threw myself into the exciting and enjoyable adventure of being not only the author, but also the publisher. And since it is still valid, I would like to reiterate the last sentence of the book on crafts that appeared four years ago. I would like to thank every buyer whose decision to purchase this book helps me to forge new plans. The plans I had then, as my reader knows, have been realized in this book.

I would also like to thank everyone who assisted me with this book: the African authorities, who never put obstacles in my path and were most helpful when I needed their advice; all the African and European friends who shared their knowledge with me, and everyone who had a part in the wonderful cooperative effort of putting the book together. The floor plans were made during the trips by my companions Urban Loher and Bernhard Gardi, among others, and the finished drawings were produced by Hans Thöni. I would like to thank my traveling companions who were always cheerful and dependable, who took charge of the expedition's car, were always helpful, cooking soups and rice and whatever was necessary, and put up with me in general. And above all, I would like to thank my wife, who always took a greater interest than anyone else, who accompanied me in thought on my journeys, and who helps and encourages me and brings everything to a happy conclusion.

René Gardi

248

Chief Mountain, Glacier National Park, Montana. **Stan Osolinski**

6:30 a.m. The Charles Choate Farm, West Barnet, Vermont. **Richard W. Brown**

3:00 p.m. On the Maybury Farm, Northville, Michigan. **Sharon Cummings** / **Jean F. Stoick**

Anderson's Grain Elevator, Champaign, Illinois. **Brad LaPayne**

Baltimore, Maryland square dancers at Cacapon State Park, Cacapon, West Virginia. **Bob Elbert**

11:00 a.m. Christopher Hutson, age 5, in London, Ohio. **Eric Albrecht**

COUNTRY USA T.M.

Photographed by 102 of America's best photographers

Park River, North Dakota. **Curt Maas**

CONTENTS

Executive Editor: Richard Brooks, Silver Image Productions, Inc.
Design and Production: William Strode and William Butler,
Harmony House Publishers, Louisville, Kentucky 40059
(502) 228-2010 / 228-4446
Library of Congress Catalog Number: 89-92274
Hardcover International Standard Book Number: 0-9624617-0-9
Printed in USA by Fetter Printing Company, Louisville, Kentucky
Color Separations by Total Color, Louisville, Kentucky
First Edition printed Fall 1989 by Silver Image Productions, Inc.
Box 6449, Champaign, Illinois 61826 (217) 398-1200,
Copyright © 1989 by Silver Image (800) 447-4135
Photographs copyright © 1988 by individual photographers

6:30 a.m. St. Mary Lake, Glacier National Park, Montana. **Stan Osolinski**

PREFACE

We have set out to produce an unusual photographic document and book about life today in the USA countryside. We sent 102 photographers to rural America on one day — October 1, 1988. Their assignment was to look at the rural areas, small communities, farms, and people, and to reveal it all through the eye of the camera during one 24-hour period. Thousands of 4-H and FFA members were invited to do the same.

As a photographic celebration of an aspect of contemporary American life, this book gives a glimpse of things rarely captured. It unveils images of particular power and beauty, and, hopefully, increases our sense of consciousness about and appreciation for the special qualities of life in the American countryside today.

A look at one day cannot provide a complete picture or definitive statement. Yet, it can show marvelous nooks and crannies, breathtaking variety, that which is exhilarating as well as prosaic, the ordinary and the extraordinary.

We hope this book will provide the kind of rich and rewarding experience for you as it has for us.

Richard E. Brooks

Richard E. Brooks
Executive Editor

9:30 a.m.   Cresco, Iowa. **Ted Mc Donough**

INTRODUCTION

By Clancy Strock

There was a time, they say, when the air was clean and clear, and the brooks ran sparkling over the sand bars.

A time when the man at the hardware store knew you by name, and the butcher knew just how you liked your steaks cut.

A time when sons learned about sawing boards straight and bringing calves into the world and fixing balky carburetors by working alongside their dads. And mothers taught daughters how to read a blouse pattern and make turkey leftovers interesting for a whole week.

A time of band concerts in the park on Wednesday night, and if you were one of those sitting in your car, you honked your applause for the sweating 16-year-old who sang "Old Man River." And the American Legion Post had a stand where you could buy soda pop, ice cream and popcorn.

There were towns where no one bothered to lock their cars, and some couldn't recall where they'd put the key to the front door.

And towns where even grandparents turned out to cheer for the basketball games, and the PTA ran bake sales to raise money for band uniforms.

There were towns where you called the mayor Jim, and the chief of police would pass along a friendly tip that your kids were getting more rambunctious than he could tolerate for long.

It was a time when flags flew proudly on Main Street for the holidays, and church bells welcomed Sunday morning. And the pastor visited the ailing and comforted the elderly.

It was a time when you didn't need a lawyer, because a man's handshake was his bond. And the neighbors came to get in the crops if you'd suffered misfortune, or put up a new barn to replace the old one leveled by a tornado.

It was a time when your worth was measured not by what you owned or how big a house you lived in or the kind of car you drove, but simply by the sort of person you were.

Yes, there was such a time. And there still is. In Country USA.

Country USA started out to be a photographic celebration of life in the country. But in the end it is a book about optimism, courage, and love. Because that's what life in the country has been about since the day the first colonists staked out their tenuous foothold on the shores of a continent filled with unknown promise and undiscovered wonders.

And those fundamentals of survival still shine brightly in the country today.

There's a song that says if you can make it in New York, you can make it anywhere. Perhaps. But there is a strong case for changing New York to Chadron, Nebraska or Dimmit, Texas or Wing, Illinois or Genoa, Nevada or Dothan, Alabama... or any of a thousand other communities no New Yorker ever heard of. Maybe it's just a matter of how you define "making it." A chauffeured limo and lunch at Four Seasons is one thing. Feeding and clothing America is another.

In a time of doomsayers and hand-wringers, optimism seems in short supply in many parts of the land. But in Country USA it is the first essential. It begins, perhaps, with such a simple — yet terribly complex — thing as the weather. Because in the end, all of your planning, work, and investment hinges on the uncontrollable,

4:00 p.m. Steve Bush and his Appaloosa Mikey head into the Snake River canyon near Pomeroy, Washington. **Gary Bye**

unpredictable whims of Mother Nature.

Yet you go ahead and do what must be done, hopeful that the rains will come, the seeds will sprout, the heat wave won't last too long, the drought will end before the pasture goes brown, and the ground will be firm when it's time to harvest.

After a year when the weather was your enemy instead of your ally, it takes a rare kind of courage and optimism to do it all another time. You just do your best, fortified with the belief that things surely will be better next year.

From all this comes a gentle compassion and love — for family, for neighbors, for strangers. You know the face of misfortune first-hand, so you readily reach out to help the neighbor with the broken hip and no one to do the work. You get out your tractor in the middle of the night to pull a stranger out of the snowdrift across the highway. You donate your hay to help some unknown cattleman five states away who has none.

You don't see many "Have You Hugged Your Kid Today?" bumper stickers in the country. The reminder isn't needed. Sometimes the hug comes in the form of an approving smile. Or in helping groom the 4-H calf when you really want to sit in a soft chair. Or in just being there when someone needs to talk. Best of all, the kids hug back, with a love rooted in respect and understanding.

Maybe it's because families are closer in the country. It comes from sharing the work and the worries and the triumphs. Country kids always know what Mom and Dad do for a living, and they learn a respect for their wisdom and skills.

Then there's the sense of continuity. You take pride in your stewardship of the land. I can recall my Dad's simple rule: If you borrow something, always return it in better shape than when it was loaned to you. And that ethic extended on to the land we owned: Work it hard, but pass it along in better shape to the next generation. Such a simple idea. And it works so well.

Oh sure, there have been plenty of technological changes. There are computers in the den. Marketing in all its complexity is a full-time concern. Farming today is big business. Operating costs are staggering. So is the debt load.

You must be a veterinarian, mechanic, geneticist, economist, agronomist, and horticulturist, sometimes all in the same day.

But the level of optimism and courage today remains unchanged. The family bonds are still strong and loving. The belief persists that "We the People" is still a viable concept on which to base a government.

Not just on the giant farms and ranches, either. The country is small towns, too. Some just a wide spot in the road. They're the places where government of and by the people still works, where people turn out for city council meetings and pitch in to plant trees in the park, or endless blocks of petunias to brighten the streets in summer. The football games may be played in a field with no bleachers, but it's still the Super Bowl to the families standing on the sidelines. Wal-Mart may be the major store for miles away, but the manager cares about his customers just as much as the Nieman-Marcus manager does in the fancy mall in Dallas.

Quite likely the newspaper comes out only once a week, but a ten o'clock stop in the local coffee shop every morning fills you in on the important news anyhow.

The country is a place of simple pleasures. You live in beauty. There is the annual miracle of rebirth — leaves budding, crops sprouting, lambs, colts and calves, the early wild flowers in the fence rows and creek bottoms.

And the daily miracles: Sunrises of infinite variety and splendor, a sky unbroken by tall buildings and uncontaminated by smog, gentle sunsets that hint at tomorrow's weather if you know their secret signals, the giant yellow harvest moon, fields glittering with

Rancher Steve Pitz with his daughter, Whitney, in Garretson, South Dakota. **Jayne Erickson**

fireflies, a twinkling ceiling solid with stars, and even the occasional eerie majesty of the Northern Lights.

Perhaps best of all are the clouds. Feathery cirrus clouds so pure white against the deep sky. The boiling black stampede of a storm racing toward you out of the west. The giant mountain range of cumulus clouds reaching up above even where the jets can fly. And, at night, the flickering fireworks far away that light up the clouds of the approaching summer thunderstorm.

There are band concerts and fairs, the quilting bees, the basketball games, the church socials, and the Fourth of July parades, the Christmas lights on Main Street and the Fireman's Picnic.

In the long, hot days of summer there are bass to be caught in the farm pond. And when the crops are in, there's time to hunt the pheasants you've watched plump up through the summer. There are hobbies to pursue in the winter. For example, the Nebraska farmer who each winter takes odds and ends from discarded farm equipment and welds a new critter for his enormous front yard — a turkey this year, a Disney character next year, and even a sea serpent from old tractor tires. People drive from miles around on Sundays after church just to see what he's added to his goofy menagerie.

Others shop antiques with their wives, and become expert restorers and refinishers. Some become wood carvers, others turn amateur travel agent — because country people are curious about the rest of the world. Especially the rest of the Country USA.

Winter is a time of planning, too. Farmers always figure they can do things better next year. And that's important, because deep down inside is a fierce, competitive professionalism. Like the man near Texico, New Mexico, who sets himself a near-impossible goal each year. Once it was to have the highest per acre milo yield in New Mexico. It took a little while, but he got there... and promptly decided he'd try for the corn-growing record. And, yes, he achieved that, too. "It just makes life a little more interesting to give yourself some challenges," he says.

The country has many faces, and you never get to know them all. Corn farmers and cattlemen, sure. But also catfish farmers. And cotton growers. Cranberry producers. And lately, men who raise llamas for profit. There are lumberjacks, Christmas tree growers, pecan producers and artichoke growers. Veterinarians and county agents and vocational agricultural instructors. Implement dealers and the man who runs the local co-op.

There are women farmers, too. And farm wives who teach school or do your tax return or volunteer at the hospital. And an all-female wheat harvesting crew that travels from state to state in the midwest.

So different. Yet so alike in their optimism, courage, and love. Country. What a place to spend a day... or a lifetime of days.

The best of all possible days, of course, are those of Autumn.

The air is crisp, the foliage burst into vivid fall colors, and the apples are ready to pick. The fields hum with the rumble of harvesting equipment and trucks, and there's a feeling of quiet triumph in the air.

That's the time of year this book captures... 24 hours across rural America in the Autumn of 1988.

If you already live in the country, turn these pages and rediscover the everyday miracles that are easy to take for granted when they surround you.

If you came from the country, this book will help you rediscover the many simple joys you treasure in your memory. And even a few you've perhaps forgotten.

And if you've always been a city dweller, let this book help assure you that out in the country are those who are the custodians of a life that some would have you believe is only a memory.

Now come along and share with us 24 hours in *Country/USA*.

Clancy Strock *was raised on a small farm in northern Illinois. Like most farm boys, he was a member of both 4-H and FFA. During most of his working years he was involved in agricultural advertising and marketing. He currently is professional lecturer at the University of Nebraska, teaching advertising copywriting.*

A general store, "Earl's Place," in Hugo, Illinois. Most of the local men have a key to the front door; first to arrive in the morning starts the coffee brewing. **Paul Hixson**

6:00 a.m. Two young bull elk at Swan Lake Flats, Yellowstone National Park. **Skip Moody / Ted Reuther / Carl R. Sams II**

Aspen, Colorado. **Jeff Stine**

OUR LAND

Letchworth State Park, Livingston and Wyoming County, New York. **Hardie Truesdale**

8:30 a.m.   Bayou Teche, northeast of Franklin, Louisiana, in St. Mary Parish. **Fred Myers**

35

Bison near Yellowstone Lake in Yellowstone National Park. **Skip Moody/ Ted Reuther/ Carl R. Sams II**

Doe and twin fawns, Kensington Park in Milford, Michigan.
Sharon Cummings / Jean F. Stoick

Yellowstone National Park, Wyoming.
Skip Moody/ Ted Reuther/ Carl R. Sams II

North Window, Arches
National Park, Utah. **Tom Till**

Canyon de Chelly, Arizona. **Scott Shaw**

Ancient Indian rock art, Newspaper Rock State Park, Monticello, Utah. **Tom Till**

Makapuu Beach, Oahu, Hawaii **Douglas Peebles**

Napali Coast, Kauai, Hawaii.
Douglas Peebles

Antler Peak, Yellowstone National Park. **Skip Moody/ Ted Reuther/ Carl R. Sams II**

South Twin Lakes, Yellowstone National Park. **Skip Moody/ Ted Reuther/ Carl R. Sams II**

Bull elk at Gibbon Meadow, Yellowstone National Park.
Skip Moody/ Ted Reuther/ Carl R. Sams II

Northern Bald Eagle at the Lower St. Mary Lake, St. Mary, Montana. **Stan Osolinski**

9:00 a.m. East Hill Road, Peacham, Vermont. **Richard W. Brown**

Rural Wisconsin. **Tom Kehoss/ Jeff Strumberger**

5:00 a.m. Cheaha Mountain, Alabama's highest point. **Ken Elkins**

8:45 p.m. Lake Cacauma, Santa Ynez Valley, California. **Frederica Georgia**

Kayaking at Harbor Island, Maine. **Kip Brundage/ Douglas Merriam**

Fishing at the southernmost geographic point in America, Ka Lae (South Point) on the island of Hawaii. **Franco Salmoiraghi**

6:00 p.m. Fly fishing on the Missouri River near Great Falls, Montana.
John Nienhuis

Jamestown, Rhode Island. **Lou Jones**

7:00 a.m. Cross Creek, Florida. **Bill R. Horne**

Guttenburg, Iowa. **David Peterson**

West coast of Hawaii. **Franco Salmoiraghi**

On the Rainbow River, near Dunellon, Florida. **Jim Jernigan**

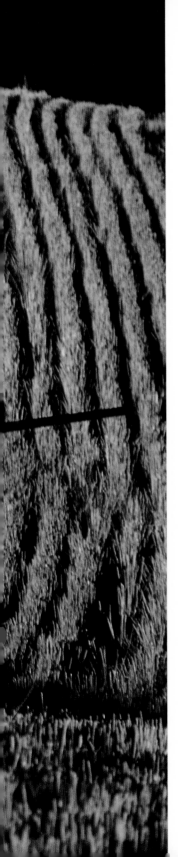

8:00 a.m. Channault Plantation, Lincoln County, Georgia. **Emory Jones**

6:00 a.m. Rob Cassetto (left) and Bart Gingerich look for game birds on the Bye farm, Pomeroy, Washington. **Gary Bye**

8:00 a.m. Channault Plantation, Lincoln County, Georgia. **Emory Jones**

Lake Cacauma, Santa Ynez Valley, California. **Frederica Georgia**

8:00 a.m. Near Baltimore, Ohio. **Eric Albrecht**

Goldenrod and asters, southern Ohio. **Eric Albrecht**

The Trout Farm/ Bed and Breakfast, Santa
Ynez Valley, California. **Frederica Georgia**

Konza Prairie, near Manhattan, Kansas. **Terry Evans**

Truman Worthy, Cragford, Alabama. **Ken Elkins**

COUNTRY LIFE

Rural Wisconsin. **Tom Kehoss/ Jeff Strumberger**

8:00 a.m. Leo Cremer, Larry Connolly and Chip Connolly move cattle near Sweetgrass Creek, east of the Crazy Mountains in central Montana. **Tom Murphy**

3:00 p.m. Elaine and Allen Kraling's dairy farm near Harmony, Minnesota. This farm site was purchased by Allen's grandfather in 1875. **Ted Mc Donough**

6:00 a.m.   A farmstead near Farley, Iowa. **Harlen Persinger**

5:00 p.m. Diane and Roger Koller's farm house near Mayview, Washington. **Gary Bye**

Sunrise over Hell's Canyon, the nation's deepest gorge. The homestead is in Wallowa County, forty miles upstream from Lewiston, Idaho. **Rick Swart**

State Center, Iowa. **David Peterson**

7:00 a.m.   Hez Somers farm, West Barnet, Vermont. **Richard W. Brown**

10:00 a.m. Henry Gregory's hammer-shaped mailbox, Trimble, Missouri. **Jim Patrico**

5:30 p.m. Stripcropping on the steep Palouse hills near Pomeroy, Washington. **Gary Bye**

Soybean field in northwestern Iowa. **Harlen Persinger**

Cattle feedlot near Dodge City, Kansas. **Chester Peterson, Jr.**

Wheel line irrigation system, Eureka County, Nevada. **Fred W. Cornelius**

Salem, Kansas. **Chester Peterson, Jr.**

First day of sugar beet harvest on the Miller Farm, Worland, Wyoming. **Ralph Sanders**

12 noon Plainfield, Indiana. **Brad LaPayne**

Stray cat at the barn door, Tremont, Illinois. **Lori Ann Cook**

8:00 p.m. April Hale, a freshman honor student at Washington State University, milks Primrose, the family milk cow, on a weekend visit home to her parents' farm in Pomeroy, Washington. **Gary Bye**

8:00 p.m. Matt Engel fills a calf bottle with fresh milk at the Engel dairy farm in Hampshire, Illinois. **David Tonge**

Sharen Devling stores milk from the family's five cows, Plattsburg, Missouri. **Suzanne Sayre**

8:00 p.m. There's always something to do on a farm, even when it rains. Elwyn and Barbara Wilson of Leaf River, Illinois tend to the sheep flock after supper. **Michael Wilson**

1:30 a.m. At farrowing time, Doug Stewart stays close to his sows and newborn litters in Waverly, Iowa. **Harlen Persinger**

Pig pens, Plainfield, Indiana. **Brad LaPayne**

2:00 p.m. Maybury Farm, Northville, Michigan.
Sharon Cummings / Jean F. Stoick

2:30 p.m. Wayne Segrera raises 3000 alligators annually on
his farm south of Abbeville, Louisiana. **Fred Myers**

10:00 a.m. Robert Branson's turkey farm, in the Lost River Valley south of Baker, West Virginia. **Tom Wachs**

Doug Scott of Wasilla, Alaska, feeds the musk oxen at the Musk Ox Farm in Palmer, Alaska. **Jane Gnass**

Gathering potatoes, Watauga County, North Carolina. **William A. Bake**

6:00 p.m. The unique call of Lester Burns brings home the cows on his farm in the highland area near St. George, West Virginia.
Tom Wachs

8:00 a.m. Feeding the pigs, Waverly, Iowa.
Harlen Persinger

4:00 p.m. Gretchen Bond hanging wash in Peacham, Vermont. **Richard W. Brown**

7:30 a.m. Janeen Stewart kisses husband Doug at their Waverly, Iowa farm, as she leaves for her public relations job at the University of Northern Iowa. **Harlen Persinger**

11:00 a.m. Picking up the mail, Goshen, Kentucky. **William Strode**

Casey Wright draws a crowd on his way to the feed bunk in rural South Dakota. **Jayne Erickson**

6:00 a.m. Farm workers strip leaves from flue-cured tobacco just south of Scotland Neck, North Carolina. **Harris Barnes, Jr.**

Goshen, Kentucky horse farm. **William Strode**

2:00 p.m. Eldredge Cranberry Bog, South Carver, Massachusetts. **Jim Raycroft**

Grape picking, Houtz Winery, Santa Ynez Valley, California. **Frederica Georgia**

Harvesting eggplant at Sun World, Coachella Valley, California. **Kelly O'Brien**

6:00 a.m. Fred Pomeroy and Chuck Kelly on opening day of the oyster hand-tonging season in Maryland. The tongers are working on the Choptank River, a few miles off of East New Market, Maryland. **David Ulmer**

Harvesting bell peppers near Stockton, California. **Joe Munroe**

8:30 p.m. Soybean harvest in Grundy County, Iowa. **Harlen Persinger**

Combining south of Friona, Texas. **Wyatt McSpadden**

Harvesting corn, Clayton County, Iowa. **David Peterson**

Herding the last of the broodmares across Split Rock Creek, Garretson, South Dakota. **Jayne Erickson**

Bull skull on the barn of "63 Ranch," south central Montana. **Tom Murphy**

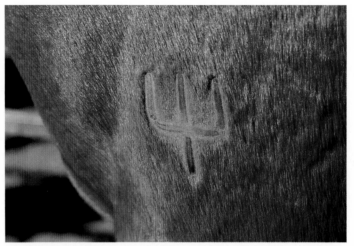

Horse brand, Pitchfork Ranch near Meeteetse, Wyoming. **Ralph Sanders**

10:00 a.m. Saddles in the barn at the Cremer ranch in Melville, Montana. **Tom Murphy**

12:00 Noon. Roadside market, Goodville, Pennsylvania. **Larry LeFever**

Ken Stewart holds a pumpkin, Presque Isle, Maine.
Kip Brundage/ Douglas Merriam

Pumpkins, Baltimore County, Maryland. **Bob Elbert**

On a pumpkin farm, Maryland's eastern shore. **Bob Elbert**

The historic Folsom House, Taylors Falls, Minnesota. **Ron Van Zee**

The Leo Casanova home, Stillwater, Minnesota. **Ron Van Zee**

8:30 p.m. The Corn Palace, Mitchell, South Dakota. **Jayne Erickson**

8:30 a.m. Charles Hogenkamp gets breakfast in Waverly, Iowa. **Harlen Persinger**

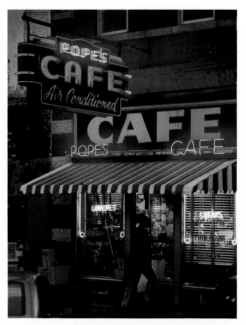

5:30 a.m. Pope's Cafe in Shelbyville, Tennessee. **Junebug Clark**

10:30 p.m. Summerland, California. **Frederica Georgia**

Four generations of the Farmer family gather for a picnic in Dumas, Arkansas. **D. Vann Cleveland**

The Finley wedding, Virginia City, Nevada. **Eugene Long**

High school football rally, Madison, Nebraska. **Bill Fleming**

Lawn sale, central Ohio. **Barth Falkenberg**

Annual quarter horse auction, Pitchfork Ranch, Meeteetse, Wyoming. **Ralph Sanders**

10:00 p.m. Arm wrestling at the Brown County Fair, Georgetown, Ohio. **Eric Albrecht**

Brown County Fair, Georgetown, Ohio. **Eric Albrecht**

Tabditha Strack with sheep, "Clinkle" at the Oklahoma State Fair, Stillwater, Oklahoma. **Philip D. Ellsworth**

The Oklahoma State Fair, Stillwater, Oklahoma. **Philip D. Ellsworth**

113

Minerva Little Hornet Cheerleaders
from Hanoverton, Ohio. **Jay Paris**

A rainy homecoming at Burlington Central High, Huntley, Illinois. **David Tonge**

Burlington Central High homecoming,
Huntley, Illinois. The Central Rockets
defeated the Valley Lutheran Ventures
of St. Charles, Illinois. **David Tonge**

5:00 p.m. Rain grounds William Nelson and James Nelson and their 1941 Stearman bi-plane at Dacy Airport, Harvard, Illinois **David Tonge**

Charles Gunnels, Choccolocco, Alabama. **Ken Elkins**

"Toby" the bear wrestles at the third annual St. Charles Wildlife Festival, St. Charles, Arkansas. **William E. Barksdale**

4-H Grand Prize Winner.   Doll Green feeds her chickens in Ambrose, Georgia. *Mandy G. Smith, 15, Willacoochee, Georgia*

RURAL YOUTH CAPTURE COUNTRY USA

4-H and FFA Photography Contest Winners

A "Country/USA" photo contest for 4-H and FFA members was held simultaneously with the professional shoot on October 1, 1988. Over 3,000 entries were received by The New Northrup King, which sponsored the contest in association with Silver Image Productions, Inc. $8,000 in prizes were awarded and the top 24 images are included in this section of *Country/USA*. An additional 52 photos received Honorable Mention recognition.

FFA Grand Prize Winner. Karen Ortmeier has a surprise for her mother below. *Daniel Ortmeier, 16, West Point, Nebraska*

Finalist. *Ann Schintz, 15, York, Pennsylvania*

Finalist. *Andy Bobb, 15, Center, North Dakota*

Finalist. *Angie Van Karsen, 11, Chassell, Michigan*

Finalist. *Lara Summers, 11, Maitland, Missouri*

Finalist. *Allan Harshman, 17, New Salem, Illinois*

Finalist. *Lisa Mullen, 21, Madison, Wisconsin*

Finalist. *Kari Rasor, 14, Anson, Texas*

Finalist *Jill Dramstad, 13, Binford, North Dakota*

Finalist. *Darin Willardsen, 18, Napoleon, North Dakota*

Finalist. *Heidi Allen, 15, Murrieta, California*

Finalist. *Justin Gabehart, 12, Minco, Oklahoma*

Finalist. *Julie Kornegay, 12, Bolingbroke, Georgia*

Finalist. *Angela Johnson, 15, Wetumka, Oklahoma*

Finalist. *Jeremiah Harding, 14, Kennewick, Washington*

Finalist. *Alfred Gosch, 12, Muldoon, Texas*

Finalist. *Brad Hardy, 18, Hawkinsville, Georgia*

Finalist. *Brian Martin, 10, Fayette, Iowa*

Finalist. *Marc Rosenberg, 15, Chenango Forks, New York*

Finalist. *Marci McKinzie, 16, Dike, Texas*

Finalist. *Jill Carey, 19, Sycamore, Illinois*

128

Finalist. *Christina Marie Nagy, 15, Cleveland, Georgia*

Finalist. *Jill Pierce, 17, Campbellsville, Kentucky*

The Gary Peterson family. **Alvis Upitis**

Carolyn teaches Snowball the cat to walk the plank.

A Farm Family

All photos in this section by **Alvis Upitis**

Breakfast after milking.

It was on the Gary Peterson dairy farm near Grantsburg, Wisconsin, that photographer Alvis Upitis spent from sunup until sunset on October 1, 1988. The farm has been in the Peterson family since 1877 and it is here that Gary and his wife, Chris, share their life with three children — Ben, 13, Matt, 10, and Caroline, 6.

Chris milks the cows, drives the tractor, and maintains the household; Gary handles the field work, maintains the machinery, and supplies the feed; Caroline helps feed the calves and take care of the family pets; while Ben and Matt fill in wherever they are needed and their school schedule allows. They all reflect a work ethic unique to family farms.

It is hard to say what constitutes an "ordinary day" on a dairy farm. On this particular Saturday, the family was busy milking and feeding the cows, plowing and disking the ground, and taking care of their many other responsibilities on the farm and in the community — typical dairy farm family life.

But on this day the Petersons also had to treat a cow for possible mastitis infection, pull another one through an especially difficult birth of an unusually large heifer calf, and rush the family's pet dog, Thumper, to the veterinarian after its paw was stepped on by a cow during milking. The cow, the calf, and the dog are all doing just fine.

The Petersons consider themselves a happy family. "We laugh a lot," Chris says. "There is a great deal of work to do on a farm, but we have a lot of fun doing it."

"That's because we are doing it together as a family," Gary adds. "This job would be too hard if we didn't work together."

What do the youngsters think of this life? Well, they grumble about the chores, but when asked whether they would rather live on the farm or in town, they emphatically choose the farm.

(Right) Chris in the milking parlor.

Gary inspects the plow before starting the day's work.

Ben and Matt scare away pigeons.

Ben loads cart with silage.

Inspecting Thumper's injured paw.

Carolyn feeds calf as part of her chores.

Family members prepare for a difficult calf birthing.

4:30 p.m. Icy and Earl Griffin, Lineville, Alabama returning from a mountain spring. **Ken Elkins**

Park River, North Dakota. **Curt Maas**

PEOPLE OF RURAL AMERICA

6:15 p.m. Richard Bertram and his corn crop, two miles south of Grundy Center, Iowa in Palermo Township. **Harlen Persinger**

Rancher Ed Bucholz in
Belle Fourche, South
Dakota. **David Bergeland**

11:00 a.m. Clint Hutson and son, Christopher, London, Ohio. **Eric Albrecht**

5:00 p.m. Russ Chatham of Livingston, Montana teaches his daughter, Rebecca, about fly fishing. **Tom Murphy**

5:00 p.m. Lloyd Allison and sons Brandon and Daniel, with their dog, Buck, Cleveland, Georgia. **Emory Jones**

Simone Evans and daughter, Amber, on the balcony of the historic Herlong Mansion, Micanopy, Florida. **Bill R. Horne**

11:00 a.m. Roaring Mountain,
Yellowstone National Park.
**Skip Moody/ Ted Reuther/
Carl R. Sams II**

6:30 a.m. A tranquil moment during a cattle drive at the Drummond Ranch, Osage Hills, Oklahoma. **Shirley Sokolosky**

10:00 a.m. Peacham, Vermont. **Richard W. Brown**

A neighborhood party, Salem, Ohio. **Jay Paris**

Ohatchee, Alabama
residents wait to try
their hand at checkers.
Ken Elkins

149

Children of the Hutterite colony, Park River, North Dakota. **Curt Maas**

Delaware County, Iowa. **David Peterson**

Amish children, Hazelton, Iowa. **David Peterson**

At Swampin Tails Ranch, Auburn, California. **Lawrence S.K. Lau**

3:00 p.m.   Carrie Somer (left) and Desiree Reames in the rain in Northville, Michigan. **Sharon Cummings / Jean F. Stoick**

Ashley Simpson and baby chick, Auburn,
California. **Lawrence S. K. Lau**

Marie Buchanan, Choccolocco, Alabama.
Ken Elkins

At the Farmer's Market, Boone, N.C.
William A. Bake

Kiffany Reid, Danburg, Georgia. **Emory Jones**

Hopie and Charlotte Strode in Goshen, Kentucky. **William Strode**

155

Isle Au Haut, Maine. **Kip Brundage/ Douglas Merriam**

"Mountain Man" Harold Cummins, Sutter Creek, California. **Dan Escobar**

Lessie McCormick reads the Bible on her 40-acre farm in Heflin, Georgia. **Ken Elkins**

11:00 a.m. 4-H'ers Leah Smith, Jerrod and Lacey David, and Bart Baudoin play with Brahma cattle between judging sessions at a livestock show in Abbeville, Louisiana, in Vermilion Parish. **Fred Myers**

Julie Shoemaker and her puppy, in Belle Fourche, South Dakota. **David Bergeland**

Gabriel Richards, Ann Arbor, Michigan. **Sharon Cummings / Jean F. Stoick**

The Hutterite colony, Park River, North Dakota. **Curt Maas**

Frankie Reid, Jr., Danburg, Georgia. **Emory Jones**

Dusty Acord, Augusta, Montana. **John Nienhuis**

Keith Duster, Holy Cross, Iowa. **David Peterson**

3:00 p.m. Lori Gathman loads alfalfa bales at the "63 Ranch," south central Montana.
Tom Murphy

7:00 a.m.   Peanut farmer Michael S. Doggett, Windsor, Virginia. **Robert Ander**

Sophie Paris with her horse, Gentle Ben, in Salem, Ohio. **Jay Paris**

Tammy Greene, North Carolina. **William A. Bake**

Soo Greiman, Waterloo, Iowa. **Harlen Persinger**

Delta, Alabama. **Ken Elkins**

Jodi Van Winkle and Mike Carter, Georgetown, Ohio. **Eric Albrecht**

Denise Hadachek at the Bridal Boutique, Atkins, Iowa. **Scott Sinklier**

163

Caralee Doak practices her dance steps in the haymow of a barn, Grundy Center, Iowa. **Harlen Persinger**

Porter Waggoner at the Grand Ol' Opry, Nashville, Tennessee.
Eric Hassler

Farmer inspecting his crops, Friona, Texas. **Wyatt McSpadden**

Tenderfoot McGowan and Scooter, Canton, Texas. **Joe Baraban**

Gregg Kringer, Garretson, South Dakota. **Jayne Erickson**

Virginia and Alvey Shagloak, Kotzebue, Alaska. **J. Stephen Lay**

Ray Krone, Augusta, Montana. **John Nienhuis**

M. W. Seymour, Wellington, Texas. **Joe Baraban**

Vivian Miller, Priscilla Schrock, Cora Crossgrove at Sauder's Museum, Archbold, Ohio. **Jeff Salisbury**

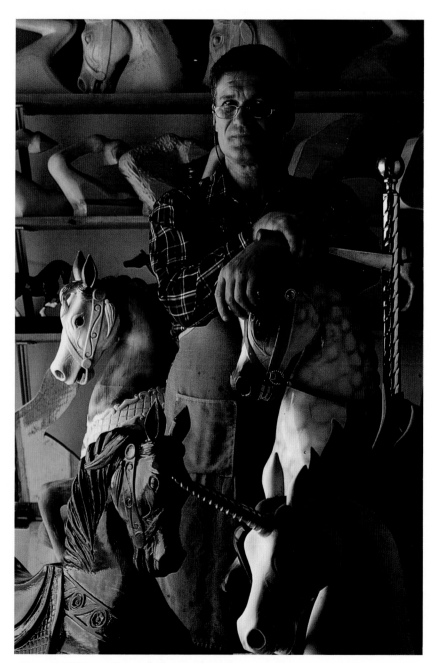

Darrell Williams farms full-time, but also carves
carousel horses in Dayton, Iowa. **Scott Sinklier**

Ernest Mostella crafts fiddles in Ashville, Alabama.
Ken Elkins

Katie, Dusty, and Cassi Greiman, Waterloo, Iowa. **Harlen Persinger**

The Nabors family has lunch with their neighbors, northeast Iowa.
Bob Coffman

10:00 a.m. Wynette, Ryan, and Larry Lindsey, and Howard
Gibbs, Pine Tree Lane, Choccolocco, Alabama. **Ken Elkins**

The George family sorts Pinon beans to sell at the Navajo trading post, Klagetoh, Arizona. **Scott Shaw**

Kelly, Larry, and Casey Wright, in rural South Dakota. **Jayne Erickson**

The Reids, Danburg, Georgia. **Emory Jones**

In Dayton, Iowa. **Scott Sinklier**

Ethel Acord, Ted Acord, Kent Mosher, Donna Mosher, Roland Mosher, and Carol Mosher at the T Bar Ranch, Augusta, Montana. **John Nienhuis**

Ryan, Susan, Hank and Chase Scott, Findlay, Ohio. **Jeff Salisbury**

4:00 p.m.   "Bessie" Irby walks a lane of cedar trees, Windsor, Virginia. **Robert Ander**

6:00 p.m. Lester Burns' last chore of the day in St. George, West Virginia. **Tom Wachs**

Richard Odom's Sohio station, Winona, Ohio. **Jay Paris**

Margaret Sherman, Archbold, Ohio. **Jeff Salisbury**

Wilford Ferguson, Bloomingburg, Ohio. **Eric Albrecht**

Louise Brown, a Navajo in Arizona. **Scott Shaw**

Henry and Eva Luker, Lineville, Alabama. **Ken Elkins**

Jim Raycroft may still be seeing red. He spent the better part of October 1 knee-deep in the cranberry bogs of Massachusetts. An international photographer, Raycroft commented, "This was one of my grandest days of shooting ever."

David Bergeland greets one of his subjects — a buffalo in western South Dakota. He also shot mules, arm wrestlers and other action in a pool hall and a night club.

Tom Murphy focuses his camera on hay handling in his home state of Montana. He also shot cowboys, ranges and cattle roundups.

Carl R. Sams II (right) prepares for take-off in the U.S. Park Service helicopter in Yellowstone National Park.

David Ulmer traveled from Missouri to the shores of Maryland to capture oyster fishermen. "Mitchener's *Chesapeake* had introduced me to the area and a previous trip whetted my desire to shoot more," he said. Ulmer reported perfect weather, calm seas, and good light at sunrise.

24 HOURS WITH THE PHOTOGRAPHERS

By Richard A. Howell

For some a picture is worth a thousand words. To others a picture may say nothing. The reaction to each photograph relies on the experience, mood, and temperment of the viewer. It also relies upon the ability of the photographer.

To bring an image to life takes perhaps a little bit of luck, but mostly a skill developed from experience, technical knowledge, and a keen artist's eye. The photographers whose work you see on these pages have spent an average of 20 years developing this proficiency. As a result, their collective works have been reproduced in thousands of books, magazines, pamphlets, and advertisements.

A photo-essay book of this quality and scope does not just happen; it takes a lot of hard work and planning by many dedicated people. Even more, it must have a steady, guiding light. . . someone who dreams the dream and then believes in it hard enough to hang on when the going gets tough and finances are difficult to find.

That someone is Richard E. Brooks of Silver Image Productions, Inc., in Champaign, Illinois. Back in March of 1987, when he conceived the idea for a book of quality photographs depicting 24 hours in rural America, he knew such a book had never been done before and that it could entail a great deal of work to bring it into being. His numerous letters, countless telephone calls and personal contacts, plus a great deal of hard work contributed by several hundred others, have made this book a reality.

"Country/USA is the first of its kind in many respects," Brooks explains. "For instance, we called upon many kinds of photographers — corporate, commercial, landscape, photojournalists, nature and wildlife, as well as agricultural. Never before has such a diverse group of professionals been involved in a single theme effort." The resulting pictures are as diverse as the photographers who took them.

The 254 photographs appearing on these pages were selected with painstaking care, scrupulously chosen from the more than 122,000 collectively shot by the 102 professional photographers and thousands of 4-H and FFA members spread across the United States on October 1, 1988.

Since the focus of this book was to be photo images of this nation's natural heritage — rural American life — the photogaphers who took these images not only had to be the best at their craft, they had to have an emotional feel for the subject as well.

One day is not a long time when over 3,615,000 square miles of a country must be covered. Not every mile of it, of

Over rice fields in Bolivar County, Mississippi. **Noel Workman**

course, but those portions of the rural area with the most interesting scenery and/or people. To find those in one 24--hour period is not easy.

"To get where you want to be, you have to start where you are," as an anonymous figure of our history once said. That is why the majority of the photographers did their shooting in the area where they live and know best. It is not familiarity bred of contempt, but understanding born out of love for the rural countryside and the people who live, work,

and play there. It shows in every picture.

It also took careful planning. Although one would like to believe the photographers just happened to find the events they recorded, it could not be left to chance that 24 hours would produce "everything you always wanted to know about the country." They needed to know where certain things would be happening, when they would be happening, and that the people involved would be there.

The logistics of synchronizing the efforts of all these photographers was handled by nine very busy regional coordinators. Some are photographers who believed in the project so much that they took on the extra obligation. Others are knowledgeable people who offered their organizational skills. Each was given responsibility for 10 to 12 photographers.

These coordinators spent a great deal of time on the telephone, prior to the day of the shoot, arranging permission for location spots, working out logistics and supplies. They shared ideas on possible picture content, alerted media in the various locales where the shooting would take place, and in some cases, helped coordinate the coverage.

Photographers in the western and northwestern USA, plus Alaska and Hawaii, were coordinated by *Eugene Long* and *Fred W. Cornelius*. After making sure their charges were fully prepared and on their way, Long and Cornelius spent October 1 criss-crossing the rural byways of their home state of Nevada, each going his separate way.

Long's day turned out to be a little more eventful than Cornelius'. And we're not even including the fact that a shot from a hunter's gun whistled by his ear earlier in the day, or that two of his cameras quit working.

Long had finished a successful day photographing two rural weddings, and several other interesting scenes, when he and a video crew ended up in a picturesque, remote tavern in the desert where they quickly found out that they were invading the sanctity of a motorcycle gang's hideout.

Ted Reuther patiently awaits the wildlife at sunset at Yellowstone National Park.

Eric Albrecht takes a breather from shooting at the Brown County Fair in southwestern Ohio. Earlier in the day Albrecht found his favorite subject, five-year-old Christopher swinging on a tire swing. "The best thing I remember was the overall enthusiasm people had for the book project," he noted. "The folks of rural America seemed to open their hearts for the idea and the photographers."

Charles Shoffner found good weather in southern Virginia along the Blue Ridge Mountains. He concentrated on hikers relaxing by a waterfall, bikers enjoying the countryside and the evening sunsets.

Fred W. Cornelius prepares to shoot cowboys at work near Eureka, Nevada, assisted by his wife, Janet. Cornelius also shot aerial views of the bright green irrigation patterns against the stark white alkali desert. "Just as we got into position we hit the only turbulence of the whole trip," he said. "A Hasselblad can leave quite a dent in your forehead."

Being a pilot helped *Chester Peterson, Jr.* take advantage of the clear weather to photograph his home state from above. Feed lots, rural churches and a small town airport were some of his subjects.

Shirley Sokolosky wanted to participate in this project so much that she brought her six-month-old baby along. The owners of the ranch she was photographing watched the baby while she worked. She experienced true serendipity when she photographed a fleeting rainbow — the only one documented on October 1.

There were a few threats and a great deal of discussion before Long and his companions were allowed to leave with their hide and fortunately, the rolls of film they exposed earlier in the day.

Debi Hassler of Evansville, Indiana coordinated the activities of the photographers in Ohio, Indiana, and Michigan before accompanying her photographer-husband, *Eric*, to Tennessee. First they spent some time with William Golden, a former member of the Oak Ridge Boys singing group, who lives on one of the oldest estates in Sumner County.

Then it was on to the Nashville area where the Hasslers finished the day at the Grand Ol' Opry. They found the performers at the show, particularly venerable Roy Acuff, to be warm and friendly. It was announced over the air that the Hasslers were there taking pictures for *Country/ USA.*

Coordinator *Diana Meyer*, was ordered by her obstetrician to stay close to her Kansas City, Missouri home. While her husband, *Bruce*, went off to shoot scenes in the state of Kansas, she was busy on the telephone with her photographers in Missouri, Kansas, Nebraska and South Dakota.

That was not the case for *Brett Knobloch* of Bloomington, Illinois, who also stayed close to the phone all day waiting to hear from his photographers in Illinois and Indiana. Not a word. Apparently they were too busy trying to stay dry or find dry locations to shoot. Knobloch produced the photo log books that the photographers used throughout the day.

Harvey M. Cook of Baltimore made good use of the telephone contacting his photographers in Iowa, Minnesota, Montana and Wisconsin. It was through Cook's contacts that the large square dance group was located and photographed by Missouri-based photographer *Bob Elbert.*

Burning up the telephone lines from his Washington, D.C. office to his photographers in the east and northeastern states was *Tom Waldinger.* Trying to make and maintain contact with a group of very busy professional photographers can be difficult, but Waldinger was able to manage it . . . with a little help from his secretary.

Walt Griffith, an Illinois native now living in Gainesville, Florida, coordinated those working in the southern states. During the day of the shoot he kept himself busy taking pictures of the photographers working in Florida.

Richard E. Brooks, the originator of this project, coordinated the photographers in the southwestern states.

Of course, it was also Brooks' responsibility to secure the services of all of the photographers in the first place. With the help of such organizations as the National Agri-Marketing Association (NAMA), the Agricultural Relations Council (ARC), Professional Photographers of America (PPA), and others, he was able to establish a nucleus of talented

Three generations of Amish near Kenton, Delaware. **John / Jennifer Harvey**

photographers. His contact with them produced names of equally capable professionals. He kept matching them to areas until the 50-state jigsaw puzzle was put together.

As a means of identification, and as a practical benefit as it turned out, every photographer and assistant was given a silver, waterproof hooded windbreaker with the project's name emblazoned upon it. With the rain in many states and an early morning chill in others, the jacket proved beneficial to many.

That first Saturday in October dawned clear and bright, or wet and miserable, depending upon where you were located. Rain pelted a dozen states in the midwest and south, a little early morning fog covered the northeast, then cleared to match the perfect weather in the rest of the country. It was sleet and low clouds in northern Alaska.

Photographers were assigned in all 50 states, but as indicated, perfect weather was not available in every state.

While that called for some quick change of plans, the professionalism of the photographers came through.

For instance, *Michael Wilson* planned to shoot farmers working in their fields in north central Illinois. "Rain poured all morning and dark clouds lingered until sunset," he says. So, "all my pictures were made with flash in grain elevators, barns, and machinery sheds. In the afternoon I was able to muck around with a farmer who was happy to show me his drought-stricken cornfields."

It was even worse for *J. Stephen Lay* who had some great shots lined up around Kotzebue near Nome, Alaska. "A rain-sleet-snow storm hit and closed the area down," he says. "Every one of my scheduled activities was canceled. I had some great ones — a reindeer herder with his deer; a musher running his dogs; and in the isolated village of Sungnak I was to shoot the entire community processing fish and caribou as they prepared for winter." Lay used only a portion of the film he carried as he settled for mostly interior shots . . . and the Northern Lights.

For *Jane Gnass*, the weather was much better near Palmer in southern Alaska. A unique musk ox farm, hay stacks, and rural scenery were among the subjects she chose to shoot.

Weather wasn't the only cause for disappointment and surprise to *William E. Barksdale* of Memphis, Tennessee. Not only did the rain cancel his planned shoot of a rice harvest, from ground and airplane, but while he was following a fisherman who was towing his expensive bass boat behind a borrowed truck on a slippery back road near Dumas, the man swerved and his truck tipped over.

"Water from the radiator apparently fell on some hot pipes and a big cloud of steam arose," Bill reports. "From 200 yards it looked like smoke. As I ran to the scene, I just knew that the fisherman, who had given up opening day of squirrel season to help me arrange a picture, was burning up! Fortunately, he wasn't even scratched, but it took three and a half hours for the police to come to take my statement and get the wreckage cleaned up."

But it was a glorious early fall day over in New Jersey, where *Arthur V. Edwards* took advantage of the nice weather to record on film the activities of commercial beekeepers and a group of produce stands.

It was bright and clear on the other coast as well, as *Kelly*

4-H Photography Contest Grand Prize Winner *Mandy Smith* of Willacoochee, Georgia with her subject, Doll Green.

Photo by Judy Jones

Emory Jones improvises a shot of a milking cow in his home state of Georgia. "Rain, fog, mist, and bright sun — we had it all," said Jones. "I didn't get to shoot anything I'd planned."

FFA Photography Contest Grand Prize Winner *Daniel Ortmeier* of West Point, Nebraska with his sister, Karen.

Photo by Ben and Matt Peterson

Alvis Upitis left his photo studio in Minneapolis to spend the day with a dairy farming family near Grantsburg, Wisconsin. "Part of the reason I elected to stay with one family," Upitis explains, "is to bring continuity to my shoot, to see them through an entire farm day."

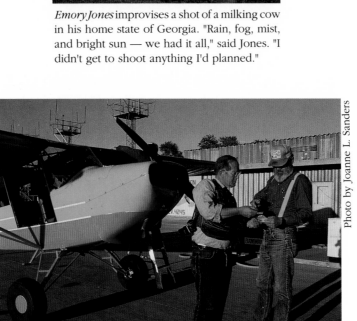

Photo by Joanne L. Sanders

Ralph Sanders gets a model release from his pilot as they return from shooting aerials of farmlands and open ranges. Sanders elected to travel from Iowa to the Meeteetse area of Wyoming where he had previously shot in the early '70s. On the ground, Sanders photographed the annual horse auction at the Pitch Fork Ranch, and a veterinarian making his rounds.

Photo by Tim Swanson

Jayne Erickson, atop a farm wagon, directs her subjects in South Dakota. Erickson spent some time on a cattle ranch, a hay farm, a sheep farm, and at a roadside melon stand. In the evening she photographed the ornate Corn Palace in Mitchell.

O'Brien set out to shoot the back roads of Orange County, California. She found much to shoot around San Juan Capistrano, San Clemente and the Coachella Valley.

O'Brien hopes her day's adventures weren't typical. "I managed to lock my keys in my car in the morning and later in the day found myself out in the middle of nowhere with a dead battery. Both times I escaped my predicament by flagging down a passing vehicle. The only place I would ever do that is in the country."

"Barefoot bacchanals boogying in the grape bins" is how *Frederica Georgia* described the grape stomping festival she photographed at the Ballard Canyon Winery in southern California. Apparently not satisfied with that exercise, the grape stompers then move on to the deck where they "dance until they drop."

Dan Escobar found a "Kit Carson Mountain Man" in northern California. He is 80-year-old Harold Cummins who owns a horse farm that provides stock for many movies and television series. He has been a "mountain man" for more than 50 of his years, dressing in fur and leather outfits he made himself and leading wagon trains over the Sierra Mountains through Kit Carson Pass.

Around Sacramento, California, *Lawrence S.K. Lau* found a camel farm, as well as youngsters doing their farm chores, and a farmer working late in his machinery shop.

Garry McMichael worked in both Missouri and Illinois as he used the "mighty" Mississippi River as his background for his shots of farm scenes, barges, the Golden Eagle Ferry, and the sternwheeler paddle boat, the Delta Queen. That was after he had been plagued by rain most of the day.

At the lower end of the Mississippi River was *Noel Workman* of Greenville, Mississippi, who captured on film barges filled with grain heading down river to the Port of New Orleans, and the country's largest cotton seed company at Scott, Mississippi.

Around Stark, Mississippi, *James E. Lytle* was busy shooting farm animals, a father and son dairy operation, a catfish farm, and wild turkeys. He also found a dilapidated post office in remote Sessuns, Mississippi.

In Pennsylvania, *Larry LeFever* concentrated on colorful produce stands, and night scenes of carnival rides. His plan

to take aerial views of rural America was canceled due to the rain. *Jim Walton* also had problems with wet weather around Indianapolis, Indiana.

Kip Brundage of Belfast, Maine, shot from a kayak on the way to a river island, but it was his associate, *Douglas Merriam*, who had to drive five hours to the northeast corner of the state to photograph potato harvesting activities, and the colorful Stewart's Pumpkin Patch.

It was a beautiful day for *Richard W. Brown* around

A rainy day in northern Michigan. **Janice Mekula**

Barnet, Vermont, from the sunrise over a cemetery to the sun slipping behind clothes hanging on a line. In between he found a quilt sale, a man in a rocking chair with a sleeping dog beside him, and such autumn activities as cutting firewood and raking leaves.

Ron Van Zee was on hand at 5:30 a.m. when the regular crowd started gathering at The Cup and Saucer restaurant in Bayport, Minnesota. He also captured the atmostphere and color of several other small towns, including Silverwater where Sherman "Sherme" Gordon, owner of Gordon Iron and Metal, "makes the buying and selling of any piece of metal a linguistic work of art."

Pulitzer Prize winner *David Peterson* left Des Moines to spend a great deal of the day with an Amish family near the Amana Colonies in Iowa. He captured a sternwheel paddle

boat on the Mississippi River, and a 71-year-old blacksmith at work, before he spent the rest of his day photographing a young boy shooting baskets and practicing his "slam dunk" into a hoop attached to a big red barn.

Bob Coffman, traveling the backroads of Iowa, managed to shoot a few overcast farm scenes, including a farm family named Nabors having lunch with their neighbors.

Ed "Skip" Weigel was up at 3:00 a.m. to photograph oyster fisherman off the coast of Florida, before moving on to the action of a rodeo. *Bill R. Horne* focused his attention on north central Florida, where he found an old church, and a fisherman on the backwaters of Cross Creek. He also photographed mansions in two of the state's oldest cities.

Jim Jernigan shot such diverse subjects as citrus trees, a race horse farm, an alligator farm, and families tubing down the Rainbow River. His participation in this project was officially recognized by his hometown of Ocala, Florida, with a proclamation from the city council.

Where else would you find the world's largest flea market except in Texas and that's where Houston-based *Joe Baraban* found it. It is held once a year on a 50-acre site, attended by both buyers and sellers who come from all over the country. "A great place for character studies," Baraban says.

Off in another part of Texas, *Holly Kuper* was photographing a family on bicycles, and cattle being rounded-up after straying onto a nearby highway. Up in the Panhandle of Texas, *Wyatt McSpadden* located sorghum harvesting, a cattle ranch at sunset, and the postmistress of the little town of Dawn standing outside her one-room post office.

Ken Elkins went to the nooks and crannies of Alabama to find his appealing people . . . an eldery couple married 76 years who still hold hands like a couple of teenagers, and a country doctor who still makes house calls. "I knew I could only spend 10 to 15 minutes with each subject," Elkins reported. "By midnight — and 68 rolls of film — I felt I had compressed one week's work into one day."

Philip D. Ellsworth spent his day in Oklahoma at the State Fair. His "biggest challenge was keeping dry," he says. Not from the rain but, "from the spray thrown by kids washing their livestock."

Photo by Harvey M. Cook

Bob Elbert of St. Louis lines up 108 square dancers for his panorama camera in West Virginia. Elbert also traveled to Maryland to shoot his favorite subject — soybean harvesting.

Photo by William Lewis

Jay Paris from Salem, Ohio shot a little league football team complete with matching cheerleaders, a fruit market, and the town of Franklin Square, where 86 of the town's population of 121 are related.

184

Photo by Robin Mortarotti

Joe Munroe documents workers gathering bell peppers in central California. He also shot tomato, almond and corn harvesting activities.

Photo by Jennifer Harvey

John Harvey takes advantage of a glorious fall day in Delaware. He was joined by his daughter, *Jennifer*, who shot solely in black and white.

Photo by Laurie Solomon

Richard E. Brooks (left), producer/ director and *Glen E. Schrof*, project coordinator, discuss logistics of the tractor panorama at Plainfield, Indiana.

Photo by Brett Lando

Jan Abbott braves the southern Illinois weather with poncho and umbrella. "After the '88 summer drought, any rain was a pleasure instead of a curse," she pointed out. The conditions bettered in the afternoon.

Photo by Colleen Kelley

Lori Ann Cook in a chicken house in central Illinois. Cook also visited a dairy farm, a commercial pumpkin harvest and a roadside vendor of plaster of Paris farm animals.

Photo by Fred Myers

Fred Myers left home for Louisiana several days ahead of time to scout locations. Finding torrential rain on shooting day, he decided, "If the Lord gives me rain, I'll shoot rain."

Two-time Pulitizer Prize winner *William Strode* photographed literally in his backyard, a horse farm near Goshen, Kentucky, with his daughters on horseback as his favorite subject. He managed to take these and other shots between rain showers.

Gary Bye and his wife, *Kathleen*, are full-time farmers near Pomeroy, Washington. They restricted their photo day to friends, neighbors and relatives. "So many scenes we shot were things we looked at every day and wished we could stop long enough to record on film," Bye reported.

"Thanks to this project we were given the opportunity." Bye went on to philosophize, "Even if we don't make the book, we had a terrific day and really discovered the reasons why we live and work in this wonderful part of America."

Salina, Kansas native *Terry Evans* took to the air to document the Konza Prairie, the world's largest continuous prairie lands, located near Manhattan, Kansas.

Brad Lapayne scouted his home state of Illinois and central Indiana with his panoramic cameras. His 360-degree photograph of tractors in a circle is the fold-out of *Country/USA*.

There is a small general store in Hugo, Illinois, that *Paul Hixson* found, called "Earl's Place." Most of the men in the area have a key to the front door and they gather there early most mornings, before the store opens, to catch up on the day's news. The first one to arrive starts the coffee brewing. Hixson also spent some time with the Amish near Arthur.

Luther MacNaughton of Omaha, Nebraska, traveled 450 miles in his home state. It was not his best day. It rained and many of the contacts he had made backed out. He did photograph a large family holding a tailgate party on their farm before going to a Nebraska football game.

Michigan-based *Junebug Clark* was on assignment in Moore County, Tennessee, shooting pictures for Jack Daniels advertisements. He extended his stay so he could be part of this photo-essay project.

Jeff Salisbury had a frustrating day in Ohio. He arose early to shoot a sunrise and the skies were overcast. He went looking for an Amish family, never found one. Had made arrangements to shoot a drainage ditch operation, but nobody showed up. Decided to look for some grain harvest action, too rainy. The final blow came when he found a picturesque Blue Grass Mountain Festival but no one wanted their picture taken. He did find elderly quilters, some barn painters, and a one-room schoolhouse.

Barth Falkenberg, who also stayed in Ohio, found several interesting items at an antique sale, and an old red barn with the famous "Mail Pouch Chewing Tobacco" still visable.

At the Big Island Rendezvous, Albert Lea, Minnesota. **Greg L. Ryan/ Sally Beyer**

In Wisconsin, *Tom Kehoss* and *Jeff Strumberger* combined their efforts and talents to photograph farmsteads, churches, windmills, and close-ups of flowers. *Janice A. Mekula* suffered through rainy weather in Michigan, but did manage to treat it artistically in her photos.

The Blue Ridge Mountain area was the photo site for *William A. Bake* of Boone, North Carolina. *Harris Barnes* slipped back and forth across the border, shooting in both North and South Carolina.

Robert Ander was busy in Virginia photographing peanut farmers, yard sales, pumpkins, laying chickens, an old matriarch of a small town, and the erecting of a large tent in preparation for an old-fashioned revival.

Tom Wachs took pictures in six counties of nearby West Virginia. He included a sunrise over a cemetery, a small general store, country church, turkey farm, and barn painting. "It was a unique day that I will always remember," Wachs says.

Jeff Stine used the snow-capped mountains of Colorado as an appropriate background for his aspen trees.

Harlen Persinger, Milwaukee, Wisconsin, was one of the two dozen photographers who traveled out-of-state to document their favorite subjects.

In Persinger's case, he was returning to his hometown of Grundy Center, Iowa, where he "knew everyone on a first-name basis." He worked his photo equipment so long and hard that his 17mm lens "just fell apart" right after he shot a teenager on a tractor at a McDonald's drive-up window.

With the help of a neighbor's daughter, Persinger was able to fulfill a dream of long-standing. In his mind's eye he saw a young girl dancing to the music of a tape recorder in the hazy dust-filtered sunlight of a haymow. It looks like a dream come true.

Curt Maas and his assistant traveled 3000 miles from Des Moines, Iowa to scout and photograph in North Dakota. "It was a challenge," says Maas. "We spent several days just scouting the area where we planned to take our pictures."

One of Maas' more attention-getting pictures, the moon rising over an old school house, is not the product of a photographic darkroom, but the result of photogapher ingenuity. It was accomplished by first taking a picture of the moon, carefully rewinding the film in the camera, then re-exposing the same frame with an image of the school house, two hours later.

Scott Sinklier, who stayed to shoot scenes in Iowa commented, "It's awesome to think that 101 other photographers were doing what I was doing at the same time on the very same day."

D. Vann Cleveland of Alabama, went to Arkansas to photograph a four-generation farm family named "Farmer." *Susan Drinker*, of Maine, packed her cameras and headed south into New Hampshire to record that state's natural beauty.

Five award-winning wildlife and nature photographers contributed their talents to *Country/USA* by focusing their efforts in two geographic areas. *Skip Moody, Ted Reuther*, and *Carl R. Sams II* left Michigan to spend the day in Yellowstone National Park. They not only recorded the varied wildlife, but also documented some of the devastation left behind by weeks of savage fires. The U.S. Park Service showed its support for the project by providing a helicopter for the photographers to use. *Sharon Cummings*

6:30 p.m. High-tension electrical towers, Arthur, Indiana. **Richard E. Brooks**

and *Jean F. Stoick* remained in upper Michigan to scout for likely subjects. They shot many warm and appealing images of wildlife, and youngsters with farm animals, before the afternoon rains set in.

Rick Swart was far away from rainy Salem, Ohio, shooting pictures in Hell's Canyon, Idaho. The shoot started at dawn on Saturday, in the deepest canyon in North America. "It was picture-perfect weather," Swart says, "when we headed the jet boat downriver and met the fishermen we had breakfast with, working the rapids. The driver on our jet boat gave the engine full throttle and with the twin 350 V-8 engines screaming, we held our position at the head of the rapids long enough for me to get the fishermen making a run at us in their open bow jet boat. It is one of my favorite shots."

Country and Western singing star *Kenny Rogers* was far away from his California home on a concert tour in northern Ohio when he switched from singing to using his photography skills to participate in the day's activities. He had been enthusiastic from the start about being part of this unique and historic event, but it was not until the last minute that he discovered his schedule would permit him to participate. Unfortunately, his landscape shooting was interrupted by the bad weather.

Franco Salmoiraghi shot on the big island of Hawaii, focusing on its people and recreational activities. His only climatic challenge was VOG, a grayish sky pollutant produced by a recent volcanic eruption. Luckily, it did not prevent him from photographing a bikini-clad beauty miles from anywhere, lounging in a softly rolling surf. The other Hawaiian "shooter" was *Douglas Peeples*, who hopped between the islands of Oahu and Kauai. His azure skies were clear and he was able to capture beautiful island scenery.

In the state of Montana there are cowboys, ranges and cattle round-ups and *John Nienhuis* came in from Milwaukee, Wisconsin to shoot them all. He also recorded a fly fisherman enjoying the great outdoors. *Stan Osolinski* of Warren, Michigan concentrated on Montana's Glacier National Park. He photographed landscapes from sunup to sundown in and around Lake St. Marys where he was even able to find a bald eagle within range of his 600mm lens.

Bill Fleming left St. Paul, Minnesota, to shoot in Madison, Nebraska, population 1,950. His subjects were a high school football pep rally, and a farm sale where he photographed people climbing over, around and under the machinery.

"Folks really went out of their way to be friendly," Fleming says. "If we didn't do anything else today, we made a whole bunch of new friends."

Pulitzer Prize photojournalist *Scott Shaw* arranged to photograph the Canyon de Chelly area of the Navajo Indian reservation in northeastern Arizona. Here the Navajo live during the winter in the valley, then move to higher ground in the summer so they can farm the lower elevation fields. The photographs of *Jim Bones* also feature Indians and their artifacts, the Pueblo Indian farmers near Tesuque, New Mexico.

David Tonge dodged raindrops as he left his home near Arlington Heights, Illinois at 4:00 a.m. By the time he returned at 9:00 p.m., he had traveled over 200 miles and photographed a dairy farm operation near Sharon, Wisconsin; a farrier working on a horse farm near Woodstock, Illinois; and a high school homecoming football game with a farmstead as a background near Huntley, Illinois.

Gregory Thorp of New Haven, Connecticut is a specalist in corn photography, so he flew to Nebraska, rented a car and started driving until he found what he was looking for. Near Dwight he found farmers unloading ears of corn from cribs and putting them in shellers, in turn loading the grain in trucks bound for the local elevator.

Alois Krenk in Dwight, Nebraska.
Gregory Thorp

Robert B. Boyd of Davenport, Iowa went the other direction, going to west-central Connecticut and Rhode Island to shoot the fall colors, country churches, and a young girl tending flowers.

Coon Rapids, Iowa, is where *Ted Mc Donough* left when he traveled to Lanesboro, Minnesota, where he found the fall foliage scenes of tree-lined streets, and traffic at night.

Traveling along the rocky coastline from Massachesetts to Rhode Island must have seemed to be a piece of cake for photographer *Lou Jones* of Boston. He had just completed an assignment at the Olympics and returned late the previous afternoon, after a 24-hour flight from Soeul, Korea. He was so dedicated to this project that he was up the next

morning to shoot the sunrise. We are not sure when his internal clock caught up with him.

While most of the participating photographers worked with 35mm cameras, several of the landscape photogaphers who took part used the larger 4 x 5 film format. *Hardie Truesdale* spent his time in northern New York state. Because he patiently waits hours for just the right lighting conditions, he only had four set-ups for the entire day. One more than he expected.

Fellow landscape photographer *Carr Clifton*, came from California to work in a nearby area of New York state, while *Jeff Gnass*, another landscape photographer from California traveled to Idaho.

Landscape photographer *Tom Till* concentrated his efforts on the scenery in his home state of Utah, particularly in Arches and Canyons Land National Forest Parks, as well as on Lake Powell, and the Colorado River.

Husband and wife teams included *Greg L. Ryan* and *Sally Beyer* from Minnesota who concentrated on the Fur Traders Festival in Albert Lea, Minnesota; and *Jim Patrico* and *Suzanne Sayre* who spent their day shooting a circus, pie baking, and assorted rural scenes along the byways of Missouri.

Not all the photographers had an "exciting" day, but some did find themselves being treated as celebrities in many areas, followed and reported on by local radio, television and newspaper reporters.

Reports from the participating photographers indicates they enjoyed the experience and while some were upset because of the inclement weather, not one complained of being bored. Those who experience the essence of country life through the photos in this book will see why.

— Richard A. Howell was born in rural Ohio, grew up in the city, and spent the next nine years as a television news reporter before moving into agricultural reporting. A former magazine editor and agricultural trade association executive, he is now a free-lance writer and operates his own public relations firm in Palatine, Illinois.

THE PHOTOGRAPHERS

Jan Abbott,
De Soto, Illinois
Abbott works as a staff photographer for the *Southern Illinoisan*. She has won several awards including, first place in the Illinois Press Photographer contest for general news in 1984, and for a pictorial feature in 1981. Her works have also been recognized by the Illinois Press Association. Abbott is a member of the National Press Photographers Association and the Illinois Press Photographers Association.

Eric Albrecht,
Gahanna, Ohio
Albrecht was named the Ohio Newspaper Photographer of the Year in 1988. He was also honored by the National Press Photographers Association as the 1988 Region 4 Photographer of the Year. His work is featured in the book, *A Day in the Life of America*. Albrecht is a staff photographer for the *Columbus Dispatch* and is a member of the Ohio News Photographers Association.

Robert Ander,
Norfolk, Virginia
Owner of a commercial photography business, Ander has featured his work in *Colonial Home* Magazine, the Knight Ridder Annual Report, the book *One Day In Norfolk, Virginia* and in many general advertising and commercial areas. Ander is a member of the Advertising Club of Tidewater, the Tidewater Society of Communicating Arts and was honored with a Certificate of Merit in 1986 from the Printing Industries.

William A. Bake,
Boone, North Carolina
As a photographer and writer, Bake is currently involved in several projects, including *A Voice From The Southern Mountains* and *Country Ways*. He is also featured in the books, *North Carolina Is My Home* and *Our National Parks*. In addition, Bake has several articles appearing in *Reader's Digest* and photographs featured in *Natural History, Life, Audubon* and *National Wildlife*.

Joe Baraban,
Houston, Texas
Before opening his own business, Baraban worked as an artist for the *Houston Post* and as a photographer for the Associated Press and United Press International. Currently, Baraban does advertising and corporate photography for such clients as Ford Motor Corporation, IBM, United Airlines and John Deere. In 1983, Baraban was honored as president of the Art Directors Club of Houston.

William E. Barksdale,
Memphis, Tennessee
Barksdale specializes in agrichemical corporations including, Chevron Chemical Co., DuPont, Dow Chemical and ICI Americas. He has held previous editorial positions with *Progressive Farmer* and *Farm Quarterly*. In addition to shooting stock and editorial photos, Barksdale has had his work featured on the calendar of Cotton Incorporated. He is a member of the National Agri-Marketing Association and the American Agricultural Editor's Association.

Harris Barnes,
Clarksdale, Mississippi
With over thiry years of professional photography experience, Barnes is currently a contributing editor for *Farm Journal* and owner of Rural Services, a free-lance agricultural writing and photographic business. In addition to *Farm Journal*, Barnes has had photographs featured in several other agricultural magazines. Barnes, who farmed for 25 years, was the first editor of the *Southeast Farm Press*.

David Bergeland,
Bound Brook, New Jersey
Bergeland is a photojournalist with the *Courier-News* in Bridgewater, New Jersey. Two of his photos were represented in the 1989 Gannett National Photo Show held in New York. A 1988 "Best of Gannett" national winner, Bergeland has also been honored by the National Press Photographers Association. Formerly, he worked for the *Argus-Leader*, Sioux Falls, South Dakota.

Jim Bones,
Tesuque, New Mexico
A photographer with 24 years of professional experience, Bones is featured in several books, including , *Rio Grande: Mountains To The Sea* and *Texas Heartland*. Bones also has an exhibit displayed in the Andrew Smith Gallery in Santa Fe. In addition, he is a frequent contributor to *Audubon, Natural History* and *Texas Monthly*.

Robert B. Boyd,
Bettendorf, Iowa
Boyd recently completed a six week shoot throughout the U.S. and Canada for a large farm equipment manufacturer. His work has been honored on a local, regional and national level. Boyd's assignments include catalog and space-ad photos for a variety of clients. In addition to being a member of APA/Chicago, Boyd serves as president of Boyd-Fitzgerald, Inc., a photography and custom lab firm.

Richard E. Brooks,
Champaign, Illinois
Brooks has twenty years experience in graphic design and commercial photography. He has received several prestigious commissions from his Alma Mater, the University of Illinois. Best known for his "Chief Illiniwek" photographs, Brooks' work appears in national magazines and corporate publications. In 1988, he formed Silver Image Productions, Inc., to produce and direct *Country/ USA*.

Richard W. Brown,
Barnet, Vermont
Brown recently completed a book project for Little, Brown & Co., entitled *Moments in Eden* which depicts gardens as an art form. A photographer for the past 18 years, Brown has spent much of his career photographing the natural and rural landscape, the people and small villages, the wildlife and seasonal changes of New England. These subjects have become photo essays for *Audubon, National Wildlife, Country Journal* and other magazines, as well as two books, *The View from the Kingdom* and *A Vermont Christmas*.

Kip Brundage/Douglas Merriam, Belfast, Maine
Combining their photographic talents, Brundage and Merriam shot as a team. Brundage's work appears in many periodicals including, *Time, Newsweek*, and *Fortune*, as well as in the book, *Middlebury College*. He is working on a photographic essay for an anniversary issue for *Down East* Magazine. Merriam is a contributor to *Country Journal, Maine Boats and Harbors* and *Down East* Magazine. His current book shooting assignment features the lighthouses of New England.

Gary Bye,
Pomeroy, Washington
Bye is a full-time farmer from rural Washington and a free-lance writer and photographer for the past 14 years. Bye has been involved with numerous professional organizations and magazines. In 1976, Bye was named Photographer of the Year by the American Agricultural Editor's Association. Bye also served as associate editor of *National Future Farmers* Magazine from 1974-76.

Junebug Clark,
Farmington, Michigan
Clark has been shooting pictures since the age of six. He is best known for his work on the Jack Daniels' Distillery advertising campaign. Clark and his father have kept the Jack Daniels' account in the family for over 32 years. He has published two books, *Virginia, A History* and *Up The Hollow From Lynchburg*. Clark is currently serving as president of the American Society of Magazine Photographers.

D. Vann Cleveland,
Birmingham, Alabama
A 17-year veteran of professional photography, Cleveland specializes in rural America and its people. His work has won numerous awards with the American Agricultural Editor's Association, of which he is a member. Cleveland serves as a staff photo editor with *Progressive Farmer* Magazine.

Carr Clifton,
Taylorville, California
Nature photographer Clifton is best known for his work in the Sierra Club and Audubon Society calendars. He has spent much of his life exploring and documenting the wilds of California. Clifton's unique photos of the landscape appear in his first book, *California, Magnificent Wilderness*.

Bob Coffman,
Hudson, Iowa
As both photographer and writer, Coffman has been capturing the essence of American agriculture for more than 30 years. His work has been featured in *Farm Journal* and other major agricultural publications. Coffman's international assignments have taken him to Japan, Brazil, Argentina and western Europe.

Lori Ann Cook,
Bloomington, Illinois
Cook is a photojounalist for *The Panagraph*. Her work has been published in *American Photographer* Magazine. Cook has won several awards from the Associated Press and from the Inland Photo Competition. She is a member of the National Press Photographers Association.

Fred W. Cornelius,
Reno, Nevada
Cornelius photographs for brochures, calendars and book assignments. He is active in several professional organizations, including the Professional Photographers Association, the Sierra Nevada Association of Professional Photographers and the Reno Advertising Club. Cornelius recently photographed the Special Olympics in Reno.

Sharon Cummings / Jean F. Stoick Toledo, Ohio / Ann Arbor, Michigan
Working as a team, wildlife photographers, Cummings and Stoick concentrate on the White-tailed deer, and the rural scenes of southeastern Michigan. Cummings has worked extensively with the Ring-necked pheasant, as well as wildlife of the Yellowstone, Everglades and Denali National Parks. Stoick's photo specialization includes the Common Loon and the White-tailed deer.

Susan Drinker,
Rockport, Maine
An enviromental and portrait photographer, Drinker has eight years of professional experience. Her images have appeared in *Wilderness* Magazine and have been exhibited at the Art Institute of Boston, and the Gallery East of Littleton, New Hampshire. Drinker has had photographs published in conjunction with the "New Hampshire Wild and Scenic Rivers" campaign.

Arthur V. Edwards,
Cherry Hills, New Jersey
Before founding Edwards Media Services in 1982, Edwards was the publisher of the trade magazine division for Harvest Publications in Cleveland and was also the public relations manager for FMC in Philadelphia. He is currently covering corporate product publicity, and is involved with the Agricultural Relations Council and the National Agri-Marketing Association. In 1982 Edwards received the Founders Award from the Agricultural Relations Council.

Bob Elbert,
St. Charles, Missouri
In addition to his duties as photo editor for *Soybean Digest*, Elbert specializes in multimedia slide presentations. His current assignments include photographing soybean production practices in the Delmarva area, and producing a slide show to celebrate the American Soybean Association's tenth anniversary in St. Louis. Elbert also serves on the photo committee for the American Agricultural Editor's Association.

**Ken Elkins,
Oxford, Alabama**

Recipient of many awards and honors, Elkins won "Best Picture of the Year" by the Alabama Associated Press a total of five times. Several of his photographs are featured in a textbook illustrating examples of excellent photography and recognized by the Columbia University School of Journalism. In addition, his work appears in the book *Alabama-The Great Surprise* and *Everybody Loves A Man From The Country.* Elkins is the photo editor of the *Anniston Star.*

**Philip D. Ellsworth,
Stillwater, Oklahoma**

As a photographer for the Agricultural Information Department of Oklahoma State University, Ellsworth documents research projects, events and activities relating to agriculture. His recent freelance projects include an album cover for CBS Records and a "Life on the Road" story about a rock-n-roll band for a local music magazine. Ellsworth is also a member of the National Photographers Association.

**Jayne Erickson,
Sioux Falls, South Dakota**

Erickson, a leading advertising and fashion photographer in the upper midwest, is best known for her 'people' shots. She has won numerous awards from the South Dakota Advertising Federation and has published several books. Erickson also specializes in documenting both local and national political campaigns. She is the owner of a Sioux Falls photo studio.

**Dan Escobar,
Millbrae, California**

Escobar provides free-lance photography for a variety of magazines and advertising agencies. In July of 1988, Escobar photographed the cover of the *Los Angeles Times Magazine.* Escobar is a

member of the Advertising Photographers Association. In 1988, he was nominated by the *American Photographer* Magazine for awards in the "Magazine Section" of the "New Faces" section for 1987.

**Terry Evans,
Salina, Kansas**

A professional photographer for twenty years, Evans is currently teaching photography at Bethany College in Linsborg, Kansas. Evans has photographs being exhibited around the U. S. in university art museums and galleries. Recent awards and honors include The Honor Book at the 38th Annual Chicago Book Clinic Book Show for *Prairie: Images of Ground and Sky* and the Prize Book Award, Illustrated Division from the Association of American University Presses, Book and Jacket Show for the same book.

**Barth Falkenberg,
Columbus, Ohio**

Falkenberg has been honored by the Ohio News Photographers Association, the Boston Photographers Association and was once awarded New England Photographer of the Year. Falkenberg has been published in *Forbes, Fortune* and *National Geographic,* as well as being featured in books, *Ohio State University: A Portrait* and the *University of Illinois: A Portrait.* Falkenberg is a member of the American Society of Magazine Photographers, the National Press Photographers Association and is currently the director of photography for the *Columbus Dispatch.*

**Bill Fleming,
Eagan, Minnesota**

Fleming has been named the American Agricultural Editor's Association Photographer of the Year four times. He was also named Farm Writer of the Year in 1977 and has served as the president of the American Agricultural Editor's

Association. Fleming was honored by having his portfolio of agricultural photography featured on the TODAY Show. Currently, he is the editor of the *National Hog Farmer* Magazine.

**Frederica Georgia
Austin, Texas**

An 8-year photography veteran, Georgia shoots stock pictures in the southwestern United States, Mexico and Asia. Her images also appear in a book on California State Parks. In addition to her photo skills, she is an editorial contributor to *Sunset* Magazine. She is a member of several professional organizations, including the American Society of Magazine Photographers, Photo Researchers in New York City and the Santa Barbara *News Press.* Georgia is a staff photographer with *Southern Living* Magazine.

**Jane Gnass,
Anchorage, Alaska**

Gnass is a self-employed freelance and stock photographer in Anchorage, Alaska. She is a frequent contributor to *Alaska* Magazine. Her photos of the landscape and people of the Matanuska Valley have received editorial and cover treatment.

**Jeff Gnass,
Oroville, California**

A photographer specializing in American landscapes, Gnass has shot in Canada, Mexico, and forty states. In eight years as a free-lance photographer, his works have appeared in *National Geographic, Natural History* Magazine and *Wilderness* Magazine. Gnass is also featured in several books, including, *Idaho, Magnificent Wilderness, America's National Parks* and *Grand Canyon, The Story Behind The Scenery.* Gnass is a member of the American Society of Magazine Photographers and the American Society of Professional Photographers.

John Harvey/ Jennifer Harvey, Wilmington, Delaware

The winner of several awards from the American Agricultural Editor's Association, where he also served as president, John Harvey currently is a communications manager for DuPont Agricultural Products Group. John Harvey's photographs have appeared on several farm magazine covers. He served as editor/coordinator of the USDA Bicentenial Yearbook of Agriculture in 1976 and has also served as president of the Agricultural Relations Council. Jennifer Harvey is minoring in Art/Photography at the University of Delaware.

**Eric Hassler,
Evansville, Indiana**

A self-employed photographer, Hassler participated in the photographing of the book, *One Day In The U.S.A.* Currently, Hassler is compiling a book entitled *Black and White Portfolio.* Hassler is involved with the Press Photographers of America, the Professional Photographers of Indiana and the Greater Ohio Valley Professional Photographers Association, where he served as president.

**Paul Hixson,
Urbana, Illinois**

A professional photographer for twenty years, Hixson has been actively involved in agricultural photography. Hixson has had several shows featuring his photography at the University of Illinois and was awarded the Purchase Award in 1983, In 1984, Hixson exhibited a one-man show at the McKinley Foundation in Champaign, Illinois.

**BIll R. Horne,
Gainesville, Florida**

Horne was honored in 1982 by receiving the "Florida Degree of Photographic Excellence" from the Florida Professional Photographers Association. Horne has been awarded seven national titles

for his pageant portraits and has had photographs displayed in such magazines as *Newsweek* and *Parade.* Horne also participated in the shooting of *24 Hours in the Day of Gainesville, Florida, A Day In The Life Of America,* and *Glamoure,* a book featuring his photographic work.

**Jim Jernigan,
Ocala, Florida**

Jernigan has spent the past 40 years capturing Ocala and north Florida in his photographs. His work has been featured in *Audubon, Florida Horse, Thoroughbred Times, Silver Springs, Oasis* and other publications, as well as in advertising brochures. Jernigan has served as president of the Florida Professional Photographers Association and the Southeastern Professional Photographers Association. Presently, he is serving as Chairman of the Advertising/ Commercial Photographers Group of the Professional Photographers of America.

**Emory Jones,
Dunwoody, Georgia**

Serving as Vice President of Public Relations for Cascino and Purcell in Atlanta, Jones photographs for 19 different newsletters, as well as doing feature articles. He also freelances for various agricultural publications and does advertising shots for numerous agricultural products. Jones is a member of the National Agri-Marketing Association and has won several awards from the American Agricultural Editor's Association and the Cooperative Communications Association.

**Lou Jones,
Boston, Massachusetts**

Dubbed "one of the top photographers in New England," Jones is a specialist in photo illustration and location photography. He has shot for many of America's largest companies, including Avon, Chase Manhattan, 3M,

and Price Waterhouse. His photographs have been featured in *Time, Fortune* and *National Geographic.* Jones is a charter member of the Advertising Photographers of America.

**Tom Kehoss / Jeff Strumberger,
Milwaukee, Wisconsin**

Working as a team, Kehoss, owner of Kehoss Studios, Inc., and staff photographer Strumberger combined their shooting skills. Kehoss has over 23 years of professional experience in commercial illustrative photography. He is a member of Professional Photographers of America, Wisconsin Industrial Photographers Association and Advertising Photographers of Milwaukee. Strumberger, a 17-year photo veteran, does all the color printing for Kehoss Studios, and works extensively with food and jewelry photography.

**Holly Kuper,
Dallas, Texas**

A free-lance photographer, Kuper has a lengthy list of clients that include *Forbes, Fortune, Ladies Home Journal, Woman's Day, Business Week,* IBM, and Kraft. Kuper has also photographed covers for *Farm Journal's* specialized dairy and beef magazines. She is a member of the American Society of Magazine Photographers and the National Press Photographers Association.

**Brad LaPayne,
Champaign, Illinois**

Owner of a photographic business, LaPayne has photographs that sell in various gallerys in New York City and Chicago. LaPayne has published several posters, including the 1986 World Series, and New York City and Chicago. LaPayne is active in the International Association of Panoramic Photographers, the Professional Picture Framers Association and the American

Society of Artists.

**Lawrence S. K. Lau
Sacramento, California**

As a commercial photographer, Lau's images have appeared in numerous ads and magazine editorial features, including *Time, Sports Illustrated, Business Week, The Wall Stret Journal* and *Playboy.* His creative photographs have been recognized by many national advertising and business organizations. Lau is a member of the Advertising Photographers of America, American Society of Magazine Photographers and Professional Photographers of San Francisco.

**J. Stephen Lay,
Fairbanks, Alaska**

As well as being a professional photographer, Lay served as Public Information Officer for the University of Alaska-Fairbanks. Lay has contributed free-lance articles and photographs to several publications, including *Alaska* Magazine, and *Sea Frontiers.* He is a member of the Society of Professional Journalists and the Fairbanks Press Club.

**Larry LeFever,
Lititz, Pennsylvania**

LeFever is a self-employed photographer, who specializes in agriculture and nature scenes. His works have been published in several major farm periodicals, including, *Horticulture, Country Journal* and *Country Ideals.* as well as in calendars and brochures. LeFever's photographs received cover and editorial treatment in the book, *FARM.*

**Eugene Long,
Reno, Nevada**

As owner of Abe's Free Lance Photography, Long does assignment work for *Nevada* Magazine. He currently has assignments which include, *Life With Mickey Mantle,* and a 300-photo assignment of U.S. legislators for New England Bell Telephone. Long has an exhibit featured at the Sternel Gallery. He also has initiated "Copy Cat" photo-finishing franchise.

James E. Lytle,
Starkville, Mississippi
Lytle specializes in agricultural photography. He has coordinated the Eastman Kodak 4-H Photo Contest in Mississippi. Lytle is working as a photographer/darkroom manager with the Mississippi Cooperative Extension Service at Mississippi State University.

Curt Maas,
Johnston, Iowa
Maas is the recipient of the prestigious Silver Award and two Awards of Excellance at the 28th Iowa Art Directors Exhibition. He travels world-wide shooting all aspects of agriculture. His work can be seen in product brochures, catalogs, magazine ads and articles. Maas is a photographer and studio manager for Pioneer Hi-Bred International.

Luther MacNaughton,
Omaha, Nebraska
An 18-year veteran photographer, MacNaughton is president of MacNaughton Graphics, Inc., specializing in advertising, marketing and multimedia services. His client list includes, Cargill/Nutrena Feeds, Precision Bearing Company of Omaha, Millard Public Schools and Tempest Company of Omaha. MacNaughton is a past member and president of Omaha American Marketing Association and Iowa and Omaha Art Dirctor Clubs. He is currently a member of the NAMA, Midlands Chapter.

Ted Mc Donough,
Coon Rapids, Iowa
Specializing in location agriculture photography, Mc Donough has been shooting professionally for 16 years. His work has taken him from coast to coast. McDonough's current assignments include,

covering the spring, mid-season and harvest activities of cotton, sugarbeets and potatoes in California, Idaho and Michigan for a Chicago-based advertising agency.

Garry D. McMichael,
St. Charles, Missouri
As a commercial photographer, McMichael does photography for Bicycle Magazine, Tours and Resorts Magazine and Farm Journal. In 1981 and 1988, he was selected Photojournalist of the Year by the Arkansas Press Association. In addition, he won "Best of Show" and the Kodak Gallery Award at the Heart of America Professional Photographers Convention. He is also a member of the American Society of Magazine Photographers and the Professional Photographers of America.

Wyatt McSpadden,
Amarillo, Texas
McSpadden, who operates a photographic business, photographs for magazines and annual reports. In 1987, he published his own audio-visual entitled, Panhandle Promise. McSpadden has been awarded numerous local, regional and national Addy Awards, National Agri-Marketing awards and a Special Merit Award for outstanding location photography.

Janice A. Mekula,
Livonia, Michigan
Mekula is a free-lance photographer, poet, and teacher. Her work can be found in the book, Frozen Sunshine. She is commissioned by various charity fundraising organizations including, Michigan Artists. Mekula is also compiling a book of poems and color photographs entitled, Worlds Away.

Bruce Meyer,
Kansas City, Missouri
Meyer, who is a veteran free-lance photographer for several TV stations, is currently working as a free-lance pro-

duction technician for KMBC TV in Kansas City. He is responsible for studio and remote camera operations, and audio and video tape production. Recently, Meyer's photographs accompanied an article in Country Woman Magazine about an all-female wheat harvesting crew that travels the Midwest.

Skip Moody/Ted Reuther/
Carl R. Sams II,
Walled Lake, Michigan/
Royal Oak, Michigan/Ann
Arbor, Michigan
Working as a team, nature photographers Moody and Reuther, and wildlife photographer Sams shot Yellowstone National Park from the ground and the air. Combined national and international credits of the three photographers include, Aireone of Italy, Audubon, National Geographic, Ranger Rick, National Wildlife, Terre Savage of France, Birder's World, Michigan Natural Resource Magazine, Sierra Club, and many other publications.

Joe Munroe,
Orinda, California
A professional photographer since 1939, Munroe has shot for Life, Fortune, and National Geographic. He is also involved in motion picture production and has received recognition for two documentaries, "Hybrid Vigor" and "Dare The Wildest River." He also has photographic essays found in eight volumes of the history book, The States and the Nation. Munroe currently has a 125-piece black and whitw photo exhibit on display at the Ohio Historical Society in Columbus.

Tom Murphy,
Livingston, Montana
Murphy's photographs have received cover and editorial treatment in four Montana Geographic books. His works have also appeared in such publications as Audubon, Outside, National Geographic

World, New York Times Magazine, Leisure, Montana Magazine, and Reader's Digest. Murphy has exhibited at several galleries, including the Danforth Gallery in Livingston, Montana, and Kodak Park in Rochester, New York.

Fred Myers,
Florence, Alabama
A thirty-year veteran of freelance photography, Myers is a member of the American Agricultural Editor's Association, where he served on the Board of Directors. Myers is also a member of the American Society of Magazine Photographers. Previously, he was field editor and managing editor of the Indiana Farmers Guide and associate editor of The Furrow. Myers participated in the one-week shoot for Alabama-The Great Surprise.

John Nienhuis,
Milwaukee, Wisconsin
A professional photographer with 11 years experience, Nienhuis shoots for Black Star and many national and international corporations. His photos have appeared in Sports Illustrated, Milwaukee Magazine and the 1985 Milwaukee Art Museum Handbook. Nienhuis is a member of the Advertising Photographers of Milwaukee and travels internationally on assignment.

Kelly O'Brien, San Juan
Capistrano, California
O'Brien is a frequent contributor to several national agricultural publications, including Successful Farming, Progressive Farmer, Farm Journal, and Dairy Today. In addition, O'Brien is a member of the American Agricultural Editor's Association and The Agricultural Relations Council.

Stan Osolinski,
Warren, Michigan
A photographer of wildlife and outdoor scenery, Osolinski is a member of the National Wildlife Federation

and in 1987 was the BBC Photographer of the Year. In addition to awards and honors, Osolinski's photos appear in several books and calendars. He is featured in the 1989 Audubon Wildlife Wall Calendar and the 1990 National Wildlife Calendar. He is represented by Marvin L. Dembinsky Jr. Photography Associates.

Jay Paris,
Salem, Ohio
In addition to being chief photographer and photo editor for the award-winning Ohio Magazine, Paris has also exhibited photographs in several galleries around the U.S. In 1987, Paris was awarded first place by the Society of Professional Journalists in the category of color features. Paris has also been honored by having prints placed within the Butler Museum of American Art. Recently, Paris photographed his twenty-fifth magazine cover.

Jim Patrico/Suzanne Sayre,
Plattsburg, Missouri
Husband and wife team Patrico and Sayre are the owners of Foursquare, a free-lance photography and writing business. They are both recipients of two American Agricultural Editor's Association Photographer of the Year Awards. Patrico was also awarded the "Oscar in Agriculture." Previously, Patrico served as editor of Missouri Realist and photo editor of Farm Journal. Sayre has worked as a newspaper photographer and assistant editor of Missouri Realist. Both Patrico and Sayre are members of the American Agricultural Editors Association.

Douglas Peebles,
Kailua, Hawaii
Owner of a photographic business, Peebles specializes in publishing photo-essay books. Peebles has published several books about Hawaii and one book about baskets of the South Pacific. He also

does a mixture of travel oriented editorial and commercial work. Peebles is a member of the American Society of Magazine Photographers.

Harlen Persinger,
Milwaukee, Wisconsin
During his 11-year career as a professional photographer, Persinger has received over forty awards from the American Agricultural Editor's Association. He has also been the recipient of two photo honors from the Badger Chapter of the National Agri-Marketing Association. Persinger is an editorial supervisor for Bader-Rutter and Associates, Inc., Brookfield, Wisconsin.

Chester Peterson, Jr.,
Lindsborg, Kansas
A member of the American Society of Magazine Photographers and a former associated editor of Successful Farming Magazine, Peterson has had photographs appear in 146 different publications in six different countries. Many of his photographs have been used by regional and national award winners associated with the National Agri-Marketing Association and the Livestock Publications Council. Peterson, who covers agriculture for several popular farm publications, is a recipient of a Certificate of Merit Award from the New York City Art Directors Club.

David Peterson,
Des Moines, Iowa
David Peterson is the winner of the Pulitzer Prize for his feature photography concerning the Iowa farm crisis. Peterson was also awarded the Iowa Photographer of the Year four times and the National Press Photographers Association Region Five Photographer of the Year three times. Peterson, who currently has a two year print exhibition touring Iowa, is a special projects photographer for the Des Moines Register and Tribune.

Jim Raycroft,
Boston, Massachusetts
Raycroft, a 15-year photography veteran, specializes in people/lifestyle and location photography. His award-winning shots have earned him numerous magazine covers, as well as honors from both the Boston and New York Art Directors Clubs. Raycroft is a frequent contributor to a variety of major national boating and leisure publications. His current assignments include shooting national ads for Peppridge Farm Products and the Sheraton Hotel Corporation.

Kenny Rogers,
Los Angeles, California
Rogers, a popular Country and Western entertainer and recording artist, has demonstrated his creative versatility in two photographic books. Your Friends and Mine is a collection of celebrity portraits. His first book, Kenny Rogers' America depicts the nation's landscapes. Both books are published by Little, Brown and Company.

Greg L. Ryan/Sally Beyer,
St. Paul, Minnesota
The husband and wife photography team of Ryan and Beyer, specialize in both location and stock photography. Combining their photo and writing skills, they have two articles appearing in the upcoming American Cyanamid publication, Farm Family America. Their photographs can also be found in their book, From This Land. Ryan and Beyer are members of the Minnesota Commercial and Industrial Photographers Association.

Jeff Salisbury,
Findlay, Ohio
Salisbury specializes in location and studio photography for ag-related clients. Shooting in all formats, this 15-year photo veteran has earned a "Qualified" rating with the Professional Photographers of

America. Salisbury is also a member of the International Association of Business Communicators.

Franco Salmoiraghi, Honolulu, Hawaii

Salmoiraghi has lived and photographed in Hawaii since 1968. He is a frequent contributor to books and magazines in Hawaii and frequently exhibits his work in fine arts galleries throughout Hawaii. He currently is a free-lance photographer accepting advertising, commercial and editorial assignments. He has taught photography in workshops and at the University of Hawaii. Salmoiraghi was a participating photographer for *A Day In The Life Of Hawaii*, as well as the book, *Hawaii*.

Ralph Sanders, West Des Moines, Iowa

A veteran photographer of twenty years, Sanders has contributed to *Successful Farming* Magazine since 1974. Prior to becoming a photographer, Sanders held editorial positions with *Successful Farming, Prairie Farmer* and the Decatur, Illinois, *Herald & Review*. Sanders also participated on a team which covered the visit of Pope John Paul II to the U.S. Currently, Sanders is operating his own photographic company that handles assignments for commercial and editorial agriculture clients in the Midwest.

Scott Shaw, St. Louis, Missouri

Winner of the Pulitzer Prize for Spot News Photography for his coverage of the rescue of baby Jessica McClure, Shaw has also won numerous awards from the Texas and Arkansas Press Association. Shaw, who is an award-winning member of the National Press Photographers Association, has also won awards at the Associated Press Managing Editor's Contest. Shaw is a staff photographer for the *St. Louis Sun*.

Charles Shoffner, Ruckersville, Virginia

A self-employed photographer, Shoffner's photos appear in the books *Indianapolis, Cincinnati, The University of Virginia: Then and Now* and a regional booklet entitled *Virginia*. He also photographed the *1988 University of Virginia Calendar* and has a photo featured in the *1989 America the Beautiful Calendar* published by the *National Geographic* book division. Shoffner is a member of the American Society of Magazine Photographers.

Scott Sinklier, Des Moines, Iowa

As a photographer for Pioneer Hi-Bred International, Inc., Sinklier has covered major agricultural projects around the world. His work has been honored by both the Arizona and Iowa Art Directors Shows and has been featured in the Smithsonian Institution. Formerly, Sinklier was a space shuttle photographer for NASA.

Shirley Sokolosky, Owasso, Oklahoma

A free-lance agricultural journalist, Sokolosky previously worked as a director of communication for the Agri Business Group in Indianapolis. Currently, she is serving as editor of *Convention Proceedings*, a 32-page publication serving the FFA. Sokolosky also wrote and conceived the photo and art ideas for the *FFA Reporter's Handbook*.

Jeff Stine, Denver, Colorado

Stine has worked as a professional commercial photographer in Denver since 1981. Always carrying camera in tow, Stine shoots stock photography wherever he travels. He spends most of his free time in the mountains, where he enjoys skiing, fly fishing and rock climbing.

William Strode, Goshen, Kentucky

Strode's prestigious photojournalism career includes two Pulitzer Prizes, of which he was a co-recipient. He has traveled worldwide on photographic assignments for such magazines as *Time, Life, Fortune* and *National Geographic*. His photographs have been exhibited in the Museum of Modern Art, and The Smithsonian Institution, as well as internationally. He is a founder and trustee of the NPPA Foundation and has taught photojournalism at numerous universities and workshops. Strode currently operates a free-lance photography business, and a publishing company.

Rick Swart, Klamath Falls, Oregon

A member of the National Association of Agricultural Journalists, Swart was a former editor and photojournalist for *Farm & Dairy Magazine*. He also edited the award-winning newspaper, *Wallowa County Chieftain*. Swart has won several awards for his feature and sports photography. He now serves as managing editor of Klamath Publishing, Company.

Gregory Thorp, New Haven, Connecticut

Thorp, who has photographed six covers for *Modern Photography*, and a cover story for *Popular Photography*, completed a photographic study of Cincinnati in 1988 that has been exhibited at the Carl Solway Gallery. Thorp has also worked as a photographer observing commercial towboat operations on the Ohio and Mississippi Rivers.

Tom Till, Moab, Utah

Till's photographs of the American landscape appear in a wide array of books and magazines. He is the author of *Utah: Magnificent Wilderness* and *Colorado: Images from Above*. Presently, Till is working on a book portraying the natural beauty of New Jersey, and a portfolio in conjunction with great American nature writers.

David Tonge, Elgin, Illinois

Tonge has been named the Illinois Press Photographers Association's Clip Photographer of the Year, five times. Tonge was also awarded as the Regional Photographer of The Year by the National Press Photographers Association in 1979. His works have been featured in *Farm Journal, Chicago Magazine, People* and *Time*. Tonge is currently a staff photographer with the *Daily Herald*.

Hardie Truesdale, New Paltz, New York

Truesdale has the cover and six interior photographs included in the *1989 Brown Trout New York Calendar*. He will also have photographs featured in the *1990 Brown Trout New York Calendar* and the *1990 Sierra Club Calendar*. In addition to calendar work and gallery shows, Truesdale's photos are featured in the books, *North From Duluth* and *The Northern Shawangunks*.

David Ulmer, Ballwin, Missouri

Owner of a photography business for the past ten years, Ulmer has had photos appear in *Natural History, Sierra, Outside, Backpacker, and St. Louis* Magazine. He was the 1988 recipient of the St. Louis Addy Award for best color poster. Ulmer is also included in two books, *Colorful Missouri* and *St. Louis in Color*. Recently, he traveled to Idaho and Oregon to shoot a whitewater trip on the Middle Fork of the Salmon River.

Alvis Upitis, Minneapolis, Minnesota

Upitis is a commercial photographer doing advertising

and corporate photography for Fortune 500 companies and major advertising agencies. He is the founding president of the Minneapolis Chapter of the American Society of Magazine Photographers and has photographs featured in the book, *MIDWEST, Images of America*. Upitis, his father and two uncles will have a joint photo exhibition in 1990 in Riga, Latvia entitled, "Upitis Dynasty."

Ron Van Zee, Bayport, Minnesota

A photographer with 25 years of experience, Van Zee has won awards from the Advertising Federation of Minnesota, the Advertising Club of New York and the National Agri-Marketing Association. He has a gallery exhibit of southeastern Minnesota geography on permanent display at the Norwest Bank Gallery in Richester, Minnesota. Van Zee also is the author of *Minnesota*, a book depicting the state's natural landscapes and quiet corners.

Tom Wachs, Alexandria, Virginia

A former geologist with the U.S. Geologic Survey, Wachs is presently a free-lance photographer. His photographs are featured in calendars, postcards, annual reports and on National Park Service brochures. Wachs also has his work included in private collections and exhibitions in the U.S. Congress, the National Geographic traveling exhibit, the Environmental Protection Agency, E.F. Hutton and Merrill Lynch. Wachs has won several awards in regional and national shows.

Jim Walton, Indianapolis, Indiana

As a professional photographer for 15 years, Walton specializes in shooting rural life and farm scenes. He is involved in several agricultural affiliations including

National Agri-Marketing Association, National Association of Farm Broadcasters and National Association of State Radio Networks. Walton is marketing manager for the Wabash Valley Broadcasting Corporation.

Ed "Skip" Weigel, Live Oak, Florida

As owner of Colonial Photography, Weigel, who has over 25 years of professional experience, photographs for companies and associations in northern Florida. Recently, Weigel contributed to the book, *Florida Rediscovered*. Weigel is a member of the Florida Professional Photographers Association, where he served as president of the Tallahassee section. He is also a member of the Southeastern Professional Photographers of America.

Michael Wilson, Decatur, Illinois

In addition to serving as managing editor, Wilson is a frequent contributor to *Prairie Farmer* Magazine. His photos have appeared in *Newsweek On Campus, Virginia Country, The Kansas City Star & Times, The National Future Farmer* and the 1986 and 1987 *Ford Heritage Award Calendar*. Wilson is involved in several professional organizations including, American Agricultural Editor's Association and Illinois Farm News Association.

Noel Workman, Greenville, Mississippi

Workman serves as president of the Delta Design Group. The 23-year veteran photographer has been commissioned by such clients as Uncle Ben's Rice, the Episcopal Diocese of Mississippi, Mars Electronic International, Mississippi Chemical Corporation and Delta & Pine Land Seed Company. Workman was the recipient of the audio visual award in 1987 from the National Agri-Marketing Associa-

tion. He is also a member of the Greater Jackson Ad Club.

THE TOP 24 4-H AND FFA PHOTOGRAPHERS

Heidi Allen, Murrieta, California

Andy Bobb, Center, North Dakota

Jill Carey, Sycamore, Illinois

Jill Dramstad, Binford, North Dakota

Justin Gabehart, Minco, Oklahoma

Alfred Gosch, Muldoon, Texas

Jeremiah Harding, Kennewick, Washington

Brad Hardy, Hawkinsville, Georgia

Allan Harshman, New Salem, Illinois

Angela Johnson, Wetumka, Oklahoma

Julie Kornegay, Bolingbroke, Georgia

Brian Martin, Fayette, Iowa

Marci McKinzie, Dike, Texas

Lisa Mullen, Madison, Wisconsin

Christina Marie Nagy, Cleveland, Ohio

Daniel Ortmeier, West Point, Nebraska

Jill Pierce, Campbellsville, Kentucky

Kari Rasor, Anson, Texas

Marc Rosenberg, Chenango Forks, New York

Ann Schintz, York, Pennsylvania

Mandy G. Smith, Willacoochee, Georgia

Lara Summers, Maitland, Missouri

Angie Van Karsen, Chassell, Michigan

Darin Willardsen, Napoleon, North Dakota

COUNTRY/USA: THE SHOOT

Producer/Director
Silver Image Productions, Inc., Champaign, Illinois
Richard E. Brooks

Project Coordinator
Glen E. Schrof

Assistant Producer/Director
Robert E. Smith

Corporate Relations
Georgia Schrof

Photographer Coordinators
Richard E. Brooks, Harvey M. Cook, Fred W. Cornelius,
Walt Griffith, Debi Hassler, Brett Knobloch,
Eugene Long, Diana Meyer, and Tom Waldinger

Publicity/Trade Shows
Domar & Associates, Danville, Illinois
Martha Curry

COUNTRY/USA: THE BOOK

Executive Editor
Richard E. Brooks

Design and Production
Harmony House Publishers, Louisville, Kentucky
William Strode and William Butler

Logotype Designer
Douglas Burnett

Contributing Editors
Richard A. Howell, Kimberly Ruff-Meenen, and Clancy Strock

Production Supervision
Silver Image Productions, Inc., Champaign, Illinois

Summer Interns
Darrell Douglass and Mark Meurer

Office Assistants
Jeana Kennedy and Reta Salmon

Marketing Distribution
Silver Image Marketing, Inc., Pontiac, Illinois
Samuel Douglass, Georgia Schrof, Glen E. Schrof, and Janet Schrof

FRIENDS

Susan Abbott
Agricultural Relations Council
Agri-News Publications
American Agricultural Editors
  Association
Marvin Black
Bloomington Pantagraph
John Brooks
Saundra Brooks
Colleen Callahan
Camera's Eye Photoworks
Melvin Daum family
Donnell's Printing & Office
  Products
Dr. James F. Evans
Max Fisher
Marilyn & John Garner
Frank & Phyllis Gladden

Terry Gowey
Grand Ol' Opry
Heartland NAMA Chapter
Lynn Henderson
Hendrick County Farm Bureau
  Women's Committee
Phil Jones
Knapp Kitchens & More
Grant Mangold
Andy Martwart
William McMullen
Carroll E. Merry
John Milewski
National Agri-Marketing Assn.
National FFA Organization
National 4-H Council
Harley Newell
Joan Olson

Premium Specialties
Printing Craftsmen
Professional Photographers of
  America
Stu Reeve
Jim Richardson
Gerald P. Rodeen
Gayle Saint
Orion Samuelson
Brian Schrack
James Smith
Dr. William F. Stagg
Thread Letters
Joan Truax
U.S. Park Service
Jerry Versteegh
John Volk
Susan Meri Witt

DONORS

Agri-Marketing, Niles, Illinois

Douglas Burnett, Urbana, Illinois

Creative Slides & Advertising/
Audio Visual, Normal, Illinois

Domar & Associates,
Danville, Illinois

Douglass-Cotter & Associates,
Pontiac, Illinois

DuPont Ag Products,
Wilmington, Delaware

Filmcraft Color Labs,
Indianapolis, Indiana

Maritz Communications,
St. Louis, Missouri

Newell Construction Company,
Inc., Danville, Illinois

Pioneer Hi-Bred International,
Des Moines, Iowa

WICD-TV, Champaign, Illinois

Image Innovations, Inc.,
Minneapolis, Minnesota

THANK YOU TO THE PEOPLE OF RURAL AMERICA!

Photo this page: Mountains above the Blue Ridge Parkway, north of Charlottesville, Virginia.
Charles Shoffner